# Requiem
# for the
# Card Catalog

**New Directions in Librarianship**
*Series Editor*: Daniel Gore

To Know a Library: Essays and Annual Reports, 1970-1976
*Daniel Gore*

# REQUIEM FOR THE CARD CATALOG

## Management Issues in Automated Cataloging

Edited by DANIEL GORE
JOSEPH KIMBROUGH and
PETER SPYERS-DURAN

*New Directions in Librarianship, Number 2*

GREENWOOD PRESS
WESTPORT, CONNECTICUT

**Library of Congress Cataloging in Publication Data**

Main entry under title:

Requiem for the card catalog.

    (New directions in librarianship ; no. 2
ISSN 0147-1090)
    Papers of a conference held in 1977 and sponsored
by the Associated Colleges of the Midwest.
    Includes index.
    1. Machine-readable bibliographic data—
Congresses. 2. Library catalogs—Congresses.
3. Libraries—Automation—Congresses. 4. Library
administration—Congresses. I. Gore, Daniel.
II. Kimbrough, Joseph. III. Spyers-Duran, Peter.
IV. Associated Colleges of the Midwest. V. Series.
Z699.A1R46        025.3'028'54       78-7129
ISBN 0-313-20608-2

Library of Congress Catalog Card Number: 78-7129
ISBN: 0-313-20608-2
ISSN: 0147-1090

First published in 1979

English language edition, except Great Britain
and Europe, published by

Greenwood Press, Inc.
51 Riverside Avenue, Westport, Connecticut 06880

Published in Great Britain and Europe by

Aldwych Press Limited
3 Henrietta Street, London, WC2E 8LU

Printed in the United States of America

10 9 8 7 6 5 4 3 2

# Contents

# Figures

# Tables

# Foreword

Joseph Kimbrough

When Daniel Gore asked me to join him and Peter Spyers-Duran in organizing a conference on management issues in automated cataloging for The Associated Colleges of the Midwest, I agreed readily. And then I had some misgivings: Why should a public librarian insinuate himself into the affairs of academe, and a rarefied academe at that? "Relax," Dan said. "We're a lot closer together than you think, and besides, public libraries are much farther along in this business of automated cataloging than are the academic libraries." If I have not quoted Dan exactly, he will forgive me. The sentiment was the same.

As it happened, the chief administrators of the Minneapolis Public Library were then (and still are) involved in the very process of decision making that the ACM conference was to address. So the timing of the conference, and my unexpected role in it, were especially fortunate for me.

When a library decides to automate its catalog, it is not a simple matter. The decision-making process is spread over many months—possibly even years—and involves many people at many levels both within and without the library. Events along the route to an automated catalog inevitably shape the final outcome. What looked feasible yesterday may very well be impossible or undesirable tomorrow. Yesterday's pipedream often becomes tomorrow's commonplace. Having watched at first hand two major public libraries struggle with the question of automating the catalog, I can attest that it is one of the most exciting and challenging endeavors to confront administrators and technical service personnel. At the same time, it is also one of the most frustrating. To those who have come through the struggle successfully, it must be one of the most satisfying accomplishments in a library career.

Most of my generation of library administrators were not formally trained to deal with automation. That is why conferences such as this one are so valuable to our continuing education and to our ability to provide better service to our publics. They put us in touch with some of the best contemporary thinkers and practitioners of the art just at the time when our need for information is greatest.

Some two hundred and eighty public and academic librarians from the United States and Canada were drawn to Chicago to hear the ten speakers and six panelists whose papers and comments are gathered into this volume. It was an exciting and satisfying conference on every level. The speakers had prepared thoughtful and stimulating papers, and they were also visible after the sessions in more informal situations, answering questions and sharing generously with the participants from their experience. It was a learning conference, and The Associated Colleges of the Midwest is to be congratulated for its sponsorship. It is my hope that more issues in library management will be explored in similar format under its banner.

The conjunction of academic and public librarians in addressing this topic sets a useful precedent. All too often in our professional associations, both at state and national levels, we split needlessly into type-of-library groups to discuss essentially the same topics. The ACM is to be congratulated for taking this step toward breaking down these absurd barriers.

The subject of this conference lends itself naturally to ecumenism, concerned as it is with networking, sharing of information, and, ultimately, sharing of economic resources. One of the major issues of the forthcoming White House Conference on Library and Information Services is almost certain to be that of a nationwide, multitype library system. The automated catalog data base is as good a base as any from which such a system could spring. In helping library managers from various types of libraries reach better decisions in this crucial area, the conference played a significant part in moving us toward that greater goal.

The conference dealt with at least five major overlapping areas of concern: technical and economic concerns, on-line feasibility, staffing and management factors, network issues, and user satisfaction. While most of the speakers touched upon more than one of these issues, Butler and Kountz stressed technical and economic concerns in their papers. Butler, Blackburn, and Malinconico addressed on-line feasibility, questioning whether an interactive cataloging mode is needed at the present time, and citing some ancillary ways in which it can be presently effective.

Staffing and management issues were explored by Berman, Spyers-Duran, Fischer, and Axford. Will automation free libraries to hire more catalogers who are dynamic, people oriented, creative, unorthodox and even "constructively rebellious," as Berman suggests, or will hard economic realities limit opportunities for catalogers? To what extent is retraining for other library activities being carried on as automation displaces conventional work routines?

Avram and Evans were concerned, among other matters, with the issues that networks raise and the many factors to consider—pro and con—in joining a network.

And, finally, how will the user—the person, presumably, for whom all this effort is being expended—respond to COM and/or on-line catalogs? Some eminently practical observations were provided by both Fischer and Blackburn from their experiences in a large public and a large university library, respectively.

A most important element of the conference was the availability of terminals and other examples of computer hardware and software for the participants to see and operate. These were provided by a number of commercial vendors whose technical expertise, guidance, and counseling are invaluable to library managers in their decision making but who are sometimes, nonetheless, undercredited. These vendors added much to our understanding of how automated catalogs actually work, and their generous support of hospitality arrangements contributed to everyone's sense of comfort and conviviality in the midst of long days of hard work and serious thought.

# Acknowledgments

Please to remember
The Fifth of November,
Gunpowder treason and plot. . . .
                    —*Anonymous*

Dr. Dan Martin, president of The Associated Colleges of the Midwest, is a brave man. This volume contains the papers presented at the second library conference sponsored by his organization. Like the first, expenses for this conference had to be paid out of receipts from registrants, a circumstance that poses a considerable financial risk for Dr. Martin, since there is no way to guarantee him beforehand that income will equal expenses. Had he not agreed to take the risk a second time, there would have been no conference, and the volume at hand would not exist. I am grateful to him for his magnanimity, and his boldness, in providing sponsorship under such risky conditions. And I think librarians generally will share my gratitude when they have read the timely contributions that make up this book. Automated cataloging is an issue that concerns everyone in the profession. Much is at stake here for virtually every library in the nation, regardless of its size, type, or mission. These conference papers should provide invaluable assistance to anyone contemplating or currently using any format of the automated catalog. Dr. Martin is the first person to be thanked for making this special assistance widely available.

Next come the conference speakers, all of whom are thoroughly experienced both in the theory and practical applications of automated catalogs in libraries. Their work needs no praise from an editor to commend it to your attention. But I do wish to record my special appreciation for the heavy labor they have undertaken in presenting to you, in clear and readable texts, the fruits of their work in this unusually complex area.

I want to thank and praise my secretary, Dorothy Barnes, for handling all the promotional work of the conference (on top of the routinely demanding duties of a library secretary); Jeanette McGrath of the ACM staff, who as conference coordinator carried the unenviable responsibility of making everything go smoothly (as it in fact did) for all the speakers, panelists, conferees, and exhibitors; Judith Anne Duncan, calligrapher to the Macalester College Library, who provided the beautiful calligraphic text for the conference brochures and program; and Joseph Kimbrough and Peter Spyers-Duran, who took upon themselves the crucial task of formulating a conference program worthy of the considerable expense of time and money borne by the conferees, many of whom traveled great distances to Chicago. The judgment of all those with whom I talked was that the program chairmen had done a superb job.

From much experience with such things, I have learned that conferences are both more enjoyable, and more profitable to their participants, when the hard work of attending carefully to a long succession of speakers is lightened by the personal pleasures of coffee and pastry service during the sessions and refreshments and informal conversations with colleagues in the evenings. Such amenities cost money (a large amount of it in a fine Chicago hotel), and I acknowledge here with many thanks the financial contributions of the following firms that underwrote the costs for all hospitality arrangements at the conference: Auto-graphics, Baker & Taylor, Blackwell North America, BroDart, CLSI, and 3M.

Finally, I note with special satisfaction that while the last day of the conference by chance fell on Guy Fawkes Day, the only fireworks set off were purely intellectual. They were ignited by our six distinguished panelists, and the reverberations from their incendiary work are recorded in the transcript of the panel session, with which this volume closes.

St. Paul, Minnesota
December 1, 1977

Requiem
for the
Card Catalog

# Collection and Resource Data Bases in Bibliographic Management

1

Brett Butler

I hope to review here the major management issues in the use of bibliographic data bases over the next decade, to stimulate some discussion and disagreement, and to provide a framework for individual library planning in the use of data bases.

## BIBLIOGRAPHIC DATA BASES

The term *data base* itself and words associated with data bases—files, records, indexes, and so forth—are not only poorly understood by many library administrators; they are not even defined within the library community as they are by data-processing managers. The literature, presentations at meetings, and general correspondence all fail to distinguish even among fundamentally different types of data bases. For the library manager one single distinction is the most crucial, and it is the one on which I will base my analysis here: there are data bases that the library owns, and there are other data bases that the library uses, borrows, or otherwise has access to. For the purposes of this paper, a data base owned by the individual library is defined as a *collection data base*. A data base used but not owned by the library is a *resource data base*.

A collection data base is a machine-readable file, maintained on an ongoing basis, which represents cataloging or indexing for a comprehensive segment of an individual library's collection. The collection data base does not include information on materials held by other libraries nor is it a general bibliography of published information. A collection data base by its nature implies the inclusion of holdings or location information, although the degree of detail may vary. At minimum, a collection data base defines the location of material held by one library (or library system). More detailed location information may include locations at individual branches or within special collections in a given physical or administrative unit.

A resource data base, by contrast, lists materials from more than one library and may or may not provide a comprehensive listing of classes of materials for any given individual library. Some data bases (such as MARC) do not represent the holdings of any particular library or system.

Location information is optional in resource data bases. For some functions, a resource data base such as OCLC is used to identify gross locations of particular material; for other functions, OCLC users are indifferent to the location of the actual document described, using the resource data base only to create their local catalog collection data base.

There are significant contrasts in the nature and uses of these two types of data bases, in their availability in the library world today, and in the benefits and limits to library managers using resource and collection data bases.

## RESOURCE DATA BASES

By providing some inventory of the major resource and collection data bases used in libraries, we can define the magnitude of current activities and also illustrate more fully the type of data base distinctions that are important to library planning.

The most important data base in the library world is also the major resource data base used today: MARC, distributed by the Library of Congress. The scope, coverage, and significance of MARC have grown to a remarkable level in the twenty years since the experimental creation of MARC records. Figure 1.1 illustrates the growth of the MARC data base and its reported uses in different types of libraries.

With MARC the nature of the resource data base can be readily seen. MARC does not represent a substantial proportion of the collection of the Library of Congress; it represents only a selection of the material currently cataloged at the Library of Congress (a proportion growing, of course, each year). Some MARC records do not represent books held by the Library of Congress at all; records from COMARC and others represent holdings of other libraries and point the way toward the eventual development of a national union catalog machine-readable data base, which would be an integrated national resource.

The non-MARC portion of the OCLC data base is the next most widely used resource data base in existence. It represents current cataloging (and in some few cases retrospective conversion of sections of total collections) from a wide variety of libraries nationwide, which have essentially no connection with each other except their common use of the OCLC on-line cataloging system. Figure 1.2 illustrates the growth of the OCLC data base, which consists of LC precedent cataloging and original cataloging input by member libraries.

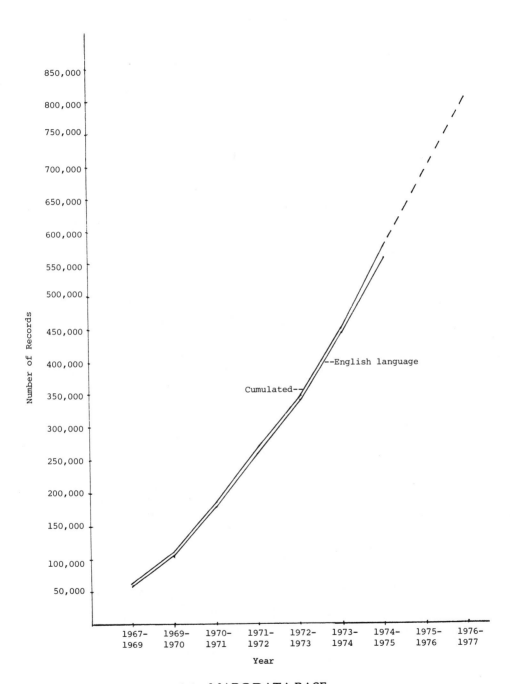

1.1   MARC DATA BASE

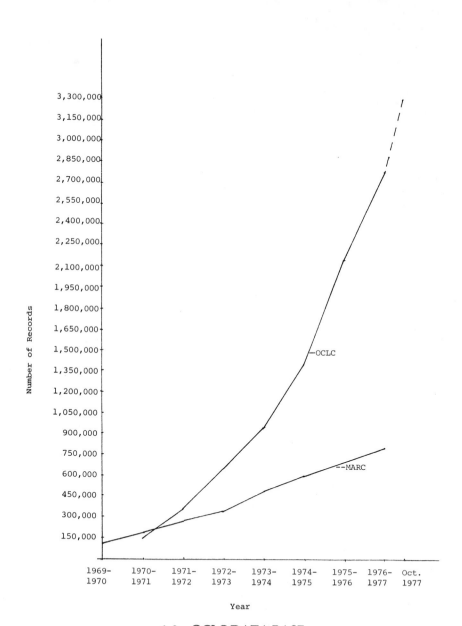

1.2   OCLC DATA BASE

While libraries joining OCLC contract to input essentially all their current cataloging, differences in defining types of materials to be cataloged, in the scope of local use of the on-line cataloging system, and other restrictions make OCLC a resource data base comprising essentially uncontrolled input from a large number of libraries. Location information at a gross level is provided as part of the cataloging process, but the data base represents a complete collection of only a few libraries and as a whole represents no single collection.

A number of other data bases are being used as resource data bases in various library applications. They are most commonly developed by local libraries or networks for individual applications, or they are developed by commercial service vendors to serve multiple library customers. A brief inventory of data bases known to have been used as resources includes University of California (*Union Catalog Supplement*), North American Blackwell union data base, CONSER participants (through OCLC), and COMARC participants (through LC).

## COLLECTION DATA BASES

By some standards, collection data bases may be considered as extremely widespread and used in many libraries for many varied applications. In a survey made in 1976 for the Library of Congress, we found some two hundred data bases of various types, which reported approximately twenty million locations or holdings of discrete bibliographic items.[1] This survey was undertaken as part of a study of the Register of Additional Locations and was aimed primarily at identifying machine-readable data that could support expanded location reporting. These data bases were in many cases incomplete in terms of bibliographic descriptors or subject access and provided only partial coverage of various local collections.

From the perspective of the local library, the potential of the collection data base becomes apparent only when the more stringent definition of collection data bases is applied: the data base must describe fully all the holdings of the library for at least a given class of material. A data base of the last three years' current monograph cataloging is not ordinarily a collection data base; a title index to periodical subscriptions in microfilm lacks the full bibliographic access that is provided for the general collection; and an annotated data base to a particular special collection, in the absence of a broader collection data base, is not a significant resource of the library.

In applying the criterion of full bibliographic description of a comprehensive local collection, we see that there are in fact very few collection data bases in use in libraries today. Among the major ones known to be operating at this time are University of Toronto, Ohio State University (partial), Florida COMCAT, Los Angeles County Public Library system, Hennepin County Library, Baltimore County Library, Rochester Institute of Technology, and University of Texas, Permian Basin. These few libraries have made the investment in comprehensive collection data bases and provide a prototype of benefits to be derived by individual libraries from the use of resource and collection data bases.

The opportunities and issues for library managers are not really centered around the question of whether libraries should run their own computer and manage their own data base, or acquire outside services. The decision relates instead to the combined use of resource data bases and collection data bases. Some of the major collection data bases listed above are managed by library administrations with their own internal system staffs and their own computer facilities; others are furnished for the libraries by data-processing departments within their parent organization; and yet others are managed for the libraries entirely by contract vendors. Many of these libraries maintaining collection data bases use resource data bases such as MARC to create their own records. The differences lie in the uses that these libraries make of their collection data bases.

## TECHNOLOGY AND COSTS

The great majority of machine-based bibliographic records produced by libraries that have built substantial collection data bases within the last ten years were created by typists or keypunch operators who read every line on a catalog card or cataloging work sheet, and locally keypunched or key-stroked that information into machine-readable form for the individual library. The costs of this kind of input were substantial and remain so given the continuing increase in labor costs in this country. Figure 1.3 shows the relative range of costs for input of bibliographic records of varying complexity.

Recent efforts in data-base development recognize the value of creating a relatively complete, flexible bibliographic record, given the ability of the computer to manipulate that record into different displays and publications. Historically, data-base creation efforts that did not result in functioning systems were most often those where incomplete bibliographic records, or abbreviated "circulation" or location records, were used.

With the growing use of the MARC format, the advantages to individual libraries of matching the MARC standard have also grown; but the cost of local input also grows, since the MARC record is a long and complex format to create. Direct cost estimates for input vary widely from library to library because of variations in requirements and direct costs charged, but the range of $1.20 to $2.80 shown in figure 1.3 indicates the relative cost magnitude for local input of reasonably full bibliographic records.

When any individual library multiplies an approximate unit cost of $2.00 by the number of cards in its shelf-list, the magnitude of the capital investment required for total conversion becomes readily obvious, and in almost every case it exceeds available funds. Some of the libraries that have built

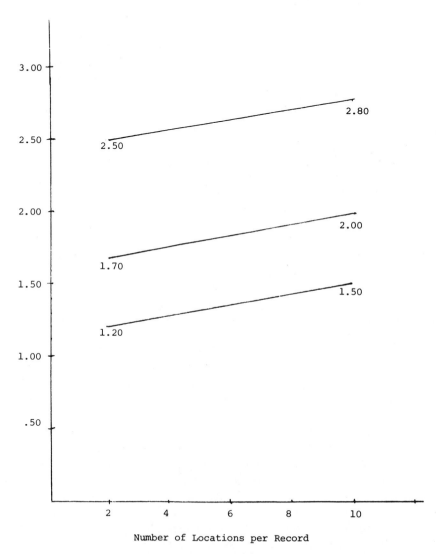

Number of Locations per Record

1.3   COST RANGES FOR LOCAL CREATION OF
      BIBLIOGRAPHIC RECORDS

collection data bases over the past decade extended the process over many years, systematically converting a portion of their files every year; Los Angeles County and King County in Washington, for instance, have been engaged in this process for more than twenty years each.

The organization and maintenance of such a lengthy conversion project is expensive and defers full benefits from the conversion until the completion of the project. The University of Toronto, for instance, has just this last year been able to utilize fully its data base for public use; conversion began a decade ago. (See chapter 7.)

Creation of a collection data base was thus beyond the reach of most libraries except the affluent. This situation has changed radically with the rapid growth in size of resource data bases and the availability of various collection data bases as resource data bases for other libraries. This is essentially a phenomenon of magnitude, because these resource data bases now contain a sufficient number of records that the average library can find in them a majority of its own catalog requirements.

This support for retrospective conversion is made even more significant by the fact that the resource data bases, provided by a variety of network and service vendor distributors, now seem to be providing precedent cataloging in machine-readable form for 80 percent to 90 percent of current cataloging. Therefore the local library investment in creating a retrospective collection data base can be maintained at minimal costs through the use of various resource data bases for current and retrospective cataloging.

Some colleagues and I have authored a detailed survey of conversion services available to libraries, which discusses in more detail than is possible here the various techniques available.[2] Total costs for a retrospective conversion (and ongoing data base maintenance) will vary widely from library to library because of local specifications, the degree to which the local collection data base can be developed from existing machine-readable data bases, and the uses to which this data base is put. Various data-base service vendors (including the networks) price their individual services in such a way that an across-the-board comparison is not possible. However, the crucial element for library managers is the range of costs associated with drawing a bibliographic record from a data base as compared to the same range of costs for original input. Depending on royalty rates for various data bases and other services attached, the size of the individual library contract and the economies available to the contractor (and other factors), the cost of obtaining a machine-readable bibliographic record of a relatively full standard nature may range between $.50 and $2.50 (figure 1.4).

The role of the resource data base (in the reduction of cost for input or creation of a collection data base) is of particular significance because input has been the one area resistant to the very rapid reductions in cost that have characterized other library automation applications in the last ten years.

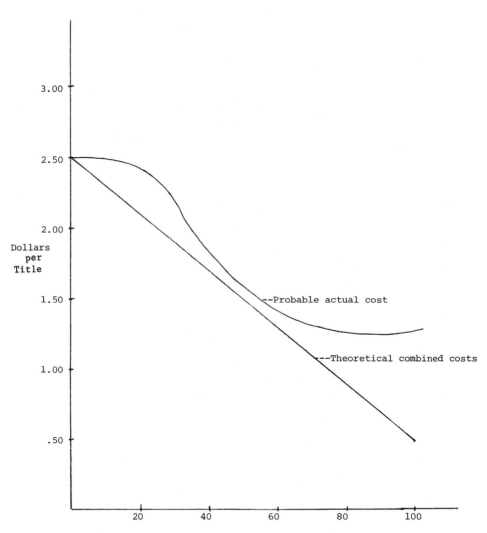

Percentage of Titles Found in Resource Data Base

## 1.4   COMBINED CONVERSION COSTS

Various projections can be found in the literature citing a decrease in computing costs to the level of 1 percent of costs for performing similar tasks twenty years ago. These projections hold an element of truth but ignore the fact that the costs of input-output devices (tape readers and CRT terminals, for example) have not decreased as rapidly as the cost of computing itself (figure 1.5). Nor do these projections take into account the fact that programming itself has not dropped significantly in cost, because of its labor-intensive nature.

Library book-catalog programs operating ten years ago could not economically accumulate and republish an entire large catalog file (even exclusive of publication, printing, and distribution costs), but today many libraries receive completely new cumulated catalogs four, six, and twelve times a year through a variety of computer programs. The rapid development of COM (computer output microfilm) has stimulated the development of microfilm-based library catalogs and catalog viewers designed specifically for public use, a micrographics application unique to the library community. The cost of basic and intelligent terminals continues to drop, and one can now buy a home computer for the price of a console television. Microcircuits such as those used in relatively inexpensive wrist-watches exceed the intelligence in many of the early computers. In fact, the power of microcircuits is so great that it seems likely that many organizations (including libraries), but particularly the home, will have not just a personal computer but may well have a whole series of personal computers dedicated to specific, well-defined tasks that require no programming or maintenance by the user.

The point of these references to related technology is that the role of the existing data base is crucial in the development of collection data bases because it so reduces input costs that the overall operating costs of a local collection data base can be justified by the number of individual applications within the local library. And this economy requires no justification based on new or esoteric services.

The problem now is to describe why an individual library should care whether it maintains a data base of its own collection or simply uses resource data bases with relatively little local planning. The following points attempt to discuss the specific uses to which a collection data base may be put in the local library—uses that are unique to the development of the local collection base itself.

## THE COLLECTION DATA BASE

The primary cost benefit of the collection data base lies in the fact that it can be used to replace and improve upon the many manual card files that dominate work procedures in most libraries. For external resource data

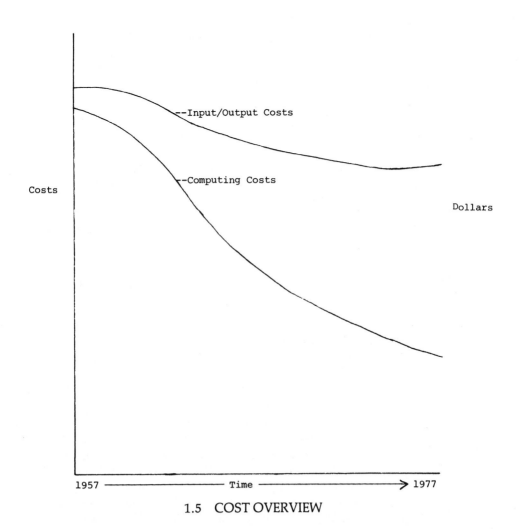

Costs

Dollars

--Input/Output Costs

--Computing Costs

1957 —————————— Time —————————> 1977

## 1.5   COST OVERVIEW

bases to support the replacement of all manual files, the information from all those card files would have to be transmitted to the resource data base and made available to each library user individually. The economics of resource data bases require sharing of common information rather than distribution of unique local information. This type of application is unlikely to grow rapidly.

With the collection data base (developed in part through use of resource data bases), local libraries can support a number of existing functions in a more efficient manner and can be free to develop new services at relatively low cost.

The costs of building the collection data base are not minor, but they should be seen as an investment in continuing library operation, at least as important as investment in stacks and reader tables. And in fact the investment in a collection data base provides some opportunities to eliminate investments in bricks and mortar.

While the strongest emphasis in library networking and development of data bases has been in the area of technical services over the past decade, the prediction Ralph Shoffner made at the 1973 Las Vegas ISAD Institute is being fulfilled: it will be the impact of library automation on public services that will, in the long run, justify capital and staff investments in the development of automated library services.[3]

I would like to divide potential uses of the collection data base into patron-related and management-related areas, and I will stress the relative importance of patron services by discussing them first.

PATRON-RELATED SERVICES

*The Main Catalog and Other Catalogs*  The first major area of application is one that has been discussed in the literature for at least a decade. With the data base, it is not only possible but practical to produce both the catalog to the entire collection and a wide variety of permuted or selected catalogs and indexes. While historical discussions have made much of this potential, real application of the computer's power to produce special and varied outputs of the data base is rarely found in practice. Most development of collection data bases, or development of specialized data bases using internal or outside resources, has focused on the creation and publication of products remarkably similar in content to the card catalog they replace.

A few examples of nontraditional indexes can be found. A particularly large and useful one is the permuted serials reference file produced by the University of California at Berkeley.[4] Most of the large catalogs produced from collection data bases have simply followed the ordering, sequencing, and display of information that characterize card catalogs. What has not been explicitly observed in published projections and discussions about the potential of the data base is that the utility of patron-related publications from a data base is directly related to the extent that the data base approaches complete coverage of a library's collections.

There are usually two sides to the shortcomings of the local library data base. It will lack information on some material newly received at the library (and almost certainly on materials on order), and few of these data bases cover retrospectively the full scope of the library's collection. The effect of these limits in coverage is to impose a randomness on patrons using publications produced from the data base. Unless patrons know precisely the basis on which materials were included in the data base, they cannot know from a search of the data base's catalog whether in fact their search has failed (that is, the material is not owned by the library) or whether the search is simply incomplete (the material may be owned by the library but is found only in a separate manual card file or a private file in the acquisitions department).

Moreover the determination of a logical basis for inclusion of material in a partial collection data base is not easy for staff or for patrons. The use of a date, for instance, seems simple and understandable, but in fact it is fraught with difficulties brought on by differences between publication and acquisition dates, initial and reprint publication dates, and the patron's lack of such information when searching. Many libraries have experienced this problem in the use of card catalogs that were split in the course of a reclassification program.

The effective public use of permuted and selected catalogs depends heavily upon the completeness of that catalog. It makes little sense to develop a special catalog of a library's Californiana if in fact it contains only material received since a given date or only material that can be found economically in a resource data base.

*The Subject Guide* Several years ago I became interested in the correlation between the use of subject terms and classification numbers in actual cataloging practice.[5] It seemed strange, but proved to be true, that little attention had been paid in the literature to the relationship between Library of Congress subject terms and Library of Congress classification numbers in actual catalog records. Through sorting a sample of records from the MARC file, we found a high correlation in practice and concluded that an index could readily be created that would relate the two for use in a given library collection.[6]

We were working at the time with the Los Angeles County Public Library system and BroDart, which were implementing a series of catalog system changes recommended in a study performed in 1975.[7] *The Subject Guide* was developed in that application to serve as a special index to the local collections in that library. It is almost totally dependent on the existence of a collection data base, for what it does is extract all the subject terms used in the county data base along with all the classification numbers assigned to titles that have used that subject term. The *Guide* is thus a list of subject terms followed by all the classification numbers used for that subject term. The first edition of *The Subject Guide* included all call numbers found and indicated the frequency with which each call number/subject term was found—that is, how many titles were held in the system with that combination of subject term and call number. A second edition in preparation attempts to make the volume even more compact.[8] Its use is almost entirely limited to patrons (or staff upon patron request), whom it guides from a subject term to the likely shelf locations of books on that subject. Although it is no replacement for the catalog, it considerably reduces catalog searching when individual items or a complete bibliography are not required.

This approach is useful only where a complete collection data base is available because partial guidance would be unsatisfactory. Conversely the local holdings of individual libraries differ so greatly that a general guide to subjects and classes (while much less expensive per copy than the custom subject guide) would not provide the precision of direction that the collection-based guide can deliver.

### VARIETIES OF DISTRIBUTION

*Limitations of Card-Form Catalog* One peculiarity of the card-form catalog and the manual systems for producing cards (or the computer-based systems used to produce catalog cards) is that the inflexibility of the card tends to force an "equality of cataloging," which may not represent the value of the material cataloged. Most use studies indicate that a small proportion of the collection is responsible for a high proportion of usage and demand.[9]

Most librarians know from experience that some books, some types of books, and some parts of books have a potential demand that justifies a bibliographic description considerably more extensive than that provided by national cataloging standards. This perception has led to local addition of annotations, local augmentation of subject headings, provision of extensive analytics for anthologies where items within the work have importance, and other varieties of extended access. (See chapter 4.) But generally the effect of manual systems has been to force catalogers to treat all items equally, even though we know that all items are not used equally and are not similar in value.

This observation is not intended as an objection to standardization, which is a necessary even if not always a cost-saving device. It points to the fact that many of the limitations in traditional cataloging systems have come about not because of standardization, or because of the unwillingness of catalogers to provide full description, but rather because of the print-bound mentality associated with the 3 x 5 catalog card. We all are aware of local decisions to curtail fullness of cataloging description because the number of cards to be filed in the catalog is a significant concern. And there was a time, early in the development of computer-based card systems, when the density of information that could be placed on the card was a significant factor in the comparative evaluation of computer-based services. The number of "second cards" as a percentage of titles cataloged was an important factor in deciding which automated system to use.

Traditional systems have also been limited in their provision for physical distribution of the catalog. It is obvious, but nevertheless significant, that a major potential function of any data base is to extend distribution of the information it contains—through computer printout, microfilm catalog, or on-line transmission.

This point has been made repeatedly in respect to book catalogs and other catalog services. Its significance here is to remind us that in the absence of a collection data base, any distribution service based on a partial or resource data base must in fact run in parallel with the existing manual distribution and filing of card files, and other manual processes. If the library does not assume the cost of parallel distribution, then we have again the situation of a partial catalog (say, a branch or department library) that makes available to patrons at that location only a fraction of the information available in the central card catalog.

*Benefits for Information Distribution* Where a collection data base provides the primary system for distribution of the library's information, the capital costs of establishing it—for equipment and printing start-up costs, terminals, and lines—can be amortized across the full use of a search covering the entire collection. And an integrated collection data base can provide variety in the form and medium of information delivery.

Using a resource data base for delivery of local information, we are restricted to what that external resource provides. For example, a library can provide a complete bibliographic entry and local call number in a catalog that it produces itself. In contrast, using an OCLC terminal for access to that portion of one's collection that has been input to OCLC provides only the information presented on the screen. Moreover if the library has utilized a MARC record, its local call number will not show on the OCLC screen. Thus a resource data-base system provides only a portion of the information needed to retrieve the desired material (unless the library always uses Library of Congress call numbers unchanged).

With a collection-based system, information delivered in any form can be made consistent, and methods of access can be standardized for the patron. A library can thus organize all types of access.

*On-line Access* The on-line public catalog is an ideal resource that still lies too far in the future for practical consideration by most library managers, partly for technical reasons but also because a large proportion of library searches require little on-line interaction, and it is on-line interaction that is the real strength of the on-line system. Nevertheless, there are three areas where more immediate on-line applications may appear.

The primary development of collection (or partial collection) data-base services is occurring in the area of microform catalogs and printed lists. Such formats always involve some lag time in publication, and there are some needs within the library that can be satisfied only by current information. It is these needs that make manual files difficult to replace because a card file (if not in arrears) is like an on-line file for purposes of retrieval. The most obvious file of this nature is the shelf-list, where classification decisions are available as soon as they are made.

On-line files can be a useful complement to off-line publication by providing a small file of current data not yet published in the off-line systems. This type of application is becoming much more practical with the development of economic microprocessing computers that provide moderate on-site storage capabilities. Although the ability of this equipment to handle whole library collections seems remote at this point, this type of on-line access can clearly handle a two-month, three-month, or six-month file in most library applications.

A second practical form of on-line access involves the maintenance of on-line files for a relatively complete collection data base but on a basis of restricted access. Here the cost of maintaining the on-line disc file is amortized against its usefulness in a particular library application. For instance, an acquisition file of materials on order can be maintained for most libraries today in standard minicomputer equipment; but the cost of distributing terminals throughout a campus or branch library system to provide the access to that file exceeds the benefits of the service. Telephones from remote locations to one terminal in the central department will provide restricted access, which may be sufficient for most of the needs of the branch or department locations. The same type of approach may work well for interlibrary loan queries.

The third type of on-line searching will be based on the capability of on-line reference service bureaus to provide time-limited access to a local or system library's data base. This approach would involve segmenting library searches to some extent, based on their difficulty, as is often done currently when local branch library requests are passed to a central reference center if they cannot be readily handled at the request site. Such a center could then provide access to an on-line file at the rate of perhaps one hour per day to search the more difficult requests, where the interactive permutative abilities of on-line indexing provide a function that cannot be obtained with the fixed-order files produced by off-line batch systems.

MANAGEMENT-RELATED FUNCTIONS

The development of a collection data base has significant implications for the management of technical services and the overall administration of library planning.

*Technical Services Needs* The impact of most automated systems on ·overall technical processing operations has been restricted by the limited nature of the data that is typically used. The data base cannot be used as a comprehensive management tool if it cannot replace the necessary technical files that have supported library operations in the past. The replacement of these files implies comprehensive data base coverage of the materials they index. The most obvious example of this problem, and the application that has so far eluded most automated library services, is that involving the shelf-list. A typical shelf-list serves two primary functions: it is the basic inventory record, and it is the classification and shelf order documentation file.

Clearly an inventory function cannot be assumed by a data base that does not include all the materials in the inventory. This aspect of the shelf-list is straightforward and obvious. The classification and shelf sequence function, however, varies widely from library to library and presents considerable demands on a computer data base because of the nature of the classification task.

A shelf-listing system must be ready to receive materials at random, identify them properly, and determine their sequence on the shelf. The accuracy of this process is important because it affects reshelving and browsing. The operation is random in nature because the daily need to assign properly sequenced numbers cannot be predicted by the nature of the material being ordered. Therefore a system that does not provide total control in one data base file or location is open to error because changes in the file can be required even while connections are being made between file A and file B.

The shelf-listing function requires verification at the time of processing, which is a difficulty with a partial resource data base (or a division between a collection file and a resource data base). This difficulty leads to the common series of steps observed in (for instance), OCLC cataloging, which could be mildly amusing if they were not so expensive:

1. The library utilizes an on-line terminal for calling up bibliographic information almost instantly across a considerable distance to Columbus, Ohio.
2. The cataloger either copies the information thus received or causes it to be printed and leaves the on-line mode of operation.
3. The cataloger physically transports the material to be cataloged and the output of the on-line system to the card file shelf-list. In a batch process of undetermined duration, the shelf-list is updated.
4. The on-line system is again aroused and the lightning process of cataloging continues. The availability to the library of a data base selection of its shelf-list is little help in this circumstance.

*Benefits for Technical Services* Integrating resource data base searching with a complete shelf-list data base would, by contrast, allow considerable efficiencies in the book-processing operation.

The same type of difficulty exists with the rest of the original cataloging

process, where verification of actual bibliographic use requires consultation of the local authority card file or a similar external or internal reference. The use of resource data bases does not support this part of original
cataloging activity in any way. The existence of a collection data base
allows the development of the library's own authority list and therefore
the integration of cataloging with the collection data base. This form of
integration is well presented in descriptions of the New York Public Library
authority control system.[10]

The collection data base is similarly useful in acquisitions management.
Since a high proportion of item requests received by libraries fall into the
two groups of data missing from partial data bases (newly received material
and retrospective collections), the existence of a partial collection data base
in on-line or print form merely provides a convenient first look, which must
then be supplemented by referencè to complete authority and inventory
files for acquisitions verification or the determination of ownership. OCLC
and automated book catalogs have not eliminated checking of public
catalogs and on-order files to verify and eliminate inadvertent duplicate
orders.

Processing control is one area where a collection data base can streamline
technical services operations and support more rapid distribution of
materials to patrons. Processing has traditionally and necessarily been
based on the premise that all bibliographic description, materials processing, and inventory control must be performed on the materials prior
to their release for public use. Some libraries have circumvented this problem in a limited way with FASTCAT systems such as those described by
Daniel Gore and others in a series of articles.[11] However, for the larger
systems, both public and academic, full and complete distribution of
materials depends upon completion of the bibliographic control process.
In practical and simple terms, this has been a necessary restraint because the
library does not wish to absorb the risk of rehandling catalog cards, processing labels, and other materials if a preliminary decision by a local staff
is changed by subsequent distribution of Library of Congress or original
cataloging. With the collection data base (pending implementation of
authority control systems that will become widely available within the next
two years, now that Library of Congress subject headings are being distributed in machine-readable form and can support the necessary data input
for machine-based authority), this link between bibliographic access and
physical availability of materials can be eliminated.

For most circulation purposes, the acquisitions level bibliographic data,
which can be obtained from the title page of the work in question, is sufficient for circulation and for inquiry about the item. With a collection data
base, a unique identification can be placed on that item, which is not
dependent upon a presumed Library of Congress card number, an OCLC

accession number, or other external bibliographic control. Copy numbering can be applied to multiple copies independent of the bibliographic description applied at the time of book receipt.

The local library can then exercise one of two options with regard to bibliographic control. It can defer input of full bibliographic data into the collection data base, waiting instead for the provision of precedent data from MARC or another resource data base; or it can proceed with partial or complete original cataloging, still leaving itself the ability to update the collection data base with network standard cataloging if it later becomes available.

Without a locally controlled collection data base, the use of resource data bases to do precedent cataloging has necessarily been tied to changes made at the time the book is processed. This, again, is because it is impossible or impractical to change the physical card files on a large scale if precedent cataloging is obtained after the book is distributed. With the collection data base, changes can be easily made.

The normal relationship of book distribution, processing, and cataloging can be varied considerably when a collection data base exists. It is then no longer necessary to determine for all time the proper subject authority, series note, or even main entry to allow the material to be used by the public. The flexibility of editing and later management of the data base, independent of the distribution of materials, can be seen in the operation of the Los Angeles County technical services department and catalog. (See chapter 6.)

Moreover with the flexibility in using the data base, we can even consider an entirely different way of managing the original cataloging function. The cost of receiving and processing external precedent cataloging (MARC or other resource data bases) is relatively low. With the collection data base, the library can, at its leisure after the receipt of the MARC records, let its subject headings newly applied to Library of Congress (and other) authority terms determine its conformance to this practice. But if the library wishes to extend the concept of variable access, the question of providing full original cataloging for materials where precedent cataloging is not found can be easily explored with the use of the collection data base. If abbreviated index information is supplied to the data base (along with appropriate status codes) at the time the book is distributed, it is always possible subsequently to compile a list of such "uncataloged" material.

I only suggest here a manual administrative review procedure. For some types of libraries, it may be desirable to review the use of materials not cataloged after the normal holding period to see whether they are likely to be worth cataloging at all. We know that the best predictor of future demand is the record of past demand; we know that most patrons request newer materials by item rather than browsing. We also know that many patrons do subject browsing by examining the shelves; but browsing can also be done using collection data base indexes like *The Subject Guide*. While we do not know how much potential demand is unfilled because complete bibliographic access is not provided, it seems reasonable to question the investment in full cataloging for materials that are not used at all within, say, a year of their original receipt.

This type of management consideration is only one of a number of economic and service management options that are opened up by the existence of a complete collection data base.

*Management and Administration* A number of administrative questions relating to the collection and its management can be addressed most effectively through the use of a collection data base.

References are readily found in the literature to the potential use of the computer for measuring profiles of the collection by subject, classification, and other parameters. Without the use of complex manual statistical techniques—statistical techniques to verify samples against the whole collection—computer analyses are only effective with a relatively complete collection data base as the analytical tool. The widespread discussions regarding the potential of circulation statistics for management information also implicitly assume that there is a profile of the collection itself against which to measure the relative use of portions of the collection.

Management use of these statistics, at least as reported in the literature and discussed by some individual librarians, is minimal.[12] This may result from the limited capability of library administrators to change radically the nature of collection development because of fixed investments in core periodical collections and departmental library funds, and the continuing encroachment of staff salaries upon materials budgets. However, the intelligent use of collection-wide data is necessary to present the case for required management change, and the collection data base provides an effective technique for gathering this data. Manual sampling and statistical techniques can be used with manual collection files to provide much of the same data, but usually the cost of developing these data exceeds their value.

These benefits of a collection data base are clearly derivative and secondary—no one would develop the data base merely to analyze it—but they should be helpful if logical management of resources is a goal of the library administration.

A final word in this area relates to inventory control, an issue commonly identified with circulation systems whose data bases typically do not provide the full access to the collection necessary for the collection data base concept. The point is that inventory control can be maintained either at the bibliographic data-base level or at the circulation level, and inventory control is equally important to management in either case.

Considerable funds are being invested by many libraries on the presumption of statistical loss figures that may not be well verified. Library administrators who have gone through the agonizing experience of taking an inventory after a hiatus of thirty or forty years would wish strongly that their predecessors had absorbed some such inventory cost over smaller periods in the past so the shock of losing 20 percent of one's collection is not absorbed all in one year.

## LIMITATIONS OF RESOURCE DATA BASES

There are at least four types of limitations that library managers will encounter when dealing with external resource data bases: control of operations, scope, authority, and quality control.

### OPERATIONS

Operations limits relate both to the fixed functions available from the resource data base manager, network, or service contractor and to the integration of those services with local library operations. An example is the limited ability of an OCLC network-type terminal to support a simple work flow in shelf-listing.

If a library wishes to enter a standing search to await arrival of MARC cataloging, this can be done with BALLOTS or commercial contract vendors, but not with OCLC. If special fields or formats are required, some contract vendors may provide these services; most networks will not. Different varieties of display and output products are available from different resource data-base management organizations.

### SCOPE

Local format needs may or may not be recognized or available in the resource data base. Local data content needs—descriptions, annotations, abstracts—may or may not be available from the resource data base and may or may not be able to be processed by the data-base system. Various ways to meet local demands for handling of location data, including circulation information, have been worked out in the various resource data bases. Integration of resource data bases with circulation systems is yet basically nonexistent.

### AUTHORITY

Problems of authority (relating to subjects, names, added entries, and other descriptive material) arise in the use of any resource data base. These data bases differ considerably in the way they handle types of entries and changes over time, in their ability to merge or integrate input from individual member libraries, and in the way they relate to Library of Congress cataloging. The significance of these issues will depend on the local library's historical and current policy with regard to authority determination and catalog entry. Although the collection data base can provide almost any level of desired cross-referencing, often the referencing is limited in existing data bases (both with regard to content and with regard to formats).

## ACCURACY

Accuracy is an issue that has both technical and philosophical overtones; quality control and data-base specification are major concerns in national network development and have been a problem in OCLC and other resource data bases.

All of the above are considerations that managers must take into account when using resource data bases. They are problems that can be managed more effectively when the resource data base is used to provide data for the local collection data base. It is worth noting again that the economics of resource data base use is the strongest factor propelling everyone toward network and collection data-base development. The economic picture will become more attractive with time, so the management of these resource data problems is not so great as to impede further progress.

## CONCLUSION

In closing, I must cite a major limitation of the collection data-base concept that I am sure is in the mind of administrators of very large research or public libraries. Even with the declining conversion and data-processing costs, and economical distribution costs, the total economic burden on a very large library developing a local collection data base is such that most will not be able to develop completely converted collections on their own initiative in the next decade.

In some areas, these large libraries are important enough to the resources of their parent organization, or their state, that conversion of their collections will be subsidized by that organization or a state network. However, many will not obtain such support and will have to face up to what it means to live with a partial collection data base coupled with the continuing existence of manual card files and catalogs.

There seem to be three approaches that large libraries can use to convert their collections to machine-readable form within their available resources:

1. Partial conversion by scope of materials: concentration on serials or other materials, on materials from a certain date, on special collections, and so forth.
2. Conversion by partial data: the most common example is conversion of circulation data to control circulation and provide some collection access as Ohio State University did some years ago.
3. The strategy identified as "closing the catalog" refers to the cessation of filing in card catalogs, with the simultaneous introduction of a machine-based catalog of materials processed after some fixed date.

With this third strategy, some libraries—Georgia Tech is one—couple a photographic microfilming of the retrospective catalog, which allows distribution of both current catalog data and the retrospective catalog to numerous locations.[13] Others plan merely to maintain the existing card catalog with minimum manual filing.

Choice of the first two strategies generally implies running a parallel production and management process, which maintains existing manual files while slowly developing the machine-based system; it generally does not provide a transition point where the machine-based system will replace the mixed system. Closing the catalog generally implies totally replacing existing operations with machine data-base management, but it still requires manual interaction steps since the retrospective card files are used as references and continue to be used generally as catalogs.

In some closing situations the ongoing data base is simply treated as if it represented the entire collection. For instance, at Enoch Pratt Library, all books cataloged by the library since 1965 are maintained in a machine-readable data base, and the catalog generated from that data base is distributed to branch libraries. No information is available in those libraries about the central library collection acquired prior to 1965. From the perspective of patrons who do not place a specific inquiry but simply use the catalogs, the collection at Pratt is represented by the microfilm catalog. (To the extent that this approach is taken, all my comments here apply to partial collection data bases as well as complete collection data bases.)

Some libraries are in a position to couple "deselection" (or weeding of collections) with the creation of the partial collection data base. That is, to the extent that the library discards older materials or sends them to storage, the catalog need not be entirely converted to machine form. The "partial" collection data base then becomes a more comprehensive "collection" data base, in proportion to the extent of preliminary weeding. This is effectively the case in some research libraries that have deferred-cataloging backlogs, where that material is largely unavailable to the public although it is in the library.

A wide variety of local issues affects the decisions that will be made in these major libraries regarding development of local data bases, and I regret that no ready comfort can be provided in a presentation such as this. I suggest, however, that two major outside activities will affect national network development and the building of local collections, to the extent that even the largest research libraries will begin to face this partial collection data-base issue because of external pressures (rather than the immediate short-term benefits to be obtained from the partial collection data base itself).

The first of the developments is the pending adoption of Anglo-American Code Revision (AACR2), which has aroused intensive debate in the profession within the last year and which should make collection data base management more attractive.[14] It will require a marked increase in the number of changes to entries and access points when AACR2-based cataloging begins to appear in MARC and in the national networks.

Unfortunately there has been no quantitative measure of this impact, but any review of the major policy changes proposed suggests that they will affect a great number of the cataloging records distributed in the next four or five years. These changes will themselves require changes—if the local library responds to AACR2—in large numbers of manual card files.

The second development is the closing of the catalog at the Library of Congress, which will affect all libraries using its copy in a variety of ways. An excellent set of studies done at the University of California Library discusses the operational impacts of Library of Congress and local library catalog closing.[15] This development will also increase the rate of catalog changes at the local level. Both of these developments together will, I feel, provide a considerable stimulus to local collection data-base development because a collection data base will eliminate many of the manual problems that will otherwise bedevil individual catalog and public service departments.

## NOTES

1. Brett Butler, *A National Location Data Base and Service* (Washington, D.C.: Network Development Office, Library of Congress, 1978).

2. Brett Butler, Brian Aveney, and William H. Scholz, "Conversion of Manual Catalogs to Collection Data Bases," *Library Technology Reports*.

3. Ralph Shoffner, "Outlook for the Future," in *Library Automation: The State of the Art II*, ed. Susan K. Martin and Brett Butler (Chicago: American Library Association, 1975), pp. 139–154.

4. Walter Crawford, "Building a Serials Key Word Index," *Journal of Library Automation* 9 (March 1976): 34–37; Stephen M. Silberstein, "Computerized Serial Processing System at the University of California, Berkeley," *Journal of Library Automation* 8 (December 1975): 299–311.

5. Brett Butler, "Empirical Relations Between Library of Congress Subject Headings and Classifications" (research paper, San Jose State University, 1975).

6. Brett Butler, "Bibliographic Subject Access: A Measure of the Relation Between Use of Library of Congress Classification and Library of Congress Subject Heading Terms," in *Information\* Politics: Proceedings of the 39th Annual Conference of the American Society for Information Science* (Washington, D.C.: ASIS 1976).

7. Brett Butler, James L. Dolby, Martha W. West, and Fran Spigai, *Improving Public Library Access: The Los Angeles County Public Library System Access Study: Final Report* (Los Altos: R&D Consultants, 1975).

8. *The Subject Guide to Books on the Shelves* (Los Angeles: Los Angeles County Public Library System, 1976).

9. F.W. Lancaster, *The Measurement and Evaluation of Library Services* (Washington, D.C.: Information Resources Press, 1977), chap. 5.

10. S. Michael Malinconico and J.A. Rizzolo, "New York Public Library Automated Book Catalog Subsystem," *Journal of Library Automation* 6 (March 1973): 3–36.

11. Daniel Gore, "In Hot Pursuit of FASTCAT," *Library Journal* 97 (September 1, 1972): 2693–2695, and his "Addendum," *Library Journal* 98 (December 1973): 3486.

12. Lancaster, *Measurement and Evaluation*, chaps. 11–12.

13. Robert J. Greene, "Microform Catalogs and the LENDS Microfiche Catalog," *Microform Review* 4 (January 1975): 30–34, and his "LENDS: An Approach to the Centralization/Decentralization Dilemma," *College and Research Libraries* 36 (May 1975): 201–207.

14. *Anglo-American Cataloging Rules*, prepared by the American Library Association, the Library of Congress, the Library Association, and the Canadian Library Association. North American Text (Chicago: American Library Association, 1974).

15. University of California, Berkeley, General Library, Future of the Catalogs Committee, *"To Close or Not to Close"*: Report—Phase I Study (Berkeley: University of California, 1975), and its *Future of the General Library of Catalogs of the University of California at Berkely: Report—Phase 3—on the Future of the Catalogs* (Berkeley: University of California, 1976).

# The Effects of Automation on Organizational Change, Staffing, and Human Relations in Catalog Departments

2

Peter Spyers-Duran

Few topics appear with greater frequency in the professional literature than automation theory or its applied technologies. Concern with this complex phenomenon is well founded; automation is considered to be the latest phase in the industrial revolution. Its impact cannot and will not be escaped by any sector of society. It is certainly becoming a dominant force in libraries, exerting a growing impact on their efficiency, services, economics, management, and staff.

Since the late 1950s, library automation charted in terms of library functions and numbers of affected staff has been moving both horizontally and vertically at an accelerated rate. (See figure 2.1.) The horizontal movement of automation appeared first in simple applications, such as circulation record management, acquisition budget control, and other record-keeping functions. Later computer-produced bibliographies and serial-periodical holdings lists arrived, followed by the major breakthrough of automated cataloging in the late 1960s. The big boom in automated cataloging came with the realization that data-base networks could provide advantages to libraries. Most recently, the on-line revolution arrived and enriched reference services by the availability of data bases in virtually all subject fields, rapidly changing the profiles of services rendered in the past.

Automation in the vertical direction has had significant impact on employment in libraries. It is not difficult to show that library automation in the early years affected primarily unskilled or semiskilled library employees by performing routine tasks. A few years later, it brought changes to many duties performed by the clerical staff. In recent years, professional librarians are being affected by the evolutionary process of automation. Indeed the changes inevitably caused by automation reverberate at every level of library employment.

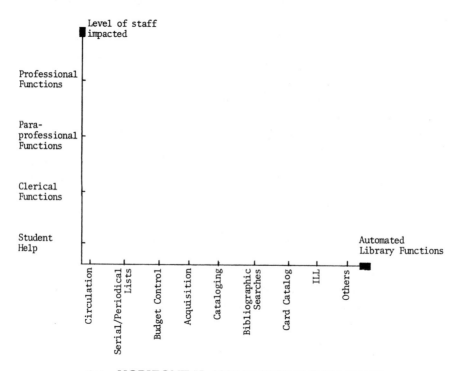

2.1   HORIZONTAL AND VERTICAL IMPACT OF
      AUTOMATION IN LIBRARIES

In August 1977 I mailed questionnaires to some 130 head catalogers serving state-supported academic libraries having an annual budget of at least one million dollars each to examine the effects of automation on organizational change, staffing, and human relations of professional catalogers and support staff. It is important to bear in mind that this project (referred to as the survey) was researched only to explore trends and experiences and not to develop statistical models that could be applied in every institutional setting. The survey also showed how the heads of cataloging view the organizational changes created by automation, and the resulting change strategy now observed and practiced. The survey found that 74 percent of the head catalogers viewed their staff as a group favorably disposed toward change. Ten percent of the group considered their staffs to be neutral on this subject. Only 16 percent clearly described their staff as having an unfavorable disposition toward any change in their department.

Eighty percent of the head catalogers reported an organizational change after automation. The most frequent type was the merger of cataloging with bibliographic searching, a unit traditionally a functional part of acquisition departments or a unit by itself. Some libraries have simply eliminated separate administrative units in technical services and have created a single department.

Catalogers reported improved work flow, more efficient work space organization, reduced backlogs, and increased productivity by their departments.

Catalog departments previously having a separate subject cataloging unit have changed to a system of sharing all categories of cataloging done by professionals and by library technicians. This, of course, had immediate implications for the subject catalogers who had to become generalists as part of this organizational change.

Staff-related changes were considerable. Probably the most significant change was reported for support staff. Changes in work assignments resulted in an expansion of duties and a greater independence for those who work on computer terminals. An increasing percentage of titles cataloged is being done by nonprofessionals, as more entries appear in the data base. This change has developed a support staff that is highly aware of the value of their contributions, although this diffusion of cataloging responsibility can make supervision and quality control more difficult.

Changes in scheduling represented a major departure from traditional catalog departmental work hours. Several libraries reported that the typical Monday through Friday, 8 A.M. to 5 P.M., work schedule had changed to a 6 A.M. until 8 P.M. schedule. Some have reported Saturday schedules as well. The need to spread scheduling over a greater number of hours per week arises from two sources. First, the computer-response time tends to be slower during peak periods of use. Consequently institutions prefer to do their search when the response time is faster, and this means a departure from the traditional workday. Second, most institutions purchase fewer terminals than they actually need. For this reason, the terminals have to be in operation ten to twelve hours a day to handle the work load. This approach understandably causes problems in terms of finding qualified staff, proper supervision, training, and motivation on a long-term basis.

Organizational changes offer numerous opportunities, as well as problems, for the administrators. Automation of a catalog department represents an opportunity to redesign the work of employees, as well as their work flow, since most catalogers find the old ways inappropriate for the new tasks. After the work and the work flow are redesigned, certain pressures are likely to develop upon implementation, and they influence four major areas: technical problems, interpersonal issues, human-relations issues, and management problems.

Technical problems arise from the seemingly limitless opportunities that on-line cataloging can offer institutions. The professional in charge of the unit is constantly challenged by the system's potential, which creates a degree of uncertainty and some guilt, by raising doubts as to whether the department is doing all it can to make the best use of technology. While the day-to-day concern may focus on hit-rate and potential downtime, the average head cataloger must be looking weeks and months ahead. Questions such as local use of archival tapes, closing the card catalog, and public acceptance of a nontraditional retrieval system call for much forethought among managers in the profession.

Interpersonal issues are likely to arise among supervisors, peers, and professional and support staff. On occasion conflict may develop because staff who cannot or will not accept automation become hostile toward those who do. In general automation of the catalog department has increased the responsibilities of the nonprofessional staffs. Increased responsibilities were the natural result of terminal work where well-trained employees work independently.

The clerical and paraprofessional staffs experienced fuller participation in departmental procedural decisions. Some libraries reported that some of their professional catalogers viewed this development without much enthusiasm. In these cases, the paraprofessionals were assigned the copy cataloging, leaving only the original cataloging for the professionals. It is not difficult to imagine the chagrin of a professional proof-slip cataloger of many years when an assertive nonprofessional assumes previously professional responsibilities on the terminal. While the importance of recognizing and understanding interpersonal issues cannot be overstated, it is equally important to realize that a truly cooperative effort is required to attain any desired goal, and this may require putting personal feelings in their proper perspective and persevering in the most productive direction for the whole organization.

There are relatively few studies available measuring staff attitudes toward computerization. One of the outstanding ones is an eighty-eight item scale test designed by Klonoff to measure staff attitudes toward computers and an automated health information system installed in a hospital psychiatric unit.[1] Klonoff's attitude scale found some alienation among the staff affected by this installation. Those involved in the automation who were knowledgeable about the system had generally positive attitudes. Conversely alienation was common, and the level of anxiety high, among staff not involved and less knowledgeable about automation.

An older study by Reznikoff complements the notion that "knowledge" and "involvement" were the two most important variables affecting staff attitudes toward automation.[2] Reznikoff also found that attitudes were associated with certain specific characteristics: age, amount of education, and length of employment.

The results of the questionnaire I sent to head catalogers support the Klonoff and Reznikoff studies. Libraries that involve their staff in the automation planning process (78 percent) had little or no human relations problem in their organization. Head catalogers by a great majority (80 percent) indicated that they do not expect alienation of staff as a general rule. Yet this same group of catalog departments reported certain common staff concerns, differing only in degree of intensity and number of staff involved.

Employment-related concerns were the most frequently reported. All libraries indicated there was some anxiety about dislocation from duties, changes in scheduling of the work week, and opportunities, or lack thereof, for advancement in a department with fewer positions.

In spite of administrative assurances to the contrary, some uncertainty about future employment opportunities in catalog departments exists. Although not openly discussed, there is some fear of layoffs, more so among the clerical and paraprofessional staff than among professional catalogers. This is not surprising since the popular belief about automation is that the bottom positions are the first to be affected. The survey indicates that fear of the future tends to be greatest prior to the the introduction of automation in a library and gradually diminishes after a year or two.

Skill- and knowledge-related concerns were reported highest during the initial stages of automation of the catalog department. The staff, both professional and support, typically worried about a new and sometimes higher level of assignment. Hewitt's study found this concern to be more prevalent in the case of support staff.[3]

Other concerns were fear of the computer and a reluctance to learn and accept a new technology and to give up old ways. Libraries responding to the survey noted that some of the older employees had difficulty learning new cataloging procedures. Some refused to learn on-line cataloging and elected instead to retire early, terminate, or seek reassignment.

Catalog department heads in the process of automating experienced varying degrees of staff ability and adaptation in this new learning experience. A proper relationship between computer technologies and employees must be achieved through an effective staff development program.

The dehumanizing effects of automation were mentioned by only a small number of institutions. Their concern was that the local authority of the cataloger was being sacrificed to the computer. It is true that the implementation of a computerized system brings with it a set of predetermined rules that must, in fact, take precedence over many local procedures and long-standing habits.

Maintenance of bibliographic quality is primarily a professional concern. The quality of shared cataloging data evoked criticism among some catalogers. Most catalogers appear to have little problem accepting Library of Congress cataloging but regard cataloging done by other institutions with some skepticism.

Concern over bibliographic quality has a broad dimension. Many systems have been established in which identical copy cataloging is now done solely by the support staff. In many libraries, 80 to 95 percent of all cataloging is now performed by nonprofessional staff working at terminals. This development has created some hostility between the support staff and the professional staff, who feel a sense of frustration.

From a managerial viewpoint, automation has a tremendous impact on staffing a catalog department. Automation can and does increase productivity. It follows, then, that the department will need fewer person-hour resources to deliver the same level of productivity. This fact alone may create enormous conflict and place pressure on the head cataloger.

Anxieties are apparent when institutions do not adequately prepare a study of the anticipated automation system. The casual introduction of an on-line cataloging system that makes adjustments piecemeal serves only to extend the period of uncertainty for an anxious staff. Most staff would prefer to have a comprehensive plan in advance that includes a position-impact study.

The increased efficiency of a catalog department after automation may depend upon many factors. It appears that the more inefficiently a catalog department operated under traditional conditions, the greater its potential for dramatic improvement.

Institutional incentives to introduce the greatest efficiency are not always present. Forty-four percent of the catalogers participating in the survey reported that they were uncertain if their library would be able to keep the "staff savings" for improved library operations, although 30 percent thought their chances were good and 11 percent excellent for retaining these savings. The uncertainty over the disposition of savings could potentially dampen the initiative and vigor with which libraries pursue catalog automation. Few library managers would willingly increase the efficiency of an organization that would shrink in size as a result of that increase. Librarians still attach prestige values to size, believing that bigger is better. This attitude may change gradually as librarians and accrediting associations come to regard productivity rather than size as a measure of efficiency and excellence. During the interim, library managers must pursue institutional guarantees that savings attributed to improved operations will not be lost to them. Several institutions have reported success in this matter. As part of the incentive program to increase efficiency, some libraries have used salary savings to finance automation and fund released time for professional librarians to pursue self-development, research, and other professional activities.

A recent study of OCLC installations reviewing longitudinal data for a three-year span indicates that terminal hands-on responsibilities had passed from the professional level to support staff.[4] The same source suggests that this switch of assignment, which released professionals from the clerical work inherent in manual operations, provided them with an institutional opportunity to engage in appropriate creative or scholarly work.

Examination of staff reduction among the survey group revealed that 51 percent of the libraries reduced their professional staff after automation. Only 35 percent of the same group reduced support staff. (See table 2.1.)

Table 2.1   **Effect of Automation on Staff Size, 1977**

| *Type of Position* | *Number of Reporting Libraries* | *Number of Positions Reduced* | *Percentage of Total Reporting* |
|---|---|---|---|
| Professional | 36 | 60 | 51 |
| Support | 25 | 43 | 35 |
| Total | 46 | 103 | 64 |

Number of libraries reducing only support staff in above group: N = 10.
Average reduction in forty-six libraries: 2.2 FTE.
Reduction of cataloging staff: 64 percent of libraries.

In 1973 in a similar study, Hewitt found that 63 percent of the forty-seven charter OCLC member libraries had reduced cataloging staff by a total of 76.83 positions.[5] Table 2.2 compares the Hewitt findings with my survey in terms of the total staff reduction recorded. Hewitt's study shows a slightly higher average reduction than this survey. The difference may lie in the fact that some institutions reporting here joined OCLC recently, and personnel reductions have not yet been realized.

Table 2.2   **Effect of Automation on Staff Size in 1973 and 1977**

|  | Number of Reporting Libraries | Number of Positions Reduced | Average Reduction per Institution Reporting |
|---|---|---|---|
| Hewitt (1973) | 29 | 76.83 FTE | 2.56 FTE |
| Spyers-Duran (1977) | 46 | 103.00 FTE | 2.20 FTE |

Hewitt concluded that the majority of libraries adequately staffed prior to automating the cataloging procedures should find it possible to reduce the size of cataloging staff. There are important factors influencing the magnitude of reduction: the size of the staff prior to automation; the relative efficiency of the cataloging system prior to automation; and the willingness and ability of a given library to optimize the opportunities an automated system can produce. Closely related to this last item are two major factors. One is the willingness of the library to reorganize in a manner that yields the most efficient results. Hewitt found that two years after automation, only 20 percent of the OCLC charter members had reorganized technical services. He noted that library administrations appear reluctant to change antiquated and inefficient structures, fearing staff unhappiness and disruption.

It would be unfair to dwell only on the problems associated with automation. The survey found overwhelming support and commitment among those who have automated. Even those who acknowledged staffing problems were eager to offer suggestions on how to prevent them or to describe how the problems were solved in their own situation. That cataloging staffs' enthusiasm and adaptability help libraries to automate successfully is a matter of record in other studies as well.[6] Catalogers, without exception, were proud of the accomplishments realized through automation at their institutions.

Libraries that have had automated cataloging for two years or more tend to look back on the problems solved with great satisfaction. It appears that time is itself a great problem solver. Libraries currently making successful organizational changes do so by increasing staff participation and staff-development programs.

For various reasons, the staff development program must extend beyond the limits of the catalog department. Significant here is the fact that shared cataloging does reduce the need for professional cataloging in a given library. While a great majority of the catalogers agree with this inevitable fact, 60 percent of the libraries surveyed indicated they are not retraining their catalogers for other professional work. Retraining catalogers for other professional assignments could reduce concern for the future from an individual's viewpoint. Retrained staff could mean new resources for the library where the staffing need may be greatest.

Francis C. Nassetta of the U.S. Office of Education reports in the 1975 *Survey of College and University Libraries* that the average annual growth of all library staffs has declined from 4 percent to 1.3 percent during the 1968 to 1975 reporting period.[7] In examining the two-year span from 1973 to 1975, he noted that the rate of growth for clerical positions was 2.4 percent (down from 4 percent growth in previous years); the professional positions showed growth at 1.5 percent (also down from 4 percent growth in previous years); and professional positions other than librarians declined at an annual average rate of 9 percent. The Nassetta study appears to support the survey in affirming the increase of opportunities for the support staff. For example, libraries often upgraded clerical positions after clerks were assigned to terminals.

Actual requirements for professional catalogers are further diminished by the apparent lack of new positions in academic librarianship. (Table 2.3 shows staff growth trends.) The declining number of opportunities for catalogers has created a situation where the supply appears to have exceeded the demand. Consequently libraries have become extremely selective and seek out only the best educated and highly skilled professionals. This is evidenced by the high expectations expressed in the few position-vacancy announcements currently advertised. These conditions emphasize again the immediate need for libraries to offer staff development programs that will provide expanded assignment opportunities. Perhaps library schools will find a new and broader role in the retraining and continuing education of librarians by participating in the staff development programs conducted by libraries.

The on-line revolution in catalog departments has been well managed by the libraries surveyed. By and large, the staff-related problems reported in the survey are preventable by proper planning, meaningful involvement, and staff-development programs. This has been clearly demonstrated in many fine institutions. Organizational change mandated by automation of the catalog department must be viewed as both an institutional and professional opportunity that can be rewarding and challenging.

**Table 2.3    Staff Growth in Academic Libraries, 1960–1975**

|  | *Fall 1960* | *Fall 1964* | *Fall 1968* | *Fall 1975* |
|---|---|---|---|---|
| Total staff | 18,000 | 25,200 | 43.500 | 55,600 |
| Librarians | 9,000 | 11,900 | 17,400 | 20,100 |
| Nonprofessional and professional staff (not librarians) | 9,000 | 13,300 | 26,100 | 35,600 |
| Libraries surveyed | 1,951 | 2,140 | 2,370 | 2,817 |

|  | *Raw Percentage Increase 1960–1964* | *1964–1968* | *1968–1975* |
|---|---|---|---|
| Total staff | 40 | 72.6 | 27.8 |
| Librarians | 32.2 | 46.2 | 15.5 |
| Nonprofessional and professional staff (not librarians) | 45.5 | 96.2 | 36.3 |

*Source:* Bronson Price, *Library Statistics of Colleges and Universities; Analytic Report, Fall, 1968* (Washington, D.C.: Office of Education, 1970), p. 2; Stanley V. Smith, *Early Release Reports for College and University Libraries* (Washington, D.C.: Office of Education, 1975).

NOTES

1. Harry Klonoff, "Measuring Staff Attitudes toward Computerization," *Hospital and Community Psychiatry* 26 (December 1975): 823.

2. M. Reznikoff, "Attitudes Toward Computers Among Employees of a Psychiatric Hospital," *Mental Hygiene* 51 (July 1967): 419.

3. Joe Hewitt, "The Impact of OCLC," *American Libraries* (May 1976): 274.

4. Anne M. Allison, "Impact of OCLC on Catalog Departments: A Study," *Network*, no. 1 (1975): 16.

5. Hewitt, "Impact of OCLC," p. 272.

6. Barbara E. Markuson, "OCLC: A Study of Factors Affecting the Adoption of Libraries to On-Line Networks," *ALA Library Technology Reports* 12, no. 1 (January 1976): 36.

7. Stanley V. Smith, *Annual Survey of College and University Libraries: Preliminary Report* (Washington, D.C.: National Center for Educational Statistics, 1975), p. 2.

# The Disposable Catalog     3

S. Michael Malinconico

An appropriate epigraph to this discussion of the efficacy of a computer output microform (COM) catalog as a potential replacement for the traditional card catalog is contained in a recent article by John North, director of the Ryerson Learning Resources Centre in Toronto. He reports the experiences of that library in converting from a card to microfiche catalog and summarizes with a rhetorical question and its answer:

> What have we gained from this transfer? A lot of staff time is now spent on public services rather than card filing; a catalog which is in a correct and comprehensible sequence; public catalogs which are 50 percent less out-of-date than before; multiple access points to our collections; [and] a 20 percent increase of our library attendance and circulation.[1]

It is perhaps significant that nowhere in this article does the issue of cost appear. This is perhaps symptomatic of a newly achieved maturity. The products of technology, having demonstrated their efficacy in the library, are no longer justified simply on the basis of potential economy, economies that in the infancy of the introduction of modern technology were often the camouflage garb for a debasement of service.

Economy and costs are still implied concerns, especially in these times of shrinking budgets. But there is a difference in emphasis. The products of modern technology are now viewed more dispassionately as means to expand the choice of instruments that can be used to facilitate the delivery of library service. The emphasis, therefore, is on the most economical means of improving service rather than on the cheapest way to provide the most spartan service.

Since the mid-1960s, computer technology has held out this promise, which is only just now being realized. Computer terminals are no longer an alien part of a library's furnishings. They have become as commonplace as electric typewriters or copying machines. It is no longer necessary to justify the efficacy of the application of computer technology to library processes. As these systems, and their costs, have stabilized, the problem confronting library administrators is not whether to venture into an uncharted realm of unknown perils but how best to exploit the rich resources of a virgin territory.

The introduction of computers into libraries has served as a catalyst, causing administrators to view library management in a new, more analytical way. The reasons are simple. Computerized systems, in general, represent a substantial financial commitment. Their introduction usually requires that operations be performed in a different way. And finally, as we are constantly reminded by their designers, the products of automated systems differ in detail from the products that have become traditional. These differences normally serve to redefine the balance that might have existed among various elements by which level of service is judged. For example, a proposed system might promise more efficient access to known titles but less efficient access to imprecisely defined items. The situation is made no less tolerable by the fact that the existing balance may be far from ideal; the need for an analytical approach is perhaps made even more necessary by this fact.

Enhancements in what we loosely call service come at some price. This price is generally monetary, but often it can be at the expense of some other component of the ill-defined rubric service. This, then, is the real management issue: balancing enhancements of service against added cost, or striking an optimal balance among its components. The intractable nature of this problem is perhaps best illustrated by noting that its solution entails an optimization equation among variables, some of which are easily quantified and others which are only qualitatively defined.

Not only do we not have quantitative measures of the value of particular components of service, but we do not even have these measures as continuous functions of the parameters that describe them. For example, we cannot define a measure of the value of providing catalog access to a title added to a collection as a function of elapsed time since its addition, or of the value of access to a cataloging record as a function of the number of ways in which access can be effected. Lacking such simple continuous measures we generally adopt discrete measures. We fix values and assume that service that falls below those levels is totally unacceptable; then we assume that if we surpass these minimum criteria, we have achieved an enhancement of service. We also, albeit implicitly, set upper bounds and assume that anything above these points contributes only negligibly to our ability to provide service. In this way we reduce the problems of assigning a continuous measure to the value of a facility to one of assigning binary values to two, often indistinctly defined, discrete points.

In this way we seek to beg the question of optimization. The final balancing of investment (generally quantitative) is effected against intuitive values assigned to each of the threshold points. In practice, we might, for instance, decide that a new title on the shelf for one month without a record in the catalog is unacceptable but that striving for a delay of less than twenty-four hours is not particularly necessary; or we might decide that subject access to materials is mandatory but that access by every word in a title invokes the law of diminishing returns.

Thus we have the dilemma of management. It is easy to determine what something will cost, and perhaps easy to determine the nature of the compromises that will need to be made, but it is not a simple matter to predict with any assurance the consequences of the variety of actions open to us. In the end, we grudgingly accept the compromises forced on us and hope that professional judgment has made the best of a bad situation. Therefore it would seem highly desirable if a course of action were available in which the constraints, or limitations, imposed were sufficiently relaxed that ample room for professional creativity is permitted, before having to capitulate to the unyielding. One of the technologies whose products are inexpensive enough to provide just such latitude is computer output microforms (COM).

COM presupposes the existence of a computer and machine-readable data. I will not attempt to justify the efficacy of the application of computer technology to library problems. This has been amply demonstrated by numerous examples from recent experience. Instead I shall be primarily concerned with the possibilities COM offers for making more effective use of a computer's ability to maintain a library catalog. A computer is an enormously powerful tool, but its effectiveness can be severely limited by the nature of the output medium used to communicate the results of its processing to a potential user. I shall assume that the use of a computerized system has been justified, but I shall not use the same arguments that justified it to justify the COM applications. I shall assume only access to a computerized facility that maintains a cataloging data base and prints catalog cards, the expense of filing those cards, and the expense of maintaining a card catalog.

A computer used in a bibliographic application is fundamentally a tool that assists in the control of prodigious amounts of data. It can rearrange and reorganize these data with enormous speed in virtually a limitless variety of ways, provided they are appropriately identified to the computer's logical faculties. It can allow us to view these data in as many combinations, and from as many perspectives, as we choose. Herein lies the rub: this ability presupposes a means of communicating the results to a human observer.

It is a painfully obvious truism that the data bases that a computer manipulates are in machine-readable form; therefore we must periodically translate the contents of these data stores into forms intelligible to humans. The most popular method for doing this is to cause the results of computer processing to be printed on paper. The larger the data base, the greater the mountain of paper required to contain an image of that data base. The fundamental problem with this approach is that such an information display is an anachronism as soon as it is created since the machine-readable data base continues to evolve despite the fact that its contents have been committed to paper.

Thus the problem confronting us—if we are to take advantage of a computer's ability to maintain a cataloging data base—is how to provide effective human-readable access to it. There is no shortage of techniques for providing access, but the operative concept is *effective access.* As soon as we introduce adjectives such as *effective,* we come up against our service measure problem; effective access must be judged within the context of the constraints implied by available resources.

Let us first consider the attributes of computer processing that are of particular relevance to the ability to maintain a catalog and to provide access to it. A computer can, with great facility, accept additions to a data base. Because of its ability to manipulate machine-readable records with enormous speed, records added to the data base are integrated instantaneously into the catalog.

Second, a computer is enormously adept at accessing all records that exhibit particular characteristics. It can with dazzling speed and indefatigable patience search through a large number of records for those that precisely match a predetermined set of conditions. Thus one can tailor retrieval criteria, and the computer will obediently provide an accurate response. The conditions specified for retrieval can be any defined within the context of the structure of the machine-readable records to be searched. These combinations of conditions can be of such degree of complexity that a human could not even expect to be able to hold them in mind while searching a manual file.

Third, a properly programmed computer can totally rearrange the structure of a catalog with unprecedented ease. This is of particular importance because a library catalog must exist in, and creates, an environment that is perpetually changing. Because of the catalog's own internal evolution and because of external changes that alter the expectations of its users, the catalog must maintain a structure that is dynamic enough to keep pace with an evolving environment. Thus, the means of access to a catalog must be varied and capable of responding to changing conditions.

There is a subtle, but important, distinction between flexibility of access and flexibility of organization. The former provides variegated access to a particular item, while the latter determines the *eidos* within which a search query can be formulated. Finally, a library catalog, since it performs a complex function, must of necessity itself be a complex instrument. If it is to serve its function efficiently—to organize and provide access to a collection—it must reveal its logical organization as quickly as possible to users. After sampling a small, appropriate part of the catalog's contents, users should be made immediately aware of the manner in which queries should be addressed. Sophisticated and varied access cannot totally compensate for a lack of consistent organization. Sophisticated access to a data base lacking a coherent structure would result only in statistical access; others would know only that they had succeeded in sampling the universe of entries satisfying their intended query, but they would never know what else might exist that would have satisfied the same query. When a query proves fruitless, if the data base being searched does not possess a coherent structure, one can never have confidence that he has indeed come to the end of an unsuccessful search. Thus the usefulness of a catalog can be directly related to the coherence of its organization and to the ease with which it can make that organization known to a user.

In summary, there are four requirements that the display analog of a machine-readable cataloging data base must satisfy:

1. It must be responsive to additions.
2. It must provide easy, flexible, and varied access to its contents.
3. It must be dynamic enough to show the effects of reorganization.
4. The display must be such that the intellectual organization of a catalog is easily revealed.

Clearly the on-line catalog provides the greatest flexibility in defining access strategies. And if coupled with an effective system to manage the data base and its reorganization, it proves enormously useful in presenting to users the effects of reorganization of the data base. Since an on-line catalog samples the contents of a data base at the instant of query, it is not at all troubled by questions of synchronism between the contents and organization of a data base, and their display.

If we now compare the requirements with the capabilities of a card catalog we would observe the following.

1. Both the card catalog and a machine-readable data base are based on a unit record concept; hence, in the absence of filing backlogs, the card catalog is quite adequate for showing additions and deletions of records. Of the known display media, a card file ranks in this respect behind only the computer terminal, provided that we carefully control the conditions by not permitting filing backlogs to develop and not substantially increasing the added access points beyond those traditionally associated with a card catalog.
2. The degree of flexibility and variety of access to a card-catalog item is severely

limited, as it is with any other static display. Because of the cost and physical space occupied by a card record, a card file is further intrinsically limited in this respect.

3. A card file is totally inadequate as an instrument that can keep pace with the metamorphoses of a machine-readable data-base's organization. The effort involved in reorganizing a card file of any substantial size is enormous. The procedures involved in synchronizing these reorganizations with those of a machine-readable file are so cumbersome that the possibility must be virtually ruled out. Although individual additions and deletions can be effected with reasonable ease, wholesale alterations of the file are quite impractical. In fact, even individual deletions require fairly awkward automated and manual procedures.

4. Because it must be reviewed sequentially, a card catalog does not readily disclose its logical organization. This limitation is slightly ameliorated by the rapid direct access it permits to ranges of limited extent.

Thus in virtually all respects, an on-line, interactive catalog is clearly superior to a card catalog. But when we review the mental optimization equation, we find ourselves faced with costs on the order of two hundred dollars and more per month per service facility. Consequently we face the inevitable management dilemma: justifying added cost against service enhancements. We inexorably come up against the upper threshold limits and inquire after an acceptable compromise.

A review of media suitable to display the contents of a machine readable cataloging data base will without doubt lead to a consideration of micrographics. The enormous information storage capacity of microforms has for quite some time presented to librarians the tantalizing prospect of a means for alleviating the constraints of austere budgets if only effective and acceptable use could be made of them. The potential of this medium has perhaps lain dormant until its coupling with the electronic technology of data processing. The synergistic progeny of these two technologies is known as computer output microform (COM). The costs associated with this form of display are low enough that it can virtually be treated as a disposable medium. Hence COM can provide a highly effective compromise between the unquestioned flexibility of an on-line system and the overwhelming inertia of the card catalog. It can provide much of the flexibility of the former at a price commensurate with the latter.

A few brief examples will demonstrate the extremely low costs of this display medium. Let us begin by comparing COM with paper. Bibliographic applications have tended to make the computer a truly prodigious printing press with a voracious appetite for paper. Consider a six-hundred-page listing. The computer paper needed for such a listing, produced in four copies, would cost approximately $15.67. The same listing in 42x microfiche would occupy fewer than three fiche and could be produced in eleven copies for $15.45 (see appendix 3.1 for details). Thus nearly three times the number of copies of the desired listing can be provided for less than the cost of the blank paper required to print it.

This hypothetical example does not include the price of the microfiche readers that would be needed before we could make use of our surfeit of copies. Let us consider a more realistic example. Assume that the six-hundred-page listing is to be produced weekly. The cost of paper for one year would amount to $815. The computer time to print a four-ply copy (assuming upper and lower case printing) would add $2,425, for a total of $3,239. If we were to produce this same listing in ten copies in 42x micro-fiche, the cost, including computer time to create a COM tape, would be $865. In one year we would have saved $2,375, enough to pay for ten microfiche readers and still realize nearly a $775 saving (see appendix 3.1).

After the first year, with the readers paid for, we would begin to realize nearly a $2,400 saving each year, or a 73 percent reduction in cost. The important point to bear in mind is not just the large saving but the fact that we have provided two and a half times as many copies of the listing—and have still realized a saving. If we are dealing with a working listing—one used by the library staff—then additional copies could themselves translate into increased efficiency and hence additional savings.

Thus the COM can render a computer-produced display so inexpensive that we need not be particularly concerned with the number of copies of it that we choose to make. In our hypothetical example, we chose to produce ten copies and to use the saving to purchase ten readers. We could have also chosen to make several more copies, which could be reserved in the event of a mishap befalling the ones intended for use.

Since we are dealing with a computer-produced listing, the amount of information included in an entry or the number of access points could each be substantially increased without exceeding our previously predicated cost. Let us assume that each entry in our previous list is produced 3.23 times by creating added entries; then the cost increases to $2,700. The savings are thus decreased to $550 per year, but we could still capitalize the readers in less than three years (see appendix 3.1).

We could consider endless permutations of this example. Instead let us address a more complex situation. Let us assume that we are maintaining a cataloging data base of a hundred thousand titles to which we add fifteen thousand titles each year. These cataloging records are such that each one creates 4.7 added entries. If we decide to reproduce an entry under each of these access points, then we might assume an average density of six records per page (including added entries). If we decide to produce a cumulative catalog at some initial time and then to produce supplements showing the additions to the data base each month, and if we were to do this for one year, we would have printed 16,667 pages at the beginning of that year and 208 supplementary pages each month for eleven months. The result is that by the end of the year, we would have 18,958 pages and twelve alphabets to consult. The cost of computer time for printing, paper for a master copy, and electrostatic reproduction of ten copies would be $8,800. If, on the other hand, we were to produce this same listing in COM but provided a complete replacement catalog each month rather than supplementary lists of additions to the data base, the cost would be approximately $8,200. (This figure includes an extra 1.5 hours of computer time each month to allow for sorting the larger list.) Thus, we would have a much more convenient catalog at less than the price of the previously assumed set of listings (see appendix 3.2).

Once again the disposable nature of a COM product is obvious. Each previous listing can be discarded because all of the information it contains is repeated in the succeeding list. In a very real sense each new display is an accurate snapshot of the data base, presenting its evolution in a time sequence of stills. If these still photographs can be made frequently enough, we would have a means of ameliorating (although not of eliminating) two of the fundamental limitations of status displays. The dynamic nature of an evolving machine-readable data base can be depicted much in the way that a series of still photographs are concatenated to produce the cinematic illusion of motion. Thus we would have a compromise solution to the problem of timely representation of new accessions if the display is produced within a period equal to an acceptable delay for catalog access to new items and a means for automatically presenting the effects of reorganization of the data base if the entire display is refreshed periodically.

There is no single answer to the question, What is the minimum size library that can take advantage of a COM catalog? The answer would be a function of a great many variables: the rate at which new titles are cataloged; the size of the existing data base, if any; plans, if any, for retrospective conversion; the number of catalogs maintained; the nature, size, and complexity of these catalogs; the amount of overlap among them; the number of COM catalogs that would be needed to replace them; the length of time allowed for capitalization of readers; and the length of time the system will be expected to be in use. It should also be obvious that the basic answer depends on the minimum size library that can benefit from a computerized system. But this is an undisguised attempt to evade the question. Although we cannot provide a single meaningful answer, we can at least provide a highly schematized model of a minimum library that can justify an automated system and demonstrate the additional savings a COM catalog could provide. This should serve to illustrate the additional economic latitude one might have in deciding to automate, or the added benefit one could derive from such a system, and indicate how the analysis might be done in other cases.

Let us assume that a library should catalog about a thousand titles per month in order to justify an automated cataloging system. Let us also construct the following model for a hypothetical library:

1. It maintains both a public catalog and a single-entry official catalog.
2. It employs student assistants at $2.50 per hour to file cards.
3. The equivalent of one half-time professional librarian, paid $12,000 per year plus fringe benefits, is required to maintain the catalogs and to train, revise, and supervise the student assistants.
4. It currently receives computer-produced catalog cards at $.039 each.
5. Each title results in 4.7 catalog cards, plus one additional card for the official catalog. (I have not included overflow cards, shelf-list cards, or cards for reporting to the National Union Catalog, which will be required in any case.)
6. It will replace its card catalogs with ten microfiche readers and twelve copies of a prospective COM catalog.
7. The COM catalog will consist of annual cumulations with cumulative supplements. (A cumulative supplement contains everything not found in the basic cumulation; hence, it supersedes all previous supplements, which may be discarded.)

Given these assumptions and ignoring the fact that both catalog maintenance and filing become increasingly costly as the size of the catalog grows, at the end of one year, we could pay for ten microfiche readers and still save $5,600. In the fifth year following conversion, even if we neglect the effects of inflation, we would be saving $4,600 and would have registered a cumulative saving of $28,000. If we were to include the effects of inflation and assume that salaries will rise at 6 percent per year but that computer-related costs will increase by only half that amount, we could also show that the costs of maintaining a manual catalog will always be greater than those associated with a COM catalog—at least in our hypothetical example. In fact, if we had included the effects of inflation, the fifth-year saving would be not $4,600 but $6,500. We could also show that with our assumed model and allowing for the effects of inflation, the savings in any single year would always exceed $2,800. (Appendix 3.3 contains the details of these calculations and the assumed costs.)

Thus COM serves as an economical alternative to traditional display media in a variety of ways. However, we should not lose sight of the attribute that keeps reappearing as a leitmotif: we have provided an alternative but the alternative generally has differed slightly from that which it replaced. These differences have two basic properties in common: first, the cost of the alternative is usually low enough that the alternative can be made larger or reproduced in a larger number of copies, and second, as a result of its low cost and mechanical creation, it can be recreated at appropriately frequent intervals.

The advantages of the first attribute should be readily apparent. We are free to determine, with sufficiently relaxed constraints, the amount of information we feel appropriate in a particular instance. The information requirements of an application can be considered with only minimal attention devoted to the limitations imposed on us by the vehicle selected for display of that information. For example, we can provide the appropriate number and variety of access points to a body of information and will not impede the user of that information. The prospect of doubling or tripling the size of a COM catalog is normally of only minimal concern. The economic penalty exacted for such a decision is generally not particularly severe nor is the simpler practical constraint of bulk. In one case at least, a 323 percent increase in the size of a listing was feasible within the economic constraints imposed for that example. The fractional increase in cost must, of course, be commensurate with the ratio by which we increase the size of the listing, but we are usually talking about costs low enough that factors as high as two or three are quite acceptable.

The minimal demand made on space by even a very large COM listing is itself an important nonconsideration. There is an enormous freedom in making as many copies of a COM listing as desired. As the number of additional copies increases, the fractional increase in cost tends to become proportional to the fractional increase in the number of copies, but we must exceed twenty copies before the fractional increase in price even approaches half the fractional increase in the number of copies. This freedom would be of little value if the space required for additional copies of the catalog precluded their consideration. For example, a 100,000-title card catalog would require 470,000 cards, 470 card trays or 8 card cabinets, which would occupy 33 square feet of floor space (even if compactly arranged). The same catalog, if typeset, would require 6,410 pages, 8 volumes, or 1.5 feet of shelf space. On the other hand, this COM catalog could be contained in 81 4 x 6 inch fiche and viewed with a fiche reader that occupies little more than a square foot of desk space. Thus we can provide information where and wherever it is needed, or desired, rather than where it can be accommodated.

The implication for increased library use is obvious. A copy of the library's COM catalog can be placed virtually anywhere on a campus that the faculty and students are apt to find it useful or convenient. Copies can also be made available off campus. Albeit a microform reader is not as glamorous as a CRT, it does constitute a relatively inexpensive form of remote access to a library collection. The same technique could be extended to provide access to the collections of several libraries. If a group of libraries were to merge their machine-readable cataloging files, they could prepare a union catalog of their joint holdings that would be automatically updated as each library cataloged its collection.

COM also offers the possibility for frequent re-creation of a file display. A catalog produced in this way is not only a disposable catalog but also a self-refreshing catalog (the entire catalog is reconstructed each time it is produced). Thus the question of catalog maintenance does not arise because it occurs automatically each time the computer recreates the catalog display.

This particular attribute ensures that recent additions to the catalog are presented without excessive delay. It can be used to advantage in other ways. It could relieve technical services administrators of their classic dilemma: "provide shoddy cataloging, and ensure timely access to newly acquired materials, but create future collection access problems; or provide quality cataloging, and as a consequence delay access to new materials, and create a cataloging backlog." If the catalog completely reconstitutes itself periodically, we could use a less than adequate record to provide timely access and rely on the automated system to replace that record with one of higher quality when it becomes available. For example, we could include an order record in the catalog until an authoritative LC/MARC record becomes available. For that matter, since we do not have to worry about having someone file order slips into the catalog and also remove them, we could even include information about material that is on order. As I have already noted, the consequent increase in the physical size of the catalog is of no particular concern.

A self-refreshing catalog lifts an important limitation imposed on catalogers by the intransigent nature of the card catalog. When user attitudes toward information and general changes in intellectual emphasis render the structure, organization, and access points of a catalog anachronisms, the cataloger can only stare at the imposing array of rodded cards, shrug, and accept the ineffable inertia of that which it should be his professional responsibility to shape. A catalog that is periodically reconstituted presents no such inertia. Each time a new COM catalog is produced, superseding the previous, we dispose of the accumulated weight of the past. The card catalog fossilizes both our good decisions and the bad ones, compelling us (like architects) to keep our mistakes always on public view.

COM technology does not of itself provide any facility that directly assists in the reorganization of a machine-readable catalog. It acts in a passive, ancillary capacity. It provides the complement to the facility to reorganize, without inhibiting a computer from performing the actual task or a cataloger from commanding it to do so.

Let us now return to the four requirements that should be satisfied by the display analog of a machine-readable cataloging data base and determine how a COM catalog compares with an on-line catalog and a card catalog:

1. A COM catalog cannot be updated as rapidly as either an on-line catalog, or a card catalog (provided there are no significant filing backlogs besetting the latter). However, the cost of a COM catalog is low enough that updated issues can be created with a sufficiently high frequency to ameliorate this problem.

2. A COM catalog cannot provide the easy and flexible access of an on-line cata-

log. It can, however, provide many more access points than can a card catalog. If enough access points are provided, we can approach (though not equal) the access capability of an on-line catalog. COM is inexpensive enough to permit a sufficiently large number of precoordinated access points, thereby compensating, in part, for the lack of postcoordinated search capability.

3. COM catalog cumulations can be produced frequently enough to reflect database reorganizations in a timely fashion. An on-line catalog can present such reorganization immediately, but one must surely question the negative effect of a delay of say one month. A COM catalog being completely reconstituted with each cumulation, and partially so with each supplement, is clearly much more simply reorganized than a card catalog.

4. A COM catalog can generally present twenty-eight or more entries at a single view. A "next screen" can be accessed with very little delay. Because of the limited size of a CRT display, an on-line catalog does not serve very well to disclose the organization underlying a file of any appreciable size or complexity because the sample of the file presented to view is too limited for one to make any sophisticated inferences from it about the rest of the file. Hence a COM catalog is clearly superior to both a card and an on-line catalog in revealing its logical organization to users.

In summary, a COM catalog can provide facilities not feasible with a card catalog. It can, with the exception of providing immediate access to the most recent additions, approach the effectiveness of an on-line catalog. The cost of such a catalog can be lower than that of a card catalog and substantially lower than that of an on-line catalog. Thus it provides a viable middle ground between the much maligned card catalog and the much praised on-line catalog.

One final point regarding a COM catalog is in order. If current trends continue, on-line catalogs will certainly be affordable by virtually any library in the not-too-distant future. This, however, will not necessarily completely replace the need for static catalog displays. Even if on-line catalogs become generally feasible economically, it will be quite some time before all of a library's catalog access requirements can be satisfied in this way. For example, it would not be desirable to provide a sufficient number of CRT terminals to satisfy peak demands and to keep them idle during less active times. COM catalogs can be used in such cases as an inexpensive way to augment catalog access facilities. John Rather, formerly of the Library of Congress, has provided a cogent analogy. The situation may be likened to the telephone company's telephone number information service. It provides both an on-line service—telephone information—and a static display service—the telephone book. Depending on the circumstances a user will select one or the other. Far from being superseded by on-line systems, the COM catalog will serve as an important complement to them.

A COM catalog can be an eminently viable alternative to a card catalog for any library that can afford access to a computerized cataloging system.

The savings effected by such an alternative can themselves be a means to justify the use of an automated system. However, the important point is not the justification of automation but that these savings can be effected while simultaneously enhancing the potential for delivery of service.

The management implications are clear: COM increases the librarian's latitude for the exercise of professional creativity. COM provides a more useful catalog, one that can be more easily maintained, or reorganized whenever necessary; it can provide many more access points; it can be used more easily; and it can exist in many more locations than a card catalog. None of these options could have even been considered with a card catalog. A COM catalog can be cheaper than a card catalog. The savings can either alleviate the pressure caused by stringent budgets or can be diverted to other desirable ends.

I should in all fairness say a concluding word about the nature of the savings. They derive only in part from the intrinsic cost of the medium used for the catalog. Nonetheless, in my final hypothetical example, I included the savings that derived from the elimination of half of a professional position. Clearly this makes no sense in practice; it is difficult, at best, to eliminate half of a position in a small library. However, we must view this half-position spared also as a means of conserving a scarce resource. That person's time that is freed can, like any other resource, be put to whatever other use is most productive; for example, that much more staff time can be made available for public service or other functions.

COM has contributed toward expanding the administrator's latitude in making decisions that could improve service. This is its principal advantage: decisions can be made that will not be enervated by economic stringencies.

## APPENDIX 3.1
## COMPARATIVE PRODUCTION COSTS: PAPER VERSUS COM

1.  Blank Paper vs. COM

      Cost of four-ply paper = \$26.11/M

      Cost of 600 pages         $= \frac{600}{1000} 26.11 = 15.67.$

      Cost of COM Master (207 frames) = \$3.50.

      Cost of Fiche Copies = \$0.15.

      Number of Fiche $= \frac{600}{207} = 2.90 \sim 3$ fiche.

      Cost of n fiche copies $= 3(3.5 + 0.15n)$ dollars.

      Cost of n fiche copies will be less than cost of blank paper, if,

$$3(3.5 + 0.15n) < 15.67$$
$$3(0.15)n < 15.67 - 3(3.5)$$
$$n < \frac{15.67 - 3(3.5)}{3(0.15)} = 11.48.$$

      Cost of 11 copies of fiche + master,
$$C(11) = 3[3.5 + 11(0.15)] = 15.45.$$

2.  List Produced Weekly

    Cost of Paper $= C_p = 52 \frac{600}{1000} 26.11 = 814.63$

    Cost of Computer time to print

        Assume:   57 lines/page,

                550 lines/minute (upper/lower case printing),

                \$45/hour (computer time to print)

    $C_c = 52 \frac{(57)(600)}{(550)(60)} 45 = 2425.09.$

    Total Cost $= C_p + C_c$

        $C_{pı} = 814.63 + 2425.09 - 3239.72.$

    Cost of computer time to produce COM driver tape

       Assume:  133 bytes/line,

              1330 bytes/block,

              0.6 in. interblock gap,

1600 bytes/in.,

125 in./second,

$150/hour (computer time)

$$C_c \doteq \left[ \frac{(57)(600)}{1600} 133 + \frac{(57)(600)}{10} 0.6 \right] \frac{150}{(125)(60)} 252$$

$$= \frac{(57)(600)(150)(52)}{(125)(60)^2} \left[ \frac{133}{1600} + 0.06 \right] = 84.84.$$

Cost of producing 10 microfiche copies and master,

$$C_m = (52)(3)[3.50 + 10(0.15)] = 780.$$

Total $= C_{c1} = C_m + C_c$

$$= 780 + 84.84 = 864.84.$$

Difference $= C_{p1} - C_{c1}$

$$= 3239.72 - 864.84 - 2374.88,$$

$$- 10 \text{ readers @ } \$160$$

$$= 2374.88 - 10(160) - 774.88.$$

Fractional Savings $= \dfrac{2374.88}{3239.72} = 0.733 = 73.3\%.$

3.    List with Added Entries

Excluding subject added entries each title will generate an average of 3.23 added entries.

Number of Fiche $= 3.23 \dfrac{600}{207} = 9.36 \sim 10$ fiche.

Cost to produce 10 fiche in 10 copies, plus master, plus computer time to create driver tape

$$= 52[3.5 + 10(0.15)]10 + 84.84$$

$$= 2684.84.$$

Difference from cost of original paper listing

$$= 3239.72 - 2684.84 = 554.84.$$

Time to capitalize 10 readers

$$= \frac{(10)(160)}{554.88} = 2.88 \text{ years.}$$

## APPENDIX 3.2
## COM VERSUS ELECTROSTATICALLY REPRODUCED CATALOG

Cost of copy = $0.038/page

Cost of 20# White Paper = $6.80/M

(See appendix 3.1 for assumptions regarding printed page, costs of computer time, and time to produce COM driver tape.)

Number of Titles at Initial Time = 100000.

Rate of Accession = 15000/year = 1250/month.

Page Density = 6 titles/page.

Total pages to be printed in one year

$$\text{Initial Cumulation} = \frac{100000}{6} = 16666.67 \text{ pages,}$$

$$\text{Monthly Supplements} = \frac{1250}{6} = 208.33 \text{ pages.}$$

Total = Cumulation, plus 11 supplements

$$= 16666.67 + 11(208.33) = 18958.33 \text{ pages}$$

Therefore, total cost,

$$C_x = \left[ \frac{(57)(45)}{(550)(60)} + \frac{6.80}{1000} + 10(0.038) \right] 18958.33$$

$$= 8808.66.$$

$$\text{Total Number of Microfiche Frames} = \frac{1}{6} \sum_{j=0}^{11} \left[ 100000 + 1250j \right]$$

$$= \frac{1}{6} \left[ 12(100000) + 1250\frac{(11)(12)}{2} \right]$$

$$= \frac{1}{6} \ 1282500 = 213750.$$

Therefore to produce 10 microfiche copies, including master, and computer time to create a COM driver tape,

$$C_m = 213750 \left[ \left( \frac{133}{1600} + .06 \right) \frac{(57)(150)}{(125)(60)2} + \frac{5}{207} \right] + (11)(1.5)(150)$$

$$= 5744.31.$$

## APPENDIX 3.3
## HYPOTHETICAL CATALOG

Assumptions:   1,000 titles/month cataloged;

$\frac{1}{2}$ FTE:   catalog maintenance; and training, revision, and supervision of clerical assistants;

$12,000/annum:   professional salary;

20 percent - fringe benefits;

1 card/minute:   average filing rate;

$2.50/hour:   student assistant salary;

5.7 cards/title:   4.7 entries/title

+ 1 card/title for official catalog;

$0.039/card

$0.05/title:   computer processing cost for production of cumulation;

$0.08/title:   computer processing cost for production of supplement;

6 percent:   salary-related inflation

3 percent:   other than personnel services-related inflation.

(See appendixes 3.1 and 3.2 for costs of COM and assumptions regarding frame density.)


Annual costs to maintain a manual card catalog, $C_{mc}$,

= Cost of catalog cards

+ card filing

+ professional time.

$$C_{mc} = 5.7[0.039 + \frac{2.5}{60} \, 12000] + \frac{1}{2}(1.20)(12000)$$

= 12717.60/year.


Therefore, the cumulative costs after n years,

$$C_{mc}^{c}(n) = (12717.60)n.$$

Annual costs for a COM catalog, assuming annual cumulations, and monthly cumulative supplements:

Total titles to be cumulated in year i

$= 12000(i-1)$.

Total titles to be included in supplements

$$\overset{=}{} \sum_{j=0}^{11} 1000j = 1000\frac{(11)(12)}{2} = 66000.$$

Therefore, total fiche to be produced in year i

$$= \frac{1}{6(207)} [12000(i-1) + 66000].$$

Hence, total cost, including computer processing time, for 12 copies of a COM catalog,

$$C_{cc}(i) = (0.05)(12000)(i-1) + (0.08)66000$$

$$+ \frac{3.5+12(0.15)}{6(207)} [12000(i-1) + 66000]$$

$$= \left[0.05 + \frac{3.5+12(0.15)}{6(207)}\right] 12000i$$

$$+ \left[0.08 + \frac{3.5+12(0.15)}{6(207)}\right] 66000$$

$$- \left[0.05 + \frac{3.5+12(0.15)}{6(207)}\right] 12000$$

$$C_{cc}(i) = 651.208i + 4910.43.$$

The cost after n years is given by

$$C_{cc}^c(n) = \sum_{i=1}^{11} C_{cc}(i) = 651.208 \frac{n(n+1)}{2} + 4910.43n$$

$$= 325.604n^2 + 5236.04n.$$

The cost difference is given by

$$\delta(i) = C_{mc} - C_{cc}$$

$$= 12717.60 - 651.208i - 4910.43$$

$$= 7807.17 - 651.208i.$$

**The cumulative cost difference is given by**

$$\Delta(n) = C_{mc}^c - C_{cc}^c$$

$$= 7481.56n - 325.604n^2$$

We can now inquire how long $\delta$ and $\Delta$ will remain positive.

$$0 < \delta(i) = 7807.17 - 651.208i$$

$$i < \frac{7807.17}{651.208} = 11.99.$$

$$0 < \Lambda(n) = 7481.56n - 325.604n$$

$$n < \frac{7481.56}{325.604} = 22.97.$$

If we were to include the effects of inflation, we would find:

$$C_{mc}(i) = (5.70)(0.039)(12000)(1.03)^{i-1}$$

$$+ \left[ \frac{(5.70)(2.5)}{60} 12000 + \frac{1}{2}(1.20)(12000) \right] (1.06)^{i-1}$$

$$= 2667.60(1.03)^{i-1} + 10050(1.06)^{i-1}$$

$$C_{cc}(i) = [651.208i + 4910.43](1.03)^{i-1}$$

$$\delta(i) = C_{mc} - C_{cc}$$

$$= 10050(1.06)^{i-1} - (4910.43 - 2667.60)(1.03)^{i-1}$$

$$- 651.208(1.03)^{i-1}i$$

$$= 10050(1.06)^{i-1} - 2242.83(1.03)^{i-1} - 651.208(1.03)^{i-1}i$$

$$= [10050(1.029)^{i-1} - 651.208i - 2242.83](1.03)^{i-1}$$

$$= \delta_0(1.03)^{i-1}$$

We now seek the point at which $\delta_0$ achieves a minimum value.

$$\frac{d\delta_0}{di} = \ln(1.029)(10050)(1.029)^{i-1} - 651.208 = 0$$

$$\frac{d^2\delta_0}{di^2} = [\ln(1.029)]^2(10050)(1.029)^{i-1}\Big|_{\delta_0} = 0$$

$$= \ln(1.029)651.28 > 0.$$

Hence, we have a minimum at

$$i = \frac{1}{\ln(1.029)} \ln\left[ \frac{651.208}{10050\ln(1.029)} \right] + 1 = 29.62 \text{ years.}$$

Because of the nature of the expression for $\delta(i)$, we can assume that if it is
> 0 in the neighborhood in which $\delta_0$ assumes a minimum, it will never cross zero.
We can examine that neighborhood by computing the following points:

$$\delta(25) = 2918.7,$$
$$\delta(26) = 2854.6,$$
$$\delta(27) = 2820.3,$$
$$\delta(28) = 2819.8,$$
$$\delta(29) = 2857.3,$$
$$\delta(30) = 2937.6.$$

We can also compute two other points of interest:

$$\delta(1) = 7155.96,$$
$$\delta(5) = 6492.64.$$

The behavior of $\delta(i)$, the difference in cost between a card catalog, and 12 copies
of a COM catalog is shown in figure 3.1. Graphs are shown for this difference (expected savings) with and without the effects of inflation. The graph ignoring
inflation (the straight line) shows the behavior one might expect: the cost of
the COM catalogs exceeding the cost of a card catalog in time; hence, the savings
becoming negative. On the other hand, from the graph in which inflation is
included, the cost of maintaining a card catalog will always exceed the cost
of 12 COM catalogs, and the difference will actually increase with time.

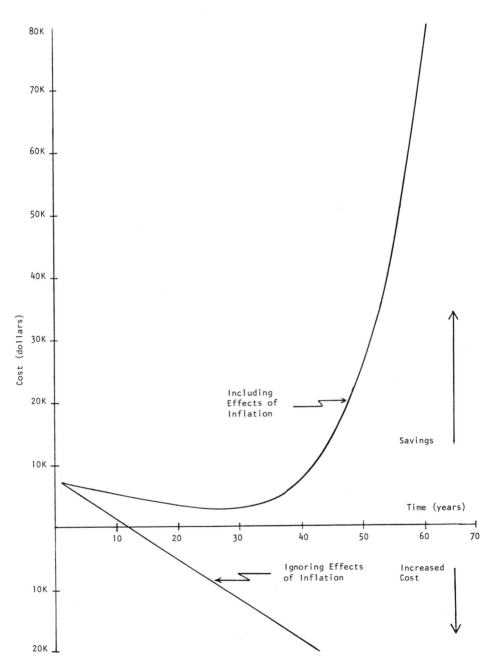

Cost (dollars)

80K

70K

60K

50K

40K

30K

20K

10K

Including
Effects of
Inflation

Savings

Time (years)

10    20    30    40    50    60    70

Ignoring Effects
of Inflation

Increased
Cost

10K

20K

3.1    DIFFERENCE IN COST BETWEEN TWELVE COPIES OF A
COM CATALOG AND A SINGLE CARD CATALOG

The same phenomenon is depicted in figure 3.2, but here the two costs are shown separately rather than their difference. This figure shows two sets of graphs. In the one excluding inflation, the cost of 12 COM catalogs overtakes the cost of a card catalog. However, when inflation is included, COM catalog costs never equal card catalog costs. And, in fact, the two diverge in time, with card catalog costs increasing much more rapidly than COM catalog costs.

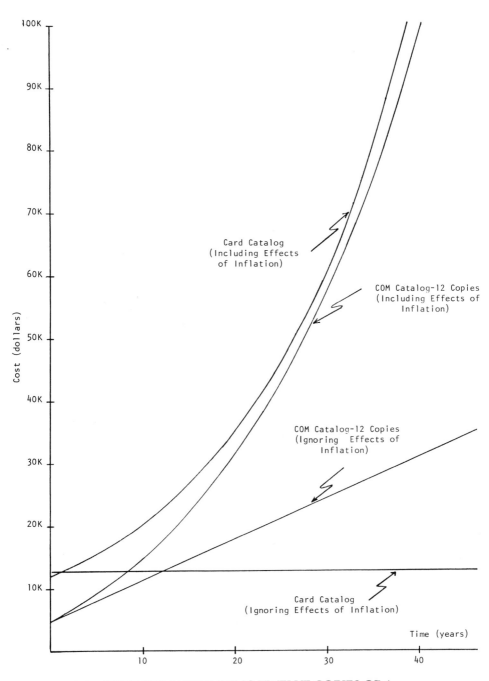

Card Catalog
(Including Effects
of Inflation)

COM Catalog-12 Copies
(Including Effects of
Inflation)

COM Catalog-12 Copies
(Ignoring Effects of
Inflation)

Card Catalog
(Ignoring Effects of Inflation)

3.2  COST OF MAINTAINING TWELVE COPIES OF A
COM CATALOG AND A SINGLE CARD CATALOG

# The Automated Catalog and the Demise of the Cataloging Mystique Or, Here Comes the Catalog the People Always Wanted . . . Maybe

# 4

Sanford Berman

Yes, Melville, there is a cataloging mystique. It may not be fully conscious and deliberate, but it is nonetheless real. And it performs a function much like mystiques elsewhere: in other, often more exalted professions—like law, medicine, traffic control, and soldiering —

- Why does the judge always appear late, in long robes, sometimes bewigged, and on a plane higher than anyone else in the courtroom? And why is so much legal discourse in Latin? Or in a jargon, presumably English, that sounds foreign to laypersons?
- Why must you always wait to see a doctor and usually find him or her outfitted in blinding white, absorbed in mysterious charts and files, and surrounded by intimidating instruments? Why do doctors transcribe notes and prescriptions in alien words and undecipherable scripts? Why do they talk about you among themselves, near enough to be seen but not to be heard?
- Why do Los Angeles motorcycle cops look like something out of *Star Wars*?
- Why the infinite layers of braid, buttons, and technicolor ribbons on major generals? Why do drill sergeants strut about with swagger sticks and speak in a strange, primate dialect whose vocabulary and syntax are known only to themselves?

In short, why all these "appearances" and "talking in tongues"?

Well, they are devices for keeping the insiders in and the outsiders out. They are mechanisms for preserving the integrity, the sanctity, and the safety of a cult or sect. They establish distance between the admitted and the uninitiated. They promote awe. And dependency. They suggest the unfathomable, the unapproachable, the unimpeachable. For those who maintain such appearances and talk in tongues, these are means to power, to security, and to ego gratification. They are ways to reinforce the differences between subjects and objects, between us and them.

Now, isn't it a bit much to claim any serious resemblance between courtrooms and catalogs, between swagger sticks and subject headings, between major generals and main entries? I don't think so.

What are brackets, slashes, and equal signs in catalog entries if not mystical markings?

Don't these abbreviations belong to an arcane language, perhaps developed by Druid priests, a kind of secret code that only librarians can now interpret:

| | |
|---|---|
| b. | ill. |
| b&w | ISBD |
| c. | ISBN |
| ca. | l. |
| cm. | mm. |
| col. | min. |
| d. | p. |
| ed. | rev. |
| enl. | s. |
| fl. | sd. |
| fr. | si. |
| s.l. | tr. |
| s.n. | v. |

Isn't there a wiser-than-thou mystique at work in the creation of personal name forms like Mozart, Johann Chrysostom Wolfgang Amadeus; Wilde, Oscar Fingall O'Flahertie Wills; Mozart, Wolfgang Amadeus; and Wilde, Oscar.

And what about subject-cataloging a work on jellyfish under *MEDUSAE,* on the Ice Age under *Glacial Epoch,* on the Asiatic wild horse under *Equus Przewalskii,* or on slipped discs under *Intervertebral Disk Displacement*? Doesn't that establish a distinct gap, a distance, a gulf between the knowledgeable ins and the stupid outs?

Why must a book on native Americans by Jamake Highwater be entered under *Marks, J.,* an author who writes exclusively on pop music? Or catalog users be shunted from Michael *Brett* to Miles *Tripp* when it is clearly "Brett" who appears as the author on the title page and in reviews?

And isn't it a form of aristocratic, high-culture mystique (or conceit) when catalogers simply cannot be bothered with the purely existential; with ideas, modes or movements that may indeed be short term, if not even faddish, but that are still meaningful to many of their less-ethereal contemporaries?

- Why haven't any Dewey numbers been specified yet for *Computer Games, War Games, Rope Skipping, Roller Hockey, Trick Skiing, Darts, Frisbee, Skateboarding, Football, Pyramid Energy,* and *Gum Chewing*? Or even for such solid topics as *Space Colonies, Appropriate Technology, Terrorism, Battered Women* and *Genetic Engineering*?

- Why did it take ten years to innovate a subject heading for *Rock Music,* forty-seven years for *Country Music,* and over sixty for *Gospel Music*? Why are we still waiting for *Rhythm and Blues Music, Trail Bikes, Kit Cars, Horseshoe Pitching, New Age,* and *Orienteering* to be validated with a holy imprimatur?

Like other mystiques, the cataloging variety also serves to keep certain kinds of lower-order creatures in their place, to remind them that this is a man's world, a Christian world, a white world, a middle-aged world, a heterosexual world, and a middle-class, profit-making world. This social mystique operates mainly through loaded words and outright omissions.

- Children are "disciplined" and "managed," not reared or guided.
- All religions but Christianity worship qualified or glossed gods (definitely not the Genuine Article).
- The position of Jews in larger societies is made permanently tenuous, questionable.
- The earth's darker peoples are ordinarily "underdeveloped," "primitive," exotically "tribal"—in essence, species of tropical wildlife.
- There is little evidence that the weak and oppressed have often rebelled. Or the moguls been called to account.
- The young, the very old, the impecunious, the boat rockers, and the despised get very little help, very little sympathy, and very little notice.

For doubters, here are a few questions:

- In how many catalogs can you find gay novels, plays, and magazines under appropriate subject headings?
- In how many catalogs can people directly and quickly find material on job hunting? On welfare rights? Or on low-cost cooking and travel?
- How many catalogs subject-trace items on family planning, national liberation movements, open housing, food co-ops, homesteading, Harlem renaissance, child advocacy, suspects' rights, patients' rights, racism, sexism, ageism, homophobia, inner city, red power, or senior power?
- Why did works severely ridiculing President Nixon—like Philip Roth's *Our Gang* and Joseph Wortis's *Tricky Dick and His Pals*—either get classed as fiction or juvenilia and in each case without any kind of "Nixon" or "Watergate" subject tracings? And why was the 1973 title, *What Nixon Is Doing to Us,* not made accessible by means of headings for *Nixon, Poverty, Social Darwinism,* and *U.S. Social Policy*?
- Why was a work titled *Effective Parents/Responsible Children: A Guide to Confident Parenting* (a book that includes material on slow learners, hyperactive children, and the "withdrawn and fearful") solely subject traced (actually mistraced) under *Discipline of Children*? And how many libraries either undid that absurdity or at least expanded the subject access with more and better tracings?
- Why are the various novels in Arnost Lustig's Children of the Holocaust series inaccessible by means of series' or subject tracings?
- Why is the anthology, *Authority of Experience: Essays in Feminist Criticism,* not under *Feminist Criticism* as either a subject heading or added title entry?

- Why can't children, parents, or teachers find anything listed in most catalogs under *New Baby in Family, First Day in School, Moving to a New Neighborhood, Overnight Visits, Cousins, Foolishness, Hiccups, Neatness and Messiness, Opposites, Tall Tales, Teasing, Unhappiness,* and *Bullying and Bullies?*
- Why does the descriptive cataloging of Helen Cyr's *Filmography of the Third World,* a 1976 Scarecrow Press volume, provide no hint that over seventy pages of annotated entries deal with North American minorities—native Americans, Asian-Americans, Afro-Americans, and Latinos? And why is there no subject access to that large block of material (the only tracings being for *Underdeveloped Areas)?*
- Why, in nearly all library catalogs, does it appear that Japanese-Americans during World War II were merely—if not even benignly—"evacuated" and "relocated" from the West Coast rather than forcibly interned in concentration camps?
- Why does the CIP treatment of New Glide Publications' upcoming *Chutzpah: A Jewish Liberation Anthology,* fail to trace "Jewish liberation anthology?" And why is the sole subject access by way of *Jews—History—20th Century,* when in fact the work does not concern history but instead deals importantly with Jewish radicalism, homosexuals, and women, with anti-Semitism and the contemporary Jewish-American scene?
- Why was *Oral Contraceptives* not assigned as a subject tracing to Natalee S. Greenfield's *"First Do No Harm . . .": A Dying Woman's Battle against the Physicians and Drug Companies Who Misled Her about the Hazards of the Pill?*
- When cataloging Cora Bodkin's *Crafts for Your Leisure Years,* why was no subject heading created and applied that would have linked this work with its intended audience—senior citizens?
- Why does the subject cataloging for John Shearer's Billy Jo Jive books ignore the obvious fact that the boy detective and most of his companions are black?
- Why is there no "Jewish" approach to Charles Reznikoff's *Poems, 1918-1936,* the first in a series of his "Complete Poems" to be issued by Black Sparrow Press?
- Why, for *Barron's How to Prepare for the TOEFL—Test of English as a Foreign Language,* was there no added entry made for "TOEFL" or "Test of English as a Foreign Language?"
- Why must over-sixty catalog users be compelled to find materials about themselves under the clinical, patronizing, and nearly lifeless rubric, *AGED?*

Having mentioned "lower-order creatures," it is also necessary to mention "lower-order media," for the mystique unmistakably favors print, placing records, tapes, films, kits, and slides in secondary, apartheid-like categories. Books enjoy the best treatment, while audiovisual media—if handled at all—are customarily branded in some way, undercataloged, and physically segregated from the print mainstream. The message could hardly be more explicit: This is ephemeral, marginal stuff, mostly stocked to pacify snotty kids or functional illiterates and surely not to be taken seriously."

On another occasion earlier this year, I posited three principles or guidelines that ought to underlie and animate all cataloging and catalogs:

- *Intelligibility*. Bibliographic data— the substance and format of catalog entries —should be helpful to catalog users, and they should make sense.
- *Findability*. Access should be quick and capacious. Among other things, this involves using familiar, contemporary language; entering works under the author's title-page name; and assigning enough added entries—for titles, subtitles, catch titles, collaborators, and subjects—to make the material findable where people are most likely to look for it.
- *Fairness*. Fairness or equity toward the material being cataloged and—with special regard to subject cataloging—to the topics themselves.

The cataloging mystique, in its various forms or trappings, violates or frustrates every one of those principles. And my thesis here is that merely replacing a manual cataloging system with an automated one, or substituting COM for cards, will not in itself undo the mystique. However, the decision to automate, if made in tandem with a decision to catalog intelligibly, usefully, and fairly, could pulverize the mystique and result in a product that is superior in format, timeliness, and content to anything we have known before, a catalog that turns on rather than alienates the user, that provides access to all media equally, and proves economically smart because it truly maximizes exploitation of the library's expensive resources and greatly enhances the library's image as a modern, responsive institution. What does this vision imply?

1. Automation is no more than a tool, a means to an end. The end requires an automated system to be multipurpose and flexible. It must not only store bibliographic records and be able to output them in desired formats—book, microfilm, fiche—but also must permit manipulation of those records and of the authorities represented by main entries and tracings. For example, it should allow the suppression or replacement of ISBD elements and other unwanted data (such as ISBN numbers and prices). It should allow the addition of "sequel" notes and award or prize headings to individual records. And it should allow the alteration of subject terms without concurrent changing of all affected records. (It should be possible, for instance, to transform the heading *Libraries, University and College* to *Academic Libraries* without also altering the subject tracing on each bibliographic record that is involved.) Outside or shared copy can never be accepted unquestioningly but must be checked—critically— against the material in hand. This is mandatory for several reasons apart from sheer mystique: there are inevitable mistakes and oversights made at central cataloging sources—including the Library of Congress—because of the tremendous materials influx, quota pressures, and overspecialization (for example, DDC numbers and subject tracings are assigned by different persons and frequently do not harmonize). And CIP records, of course, are at once incomplete and too often wrong. Further, a given work may contain material of significant local interest that is worth highlighting through notes and analytics, but is hard to highlight what you do not see.

3. Standard cataloging authorities or schemes—like DDC, AACR, Sears, and LCSH—can no longer be regarded as sacrosanct or immutable. Rather they should be considered as cataloging aids, to be tailored or transmuted as necessary to meet the requirements of the library's collection and clinetele.

4. Catalogs deserve careful and thorough maintenance which can best be done locally. This encompasses adding and deleting "see" and "see also" references, introducing links to variant name forms (especially pseudonyms), composing scope and history notes, closing authors' dates, and resolving authority confusions or discrepancies.

5. Probably most startling to administrators as well as library educators, this vision implies that libraries may need more, not fewer, catalogers and that they should be of a somewhat different breed than in the past: dynamic and autonomous instead of passive and acquiescent; people rather than punctuation oriented; alive to the world outside; and friends—at least in spirit—to all media, ages, colors, classes, and life-styles. They should be creative, unorthodox, and constructively rebellious. (Few library schools have thus far geared their admission policies or curricula to produce such graduates.)

To wrap it up: New software and hardware alone will not necessarily or automatically undo that ancient, wasteful, alienating mystique. But if the new technology were fused with a small revolution in attitudes, we could enter a golden age of cataloging. Do we want to? Or is the old mystique too comfortable?

# Effect of National Networking on Catalog Management Decisions

**5**

Henriette D. Avram

---

Webster defines *national* as "of or relating to a nation."[1] Based on that definition, a national network is a network of a nation, or a nationwide network. It is in this context that I use the term *national network* as opposed to a second definition by Webster of the term *national*, that is, belonging to or maintained by the federal government.

A national library network is the organization of libraries and other information services on a nationwide scale in such a way that member institutions and their users have access to the bibliographic data pertinent to, and thus to the materials available in, any other member institution through that institution's own system or through a system in which it participates. The network can exist only through the use of computer and communication technology. The increased cost of resources and the lack of funding to meet this increased cost, all too familiar topics of the past decade, have resulted in the acknowledged need for sharing or networking, and the technology has provided a possible solution.

Existing library network organizations in the United States are principally of two types. The first type, which I shall call a utility, is made up of organizations that maintain large on-line files of bibliographic data and provide various technical and public services to individual institutions. Examples are the Bibliographic Automation of Large Library Operations Using a Time-Sharing System (BALLOTS), the Ohio College Library Center (OCLC), the Research Libraries Group (RLG), and the Washington Library Network (WLN). The second type of library networking organization brokers computer-based services from one or more of the utilities for its member libraries and may operate other bibliographic services, such as a union file of location information, a photocopy center, or computer-based information retrieval services. (The information retrieval services at this time are mainly commercial services.) The New England Library Network (NELINET), the Southeastern Library Network (SOLINET), the Federal Library Network (FEDLINK), the Indiana Cooperative Library Services Authority (INCOLSA), and the Bibliographic Center for Research (BCR) are examples.[2]

Within the utilities, two major approaches toward "automated cataloging" can be seen.[3] The first is that cataloging data representing the collection of an individual institution are not maintained in the utility's on-line file. The system maintains in its master file only the first record input for each bibliographic item. An exception to this could be the case where a Library of Congress record, if available, overrides any other record. Thus if an institution finds a record in the system representing the bibliographic item in hand, any modification made to that record to represent the specific bibliographic item according to the cataloging conventions of the institution is not maintained in the master file but is sent to the institution as a catalog card or as a record of magnetic tape. The main point is that the catalog of the individual institution is maintained by that institution and does not exist in its entirety in the on-line file. Institutions using this type of system are primarily those that maintain a card catalog, although the individual institution could conceivably set up its own automated system using records supplied by the utility.

In the second approach, cataloging data representing an individual institution's collection are maintained in the utility's on-line file. Printed cards, book-form catalogs, or magnetic tape records may be produced, but the significant characteristic is that the institution's catalog is available in the utility's on-line file. The design of such a system permits either multiple records representing the different cataloging conventions of different institutions or, through the use of an authority control system, local variations within the single record.[4]

OCLC is the largest utility in existence today with the greatest number of institutional members. It uses the first approach to automated cataloging. The catalog of the institution is not maintained in the on-line file.

In 1975, Sue Martin, addressing the library networking activities of that year, stated that "the centralizing role abdicated by the Library of Congress and/or NCLIS remains vacant," and "libraries and networks have entered cooperative efforts without concrete plans for using the system, expanding the usage within each library, and interfacing the system to other similar systems. They may operate successfully in this manner for a time, but there will be in the future a nationwide need for additional standards and practices to accommodate the complexities of our growing bibliographic and technological apparatus. When this time comes, it is to be hoped that the lacking plans and guidelines will have been provided."[5] It was exactly this lack that created the environment for the Librarian of

Congress to establish a Network Development Office (NDO) in order for the Library of Congress to participate more actively in national network planning with other network-related organizations and maintain closer cooperation with the National Commission on Libraries and Information Science (NCLIS).

Over the past year, the activities of NDO and NCLIS have been varied, but all have concentrated on trying to bring the disparate networking efforts into some kind of cohesive whole while providing some of the missing links. The Network Advisory Group, made up of the policy makers of major networking organizations, provides guidance to NDO.[6] The Network Technical Architecture Group, established by the Network Advisory Group, is concerned with the design and the implementation of the interconnection among the utilities and with the configuration of the national data base. The linking of the utilities will be an important first step toward a nationwide system because it will enable the members of one utility, who are currently restricted to the records existent in one data base, to have access to records in other large data bases. The linking will also allow the utilities more flexibility with respect to which records to keep on line. The results of an effort currently under way in NDO to find solutions to the problems of building a logically consistent national library network union catalog created by many institutions will be input to the Network Technical Architecture Group.[7] This work deals with authority, bibliographic, and location files in a national setting.

A subcommittee of the Network Advisory Group has been formed to write a work statement to seek a consultant to recommend a method of determining the legal and organizational structure of the library bibliographic component of the network.[8] This subcommittee will submit the work statement to the parent group for review and evaluation, and the work statement will receive wide distribution.

In addition to these efforts, work is under way to develop several standards required for computer-to-computer communications. These standards are being developed under the auspices of various organizations in full coordination.

In summary, the centralizing role advocated by Sue Martin is being performed by a variety of organizations working cooperatively toward a common goal.

## MANAGEMENT CONSIDERATIONS

The national network will be a network of networks. It appears likely that individual libraries will join regional or other networks, which in turn will become members of the national network. One of the major decisions managers have to make is whether to join any network or remain unaffiliated. This decision may be tempered by the importance they assign to the evolving national network. The very fact that there may be a national network may sway them in favor of or against joining a network.

Once libraries have decided to join a network, the decision becomes which one. Asking (and answering) some questions may help managers to make the selection:

Does the purpose of the network match the goals of the library?

What other institutions are participating in the network, and what have been their experiences?

What is the network's attitude on technical and cataloging standards?

Will the network provide the services needed to satisfy patrons?

What are the costs of joining the network and the cost of the services?

What is the network governance?

Does the network provide all the training required?

What will be the manager's involvement with technical matters?

Will the network keep current with changing technology?

Is the network system reliable? Are there back-up facilities?

Are there provisions for data base integrity?

Decisions may be influenced by the importance the manager assigns to the national network and whether the network under consideration intends to join the national network.

Management's planning function has changed drastically over the past several years. There are new options and new tools, and managers must remain aware of what the technology means to their institutions in order to exercise management responsibility to plan. Institutes are becoming increasingly available. Articles and reports assist managers in evaluating whether an institution should join a network and, if so, which one. The two most recent that I have seen are those issued by the California Library Authority for Systems and Services (CLASS) and the Markuson report in the American Library Association's *Library Technology Reports*.[9] The CLASS report is a comparison of the BALLOTS system and the OCLC system, and the Markuson report concentrates on the OCLC system.

A national network will have an impact on catalog management decisions in a variety of areas. For each decision, there may be pros and cons. In the final analysis, there will be a trade-off but one thing should be kept in mind: a network does not negate management responsibility to incorporate innovative ideas in library operations in order to provide new and better services in the absence of increased funding and in the face of rising costs.

## LIBRARY OF CONGRESS

Any discussion of the catalog management decisions must include at least a brief description of the Library of Congress's operations and future plans since its services will be a major component of a national network.

The library's plans have not changed substantially since 1971 when the Librarian of Congress, L. Quincy Mumford, approved two systems: a core bibliographic system for the control of bibliographic information for internal processing within the library and a national bibliographic service for the support of the nation's libraries. The national bibliographic service is being built using data generated by sources external to the library (national and international), as well as data generated by the core bibliographic system, and these data will be available in a variety of forms, including hard copy, microform, magnetic tape, and on-line.

The Library of Congress distributes approximately two hundred thousand MARC records per year covering books in all roman alphabet languages (including COMARC records), and serials (including CONSER records), films, and maps in all languages. Canadian MARC records for books are converted to the library's MARC format and made available for distribution. Library subject headings are also included in the distribution service, and name authority records will be available in the near future. Printed cards, the films book catalog, library subject headings in hard copy and microform, and the Register of Additional Locations in hard copy and microform are produced from the automated system. Internally, the MARC files, the in-process file, and the Register of Additional Locations are available on-line, and the MARC files are available to Research Libraries Group in a data communication link between the Library of Congress computer and the computer at the New York Public Library.

Plans include adding the in-process records to the MARC Distribution Service, making all bibliographic, authority, and location files available on-line with additional types of access, expanding the remote input of records beyond the present CONSER and COMARC projects, and making available the data from the various countries with which the library is entering into international exchange agreements. On-line bibliographic, authority, and location files will be available to a selected number of organizations in a pilot project that is in the process of definition. The expectation is that operational on-line services will be available principally to networks.[10]

A recent study performed on contract to NDO and funded by NCLIS compared these operational and planned services with those of the various networks and library systems around the country in order to assist in the determination of the role of the Library of Congress in the evolving network.[11] There was great interest expressed by those surveyed in having remote on-line access to the library's files with computer-to-computer transmission of requested records. One of the suggestions coming out of the study was to develop the capability to search the library's in-process file to determine if an item is in the cataloging process and to post to the record a request to upgrade the processing priority. The result of such a capability could be that needed items would be cataloged more quickly. An expansion of this idea would be to make available the MARC international records for users to post requests for cataloging by the Library of Congress. One of the principal findings of the study was, however, that the Library of Congress's cataloging service was the most important it provided to the nation's libraries and that all efforts should be made to make this service more timely.

The Library of Congress's commitment to national networking and to making its cataloging services available through networks should have a bearing on the future direction of American libraries.

## AACR2 AND CLOSING THE CATALOG

The adoption of AACR2 by the Library of Congress and the closing of its catalogs in 1980 will have an impact on institutions using the library's cataloging products. Regardless of the form of these catalogs, libraries will have to decide whether to close the old catalog and start anew or incorporate new headings into the old catalog.

If the decision is to close the old catalog, will a reference structure be set up to interrelate the old (all past rules, including AACR1) and the new AACR2), or will the new catalog be wholly new? If the prospective catalog is to be maintained in machine-readable form, will the old catalog be converted to a machine-readable catalog? If so, will the old catalog be updated to the new rules? And what will libraries already maintaining a machine-readable catalog do with the pre-AACR2 cataloging contained in it? Many of these problems could be alleviated through the use of a sophisticated automated authority control system, but libraries are just beginning to develop these systems.

These considerations have been aired at several American Library Association Information Science and Automation Division conferences. The closing of the Library of Congress's catalog and the implementation of AACR2 will affect the MARC data base, which, it is anticipated, will be modified over time to reflect the change in headings under AACR2. As the proverb states: "The word is quickly spoken but the deed takes longer."[12]

The closing of the catalog, the implementation of AACR2, and the updating (or not) by the Library of Congress of the approximately one million MARC records will involve all libraries and their budgets. From a nationwide perspective, the adoption of AACR2 by the Library of Congress appears to imply that the future national library network union catalog data base will have records cataloged according to AACR2. This will have an impact on networks (as well as on individual libraries) that receive Library of Congress data and/or report to the national union catalog, and, of course, there are implications for staffing to implement whatever decision is made.

## STANDARDS

The existing utilities differ in their approach to the storage, retrieval, and manipulation of bibliographic data. The problem is to so interconnect these systems that data can be shared across the systems. There are three areas where standards are required to make this interconnection effectively.

First, the majority of utilities have specified their input procedures to approximate closely Library of Congress cataloging practices and MARC procedures for content, content designators, and character sets.[13] MARC records are rich in content and content designation since they were designed for a multiplicity of users and a multiplicity of uses rather than for any single purpose—catalog cards, book catalogs, circulation, and so forth. Adherence to standard cataloging conventions, standard subject headings, and standard classification systems brings closer the day when there will be a consistent, and therefore more usable, national data base.

Second, if the utilities were interconnected within the present state of the art, the burden of using the multiple data bases would be placed on the user, who would have to know the command language and search arguments for each system in the network. This would be no different than the problems an operator would be faced with if his library were a member of OCLC or BALLOTS, for example, and had access to Library of Congress files as well. Searchers would have to be trained in and remember the access methods of each system used. Research is under way toward solving the problems of multiple command languages. This particular problem is created by the design differences between systems, and there is no reasonable possibility that all the systems will be redesigned. One solution might be the design of a common command language that would be converted to the particular commands of the system being accessed. Other approaches are also being investigated, all aimed toward making the use of multiple on-line data bases simpler for users.

Third, in order to interconnect the utilities, standard communications protocols are needed to transmit data from one computer to another. Each utility will have an interface configuration (hardware and software) into the network, which, among other procedures, will translate to and from the network protocols. Currently these protocols are being worked on by various groups.

All of these communication protocols are being developed based on the concept of layering. By isolating individual groups of functions and allowing them to be implemented independently in a separate layer or level, analysis of computer systems can be greatly simplified. Each level makes use of the functions contained in lower levels and may perform functions that are used by higher levels of protocol. The concept of protocol layering is often illustrated by a simple analogy. Letters are mailed using envelopes. The letter and envelope are interrelated yet independent. The envelope has a very strict format, with certain information required to be in a certain position for correct routing of the letter (the address in the center, the return address in the upper left, the stamp and cancellation mark in the upper right). Inside the envelope is the letter, which has its own format based upon the type of letter it is—business or personal. It contains the date, inside address (if business), salutation, text, closing, and signature. This information appears in a different format for different types of letters, yet whichever format is used in the letter, the envelope format is unaffected.

The envelope is comparable to a network protocol, used to route information from one location to another, independent of the information it contains; the letter is comparable to an application level protocol used to convey the text to its destination in the appropriate format—hence, the two level or layers of protocol. This is another instance where the individual utilities will retain their unique characteristics but must add the interface required to become part of the network.

By committing itself to the use of these standards, each library has access to the data base of the entire national network, which will make available a source of bibliographic data without the costs or other problems of creating that data and a source of location information for interlibrary loan or other resource sharing programs. There is no doubt that there is a price to pay. With the standards described in the first point above, there will be the higher cost of inputting a full MARC record as opposed to a simpler record. And with respect to the other two protocol standards, libraries will no doubt be paying the network for some part of the developmental costs. However, there could very well be a price to pay by not ahering to standards. Dougherty makes this clear with respect to standards for machine-readable records.[14]

## COOPERATIVE CATALOGING

The Library of Congress has already stated that it cannot catalog the volume of records needed for the nation's libraries, and it is investigating the concept of cooperative cataloging and/or conversion in projects such as COMARC, CONSER, the Government Printing Office authority project, and the Northwestern University Africana project. The interconnection of utilities will mean that the nation's data base is available to all members, including the Library of Congress, and each time one library catalogs and converts a record, it will be contributing a record for the benefit of some other library or libraries within the national network.

The development of the interconnection among the utilities to provide a national resource is only in the planning stages. The costs of this activity (and any other costs resulting from the configuration of the projected national data base) are still unknown, but they eventually they will have to be compared against the costs of duplicated acquisitions, cataloging, conversion, and so forth.

## STAFFING

The national library network can exist only through the use of computer and communication technology. On-line technology is far more complicated than the off-line systems of the late 1960s and early 1970s. The knowledge required in most cases cannot be self-taught. Library automation has in a way gone full circle. In the late 1950s and early 1960s computer technicians who designed systems lacked enough background in the complexities of bibliography. We then trained librarians either to become technicians or to work with technicians. And now, with all the complexities of networking, we are back to requiring individuals with advanced training in the technology. One cannot make a generalized statement as to the type of staff required in each institution or each network that is a participant in the national network. It is too early to state with any certainty staff requirements at individual institutions resulting from national networking—but network organizations will bear the cost of staff working on national networking, and all or part of this cost will most certainly be passed on to individual libraries as part of their service charges.

## AUTONOMY

Participation in networking will mean a certain loss of autonomy to individual institutions. In order to reap the benefits of using bibliographic work done by others and having greater access to materials outside one's own library, each library must be prepared to accept the fact that the network will not be dedicated exclusively or primarily to the needs of the individual institution and its clientele, and that it will have to accept decisions made in committee or by a higher level of management. By the same token, a national network will put some contraints on the policies of the various individual networks.

## NETWORK MANAGEMENT

National library networking has ramifications beyond those of catalog management. The technical feasibility of network resource sharing has been established. Library networking will provide wider access to a greater number of resources for a larger number of users, but there are problems associated with this resource sharing, the major one being those "of conflict resolution between major organizational units which have become dependent on each other's resources."[15] For example, network operational management involves network measurement and control. Measurement is essential so that the performance of the network can be monitored and improvements installed when needed. Control involves the everyday operation of the network, analogous to the day-by-day support essential to every data-processing installation. It includes the maintenance of network hardware, software, and communications. Will the operational management of the network be centralized or decentralized?

There are many such issues to be resolved. The legal, economic, and administrative aspects of networking will affect all levels of management in the organization involved. If I were to assign a level of difficulty to each of the major areas where solutions are required, the lowest level of difficulty would be given to the technical areas, the next higher to the bibliographic area, the next to the legal, economic, and administrative areas, and the highest of all to the human and psychological area.

There is no doubt that a governing body will have to be responsible for the administration of the national library network. Managers will be very much affected by future steps in this direction. They should become involved to see that the library profession faces up realistically and promptly to resolving the issues of network management.

## CONCLUSION

I began by stating what a nationwide library network implied: access to bibliographic data pertinent to, and thus to the materials available in, any member institution through the institution's own system or through a system in which it participates. We have not yet accomplished such a service, and much work remains to be done before we reach this goal. The MARC Distribution Service from the Library of Congress provided the initial impetus for library networking. Kilgour and his vision of a shared cataloging service created the first utility, the Ohio College Library Center. The library community, working together, has made great progress in resource sharing.

It is important for managers to be aware of the effect of a national library network on their institutions, and equally important for them to recognize a prerequisite for building an effective system: commitment of time and resources on the part of everyone.

## NOTES

1. *Webster's Seventh New Collegiate Dictionary* (Springfield, Massachusetts: G & C Merriam Company, [c. 1963]), p. 562.

2. Categorizing network activities by types is not all that straightforward. A finer breakdown (still not entirely definitive) might include multistate service centers, statewide intrastate service centers, resource libraries, national libraries, the private sector, and communication carriers.

3. I have put quotation marks around the phrase "automated cataloging" to distinguish between the input and the maintenance of cataloging data in an on-line file and the automated production of bibliographic tools (printed cards, book form catalogs), and what some call automated cataloging—the act of cataloging using the machine as a tool, which requires the linking of the bibliographic files with the authority files (both names and subject headings).

4. There are various techniques for accomplishing this, but such a discussion is out of scope for this paper.

5. American Society for Information Science, *Proceedings of the Annual Meeting*, vol. 12 (1975), pp. 16–17. "Administrative Consideration of Library Networking," by Susan K. Martin, University of California at Berkeley.

6. The Network Advisory Group has been succeeded by the Network Advisory Committee established by the Librarian of Congress in April 1977 to advise him on matters related to network development. The deputy Librarian of Congress serves as chairman and the director of the Network Development Office as executive secretary and vice-chairman of the committee. At the time of this presentation, the Network Advisory Committee has not yet convened, and therefore for this paper, the name Network Advisory Group is used.

7. The first phase of this work, funded by NCLIS, to determine the tasks leading to the design of the national library network union catalog, has been completed by Edwin Buchinski of the National Library of Canada under the administrative and technical supervision of the Network Development Office. An evaluation team consisting of individuals from several institutions, including the Library of Congress, provided guidance and support throughout the investigation.

8. Following the NCLIS program, we are actually concerned with the National Library and Information Service Network. The Network Advisory Group and the Library of Congress Network Development Office recognized that they were limiting the first efforts to what they called the library bibliographic component. The term "library bibliographic" was used to indicate an emphasis on this component of the larger network as opposed to "library resource sharing" (collection development, document delivery, and so forth) or the overall concern of the total information community. While recognizing the equal importance of all components and information agencies in the network, the Network Advisory Group felt that the library bibliographic component should be given the first priority at this time. It was acknowledged that a basic purpose of the library bibliographic component was to make known what library materials are available. See *Toward a National Library and In-*

*formation Service Network: The Library Bibliographic Component*, prepared by Henriette D. Avram and Lenore S. Maruyama. Preliminary edition. Washington. Library of Congress (June 1977), p. ii.

9. Jamie J. Levine and Timothy Logan, *Online Resource Sharing: A Comparison of BALLOTS and OCLC; A Guide for Library Administrators* (San Jose, California: California Library Authority for Systems and Services, June 1977). Barbara Evans Markuson, "The Ohio College Library Center: A Study of the Factors Affecting the Adaptation of Libraries to On-Line Networks," *Library Technology Reports*, 12, no. 1 (January 1976).

10. William J. Welsh, "The Library of Congress as the National Bibliographic Center," *Library of Congress Information Bulletin* 34 (June 27, 1975): 268.

11. "The Role of the Library of Congress in the Emerging National Network." Prepared for the Library of Congress under contract by Lawrence F. Buckland and William Basinski, Inforonics, Inc. (forthcoming).

12. M.M. Botvinnik, *Computers, Chess and Long-Range Planning*, trans. Arthur Brown, Heidelberg Science Library, 11 (New York: Springer-Verlag, 1970).

13. The content designators are the tags, the subfield codes, and the indicators used in MARC records.

14. Richard M. Dougherty, "Data Base Pollution," *Journal of Academic Librarianship* 3 (July 1977): 127.

15. Einar Stefferud, David L. Grobstein, and Ronald P. Uhlig, "Wholesale/Retail Specifications in Resource Sharing Networks," in *Computer Networking*, ed. Robert P. Blanc and Ira W. Cotton (New York: IEEE Press 1976), p. 334.

# The Flexibly Automated Catalog: Budgets, Services, and the Varied Catalogs at the Los Angeles County Public Library

**6**

Mary L. Fischer

Los Angeles County Public Library published its first book catalog, a children's catalog, in 1953, using punched cards and unit record equipment. That first catalog, crude by contemporary standards, was later to be called a child of necessity. Almost a quarter-century later, a flexible, computer-supported collection access system was defined and integrated into both the technical-support and direct public-service functions of the nation's largest county library.

To understand the problems and strengths of that collection access system and the pressures that led to its definition, one needs first to examine briefly Los Angeles County, the library, the necessity of 1953, and the subsequent quarter-century of development. With seven million residents, Los Angeles County today is the most populous county in the nation. Geographically large, its urban area would comfortably hold the cities of Denver, Chicago, St. Louis, Philadelphia, New York, Pittsburgh, and Detroit. The total county area equals the area of Rhode Island and Delaware combined. It is politically complex, with seventy-nine incorporated cities and numerous variations in city-county relationships. It is rich in public library resources; it contains the nation's largest county library, one of the largest city libraries (Los Angeles Public Library), and thirty-four other public libraries offering services independently or through the twenty-five-member Metropolitan Cooperative Library System.

Los Angeles County Public Library was founded in 1912 under provisions of the 1911 County Free Library Law. While it is an integral part of county government, operating under the board of supervisors, it is financed by a separate tax levy imposed on all properties within the service area. Both joining and withdrawing from the county library system are relatively easy.

Currently the county library, with ninety-three regional and community libraries, ten institutional libraries, and six mobilibraries, serves forty-three incorporated cities and most of the county's unincorporated territory—a service area of 3,020 square miles containing 2.4 million people. Administration and centralized technical processing are provided from a system headquarters, but there is no large, public central library. For administrative and service effectiveness, the system is divided into six regions, ranging from North County, with twelve libraries and three mobilibraries spread over 2,000 square miles with a service population of 262,157 people, to Southeast County, with seventeen libraries and one mobilibrary in 250 square miles with a service population of 607,837. The average community library has two librarians, 35,272 volumes, and 8,482 square feet; regional libraries average seven librarians, 138,750 volumes, and 31,551 square feet. Collections are generally permanent, and an attempt is made to tailor them to the region and local community.

In contrast, the Los Angeles County Public Library began operations in 1913 as a rural library service to 100,000 people spread thinly over 3,300 square miles. Service was directed by a small, centrally located professional staff and delivered through many small branches staffed by paraprofessionals. Branch collections rotated at six-month intervals. A dictionary catalog and location records were maintained at system headquarters. By 1925, a few communities had grown and stabilized and demanded more intensive library service. Branches serving them developed permanent collections and card catalogs. These were exceptions, however; branch card catalogs were not generally developed.

Overall, the county library remained an essentially rural service until the westward tilt of the 1940s. Then, beginning with the war years and continuing well into the 1960s, Los Angeles County had an average growth rate of one person every ten minutes. Orange groves were replaced by housing tracts and shopping centers, and the county library scrambled to build libraries and book collections, recruit librarians, and develop the techniques and tools of modern urban library service.

By 1952, the midway point in the Los Angeles County population boom, only 26 of the (then) 114 service outlets had card catalogs; the only union catalog and location file were at system headquarters, which was closed evenings and weekends. The library estimated the cost of installing a card catalog in every branch at over $400,000; were that step to be taken, there would still be no distributed union catalog. It is important to realize that, essentially for budgetary reasons, developing a card catalog at every branch was not at any point a probable action.

Faced with the mounting pleas for catalogs from branch librarians, the necessity to sell county library services to growing, restless cities, increased service demands from the postwar generation, prospects of continued growth, and budgetary constraints, the library sought an alternative to the branch card catalog. That bibliographic child of necessity was published in 1953 not as a cost-saving alternative to existing card catalogs but as an achievable alternative to no public catalog at all in most county branches.

Although early Los Angles County Library catalogs are described in the literature and their specific technologies are not the issue here, it is nevertheless useful to review a history that is, at the least, unusual in length and variety. Unquestionably that history shaped the catalog product and staff attitudes that were addressed in 1975. Thus the history is necessary background.

In 1952, following a feasibility study and a report on the King County (Washington) Library products, the library developed procedures for book catalog production, utilizing unit record equipment owned by the county assessor and the registrar of voters—on an off-hours, time-available basis that was to become increasingly irregular as demands from various county departments grew. Data were punched on tab cards, processed on an IBM 407 accounting machine, and printed on multilith masters for duplication. The first catalog, a children's catalog, was produced in 1953; the adult catalog was completed in 1955. The library's share of the cost for the first systemwide catalog was less than $50,000.

The end product of this unit record system was a legal-size volume, printed in unvaried, upper-case type, with a limited character set, in a single-column format. Volumes were spiral-bound. In 1975, book catalog "as-used" subject terms still reflected the limited punctuation symbols available in this and other early catalog production systems.

By 1964, now accustomed to the availability of a public catalog and anxious for a better-looking product, the library tried a sequential camera process, contracting with a commercial supplier. A single line of data was typed at the top of a tab card, using a typewriter with variable fonts and spacing. Manually assigned code numbers identifying various parts of the catalog entry were keypunched on the tab card. Tab equipment was used to sequence decks of cards, which were then photographed, one line at a time, by a sequential camera. Negatives produced by the photographic process were used in offset printing.

Although the product showed substantial cosmetic improvement, there were fundamental weaknesses. Editing was difficult, the methodology tended to result in artificially abridged entries, and data were not readily manipulated—what was input was what was output. In 1975, after eight years of experience with a computer-supported catalog, staff still basically perceived the input process as defining the output product. The end of this short phase was hastened both by poor library-vendor relations (and the eventual financial failure of the vendor) and by the growing popularity of library automation.

In 1965, already dissatisfied with the sequential camera process, the Library and Management Services Division of the Chief Administrative Office began investigating computerization. This investigation was encouraged in 1966, by receipt of a grant from the Council on Library Resources, which resulted in a study and report on use of optical character recognition for converting catalog data to machine-readable form. By 1967, the library specifications were written for the first Los Angeles County Library computer-produced catalog. Among the specified requirements were an expanded character set (upper and lower case, Arabic numbers, standard punctuation) and variable-length records (up to a limit of thirty-one typewritten lines).

## THE CATALOG: MAY 1975

By 1975, almost a quarter-century after the first Los Angeles County Library book catalog had appeared, the catalog had evolved into a massive tool with familiar outlines. A master (or complete) book catalog was published annually, with separate volumes listing adult nonfiction books by author, title, and subject; similar volumes for children's books; and separate volumes for adult fiction and all foreign-language materials. Entry content varied with the type of entry. The last printed master, cumulated in October 1974, was published in forty-seven photocomposed volumes. Between annual publications, newly cataloged titles were listed in cumulative paper supplements, at varying intervals, in the same organization as the master catalog.

The data base supporting the production of this catalog contained, by 1975, some 300,000 titles, the library's entire book collection. Records were not MARC-like. Tagging was limited, with subelements largely unidentified. A six-character alphanumeric identifier was assigned to each record.

At this point, several problems in management and use of the book catalog could be identified by administrators and staff.

First, from 1961 to 1975 the contract book catalog production budget had increased by 35 percent from $260,000 to $350,000. Paper costs in particular were increasing rapidly; in addition to budgeted increases, the 1974-1975 billings included an unanticipated $4,206.05 for increased paper cost due to "environmental" factors.

Second, the lag between the acquisition and processing of a new title and the appearance of essential access data in the book catalog was six months. In an attempt to compensate for this demand-period delay, community library staffs were compiling and typing their own new title lists, a duplicative effort costing $40,000 annually in labor alone (table 6.1).

Table 6.1    **Catalog and Bibliographic Access Subsystem
Costs, May 1975**

### TOTAL ANNUAL COSTS

| Operating Function | Projected Total Costs |
|---|---|
| Book catalog input | $ 72,200 |
| Vendor catalog contract | 320,000 |
| Book catalog distribution | 10,400 |
| Community library supplements | 40,800 |
| Government publications catalogs | 44,100 |
| Total | $487,500 |

### COSTS BY SYSTEM LOCATION

| Operating Function | System and Systems Headquarters | Community Libraries | | |
|---|---|---|---|---|
| | | Large | Medium | Small |
| Catalog input | $ 72,200 | | | |
| Catalog contract | 320,000 | | | |
| Distribution | | $ 1,500 | $ 4,500 | $ 4,300 |
| Supplements | | 37,800 | 800 | 2,100 |
| Government catalogs | | 1,600 | | |

Third, while the broad distribution of the book catalog provided all county residents with a list of the entire book collection, it did not tell them where individual copies were housed. A hierarchy of card files was used to record item locations. With the pressure of rapid growth and the shift to strong regional organization, maintenance of a centralized union location file showing branch holdings had been discontinued by 1960. The union shelf-list, in the Catalog Section, showed copies but not locations. A system headquarters location file pointed to the holding region only. Regional location files carried branch holdings for a single region only. Branches maintained local shelf-lists (table 6.2).

Table 6.2   **Location Access Request System Costs, May 1975**

| Operating Function | Systems Headquarters | Region | Type of Library | | | Estimated Average Annual Cost |
| | | | Large | Medium | Small | |
| --- | --- | --- | --- | --- | --- | --- |
| System location files | $ 43,098 | $ 60,635 | | | | $ 103,733 |
| Library shelf-lists | 7,441 | | | $ 10,708 | | 18,149 |
| Interlibrary requests | 48,600 | 77,171 | 111,318 | 62,025 | 81,534 | 380,648 |
| Intersystem requests | | | | | | 12,636 |
| Request delivery | | | | | | 9,100 |
| Total | | | | | | $ 524,266 |

Interregional requests—130,000 annually—moved from branch to regional to system headquarters and on to a second regional headquarters. Further, because interagency loans were considered shelf-list transactions, not simple circulation transactions, this path was reversed, temporary—or permanent—location changes being noted in all files. A minimum of one month was required to move a request through the files, and delays of six months were common.

Fourth, Technical Services was using multiple and overlapping files for the control of the cataloging process and the book catalog publications. Developed as a means of economically duplicating and distributing the union card catalog, the book catalog and supporting data base had never become the official catalog. The union card catalog was officially transformed into a name authority file in 1967, but there was no fundamental change in attitude or practice. With the development of the computer-supported catalog in 1967, a control card file was created and maintained as a card-form record of the book catalog, existing parallel to the offical catalog-name authority file. Cataloging copy in the two files was not identical. Variations in county library cataloging practice developed in response to real or assumed limitations in early book catalog production systems and book catalog economics. Variations occurred most notably in use of punctuation, dates, and other numbers and in elimination of tracings and abbreviation of other data. Variation from official library practice also resulted in maintenance of dual subject authority files—one for the correct terms and another for book catalog as-used terms. Finally, a complete file of OCR input sheets returned by the book catalog production vendor was defensively maintained.

Fifth, if Technical Services regarded the book catalog as a subsidiary effort, to Public Services it was an essential tool defined by and issuing forth mysteriously from Technical Services with inadequate subject headings and cross-references and most imperfect perfect binding, which often disintegrated within the first quarter of use.

Sixth, significant parts of the collection were not included in the distributed catalog: periodicals, government documents, 16mm films. Each region manually prepared an annual regional periodical union list, but no systemwide list existed. Card catalogs were maintained at branches housing document collections, but no bibliographic data were distributed to other branches. Film catalogs were irregularly produced.

In 1975, under the leadership of the newly appointed county librarian, Carol Moss, library administration contracted for a consultant study to review the book catalog and all associated files and procedures, a combination of operating resources that became known as "the access system." The study was financed by $20,000 from the annual California Public Library Services Act grant, a per-capita-based award.

The following study guidelines were established:

1. The contract book catalog services budget would not exceed the current $350,000 level over the next three budget years, ending June 1978.
2. Emphasis would be placed on eliminating duplicative manual file maintenance tasks.
3. Regional and national bibliographic resources, including developing networks, would be used wherever possible to minimize local costs.
4. Planning would anticipate and employ new technological resources. The overall goal of the study was to produce a workable management plan for increasing service while reducing unit costs over the succeeding three to five years.

An intense six-month study schedule was established so the study recommendations could be reviewed before specification of a new or revised book catalog services contract in October 1975. An advisory board of senior administrative staff, headed by the county librarian, was established to meet regularly with the consultants to review alternatives and to guide the schedule of field investigations and data collection. The Library Systems Group was assigned to assist in investigation and data collection, and the special assistant to the county librarian coordinated these various efforts.

The consultant studied the distribution of titles and volumes within the system, the operation of the location-information and book request system, and (using labor and time data supplied by the Library Systems Group) the cost of all elements of the access system. In addition, an intensive examination was made of patterns of catalog use and available network resources.

The study reported two general conclusions and a set of specific recommendations for changes in the access system. Implementation of these recommendations began on a limited basis while the study was in progress, gaining full force with publication of the final report, *Improving Public Library Access*, in November 1975.

While the conception and inauguration of the consulting study were major steps toward change, the impact of the study was greatly intensified by other, concurrent developments. In early 1975, the position of special assistant to the county librarian was created as a high-level staff position with the specific charge to recommend and guide change in library operations. Further, in support of this effort, a Library Systems Group (now including four budgeted positions) was developed, pulling together systems analysis, industrial engineering, and library skills. The access study thus was made in an environment of both strong administrative and technical support.

## THE ACCESS SYSTEM

By November 1977, two years following completion of the Access Study, all recommended products had been developed, and the role of the published catalog in the technical and public service functions of the Los Angeles County Public Library had been fundamentally and permanently altered. The access-related changes may be typed as product developments, drawing heavily on access study recommendations, or organizational and procedural modifications, based primarily on studies by the Library Systems Group and aimed at increasing productivity and integrating the access system in library internal operations. Alternately these changes can be categorized by affected functional area—for example, bibliographic access, location access, or catalog management.

### CHANGES

*Location Access* The most sweeping change recommended by the consultant study was in the handling of location access. The Access Study demonstrated that while each local library has only 10 percent or less of the titles owned by the county library system, over 98 percent of the system-wide circulation (now more than eleven million) is provided by titles located within the local library's collection. It appears, then, that the published union catalog provides bibliographic access to systemwide holdings, but the book-location and book-delivery portions of the access system are essentially unused. During site visits, it was quickly apparent that because of the excessive delays in moving requests through the hierarchy of location files, staff were actively discouraging use of the request process. Further, although no statistics on request fill are available, sampling showed that an average of 20 percent of the requested titles supplied were not claimed. In reply to a questionnaire, most staff stated that requests were unclaimed because it took too long to fill them.

To provide community libraries with location information, eliminating the hierarchy of card files and permitting the development of radically simplified request procedures, a microfiche *Location Index,* listing the location of each volume in the library system, was developed. The necessary conversion to machine-readable form of the county library's four million location records began in mid-1976 and is scheduled for completion by the end of 1978. The first *Location Index* is currently being produced and represents complete holdings of five regional libraries as well as systemwide acquisitions since January 1976.

Staff to perform the location file conversion was made available by work simplification in existing units, as recommended by the Library Systems Group. Both system and regional headquarters location files were closed, and interim procedures, utilizing TWX communications, were developed by the Systems Group and a task force of community library staff. Request volume has increased marginally.

*Catalog Management* The second major body of Access Study recommendations concerned the utilization of the bibliographic data base in library internal operations. During the preceding quarter-century, the book catalog had been an effort subsidiary, sometimes parallel, to the primary cataloging control of the collection. Now, however, existing data bases, software, and network resources make it feasible to invert the relationship, making the bibliographic data base the method for managing the collection: for determining name and subject authority, filing order, and eventually classification. Internal economics and available contract resources make it appropriate to accept Library of Congress MARC cataloging with minimal editing—an internal policy shift clearly compatible with the rapidly developing California State network situation. Following thorough systems analysis and work measurement by the Library Systems Group, extensive organizational and procedural changes were carried out in the acquisitions section in 1976 and the catalog section in 1977.

*Catalog Publication* The third major area of change was the concept of the published catalog. Access Study recommendations moved beyond the concept of the single catalog to the collection, recommending that it be published as several catalogs as needed for different users and types of library materials. The catalog package could economically expand the scope of bibliographic access to include nonbook media and materials on order or in process. Multiple catalogs could provide for more rapid publication of commonly needed catalog information and more elaborate publication of detailed information on a less frequent basis. Further the recommended changes expanded the total scope of the catalog, deemphasizing traditional lines between the catalog system, and acquisitions and inventory control systems.

Changes in each of these three areas required developing new catalog products and revising organizational structure and procedures. The lines

Table 6.3   *The Weekly Index*

---

*Scope:* Items on order, items received and in process, and items cataloged subsequent to latest *Master Catalog.*

*Frequency:* Weekly, cumulative.

*Format:* 48X microfiche with header, index.

*Organization:* Author-title entries, interfiled.

*Contents: Header:* Report title, distribution date, fiche number, first author or title on fiche.

   *Index:* First word on each frame, plus grid coordinates.

   *Entry:* Author, title (excluding subtitle), edition, publisher, publication date, call number (if available), bibliographic access number (BAN), status code; location codes.

*Use:* Primarily internal (reserves, interlibrary loan, reference).

*Distribution:* 120 copies (community-regional-institutional-mobilibraries, regional offices, systems headquarters). Mailed directly to individual locations by COM processor,

*Cost:* Production: $56.25 set-up,
       $.0810 per frame.
   Delivery (mail to each agency): $30.00 set-up plus postage.
   Cost per copy (delivered) at 1,334 frames: $1.76.

*Publication status:* In regular production since April 12, 1976.

---

do not always flow clearly from product or procedural change to a single area of impact.

## PRODUCTS

*Weekly Index* A tenet of community library service is that new books and essential access records must be made available quickly because demand for most titles peaks very soon after publication. In an effort to meet that demand and to increase the return on book budget dollars in measurable collection use, the library has made extensive policy and procedural changes since 1975, many relating only peripherally to the access system. One decision was to add a short record to the catalog at time of order rather than after cataloging. One effect of that change is to minimize the negative impact of catalog publication lag, noted in the charge to the Access Study team. That problem is additionally addressed by rapid distribution of new title information through *The Weekly Index* (table 6.3).

Several points may be made on the basis of the Access Study investigations and experience with this tool, which has been in regular production since April 1976. First, a frequent observation in 1975 site visits was that branch staff could not respond to patron queries about anticipated acquisitions. They did not know what titles were selected or for which branches they were purchased. While aimed principally at the publication lag problem, the addition of on-order records to the catalog file and their publication, with branch codes, in *The Weekly Index* effectively provided community libraries with a distributed open-order report, as well as a frequent catalog supplement. Second, addition of even a short record at time of order implies a fundamental change in the book catalog production cycle. Third, the requirement to show status—on order, received, cataloged—was a marked extension of the capabilities of current book catalog software. The recognition that *The Weekly Index* could be a distributed open-order report, as well as a fast catalog supplement, meant that status must be shown at the copy rather than the title level, allowing multiple appearance of a title on the report, with a variant status for each entry.

*The Digest* As traditionally conceived, the book catalog supplement served only as a subsidiary of the master catalog. During most of its life the supplement contained too few titles for it to be a useful tool. All users were faced with using both the supplement and the master catalog, regardless of how limited or specialized their needs might be. Further, the titles in the traditional supplement were not necessarily new titles, having been published from one to eighteen months or more before supplement publication.

To provide a compact and portable tool, the study recommended that the traditional supplement be discarded and replaced with a selective catalog, including new items and older titles likely to be wanted in a small branch basic collection. This *Digest*, similar in concept to a desk, or abridged, dictionary, was to be updated and printed quarterly (table 6.4).

Table 6.4   *The Digest*

---

*Scope:* Titles received and being processed, titles cataloged subsequent to latest *Master Catalog,* and selective high-use older titles already included in the *Master Catalog.*

*Frequency:* Quarterly.

*Format:* Print (photocomposed), four-column, with "Notes to the User."

*Organization:* Author-title entries, interfiled; subject entries.

*Contents:* Author, title, edition, publisher, publication date, call number (if available), bibliographic access number (BAN), subject heading (subject entry only).

*Use:* Staff and public use. Aimed at users seeking primarily current materials or retrospective titles likely to be in a small branch basic collection.

*Distribution:* 500 copies (community-regional-institutional-mobilibraries, regional offices, systems headquarters). Distributed from systems headquarters.

*Cost:* Production: $10.92 per page.
             Delivery to SHQ: no charge.
             Cost per copy at 750 pages: $16.38.

*Publication Status:* Temporarily suspended.

---

After one year, publication of *The Digest* has been suspended, pending reevaluation of its management and utility. Several issues led to that decision. First, in spite of positive reactions from individual users, patron interviews have thus far indicated a minimal level of use. Second, the decision to produce a microform, instead of book-form, master catalog significantly alters the economics involved, and as a consequence the catalog package must be reconsidered. Third, the selection of high-use retrospective titles is, until completion of the shelf-list conversion, a very labor-intensive and judgmental process. Reference staffs have compiled lists of titles that they believe are appropriate for a small branch basic collection. After a year, basic reference titles in all Dewey classes have been added, as well as a basic fiction list, with compilation of other lists in progress. Added-copy acquisitions lists have been used as one indicator of high-use status. Completion of the location data conversion, allowing for identification of broadly held titles, will facilitate this process, as will eventual implementation of a computer-supported circulation system. Reevaluation of *The Digest* concept is expected to result in redefinition of the product.

*Master Catalog* The *Master Catalog* has historically been the high-cost item in the book catalog package. In 1974–1975, the county library's book catalog budget was $340,000, of which $210,000 was the cost of producing four hundred copies of the *Master Catalog*. The large percentage of catalog budget dollars allocated to the *Master Catalog* had severely limited the library's ability to produce other catalog products, and yet no clear indication existed that the utility of the master catalog justified such overwhelming commitment of funds. The study recommendations were that the library achieve increased budget flexibility and increase the utility of *The Digest* by publishing the *Master Catalog* biannually, spreading the cost over two fiscal years, and that the library evaluate the use of a computer-output microfilm instead of print-form *Master Catalog.*

Publication of the book-form *Master Catalog*, scheduled in October 1975, was suspended as implementation of the study recommendations began. While the Book Catalog Services and Products contract specifications released in October 1975 assumed continuation of a book-form *Master Catalog*, the ability to produce a COM master was a required vendor capability, although price quotations were not specifically demanded. By the start of the 1976–1977 fiscal year, it was apparent that the economic arguments favoring the COM master were substantial. Further, it was recognized that the cost of required hardware could be spread over two fiscal years and (even adding the cost of COM catalog production) still not greatly exceed the cost of publishing an annual book-form master catalog.

To test the utility of the COM master, determine its acceptability to staff and patrons, and identify problems in its implementation, the library determined to produce a COM master, install rented hardware, and observe the use of that master catalog format in various branches and sections. Eighteen branches were selected, distributed evenly across the service area—generally one small, medium, and large library in each geographic region. Ten control branches were also selected, all still using the print-form master and having a comparable spread of size and geography. In addition, the COM catalog was to be used in all regional headquarters and at system headquarters in the acquisitions, cataloging, and interlibrary loan sections (table 6.5).

A test master catalog, a complete master cumulated December 1, 1976, was produced. COM catalogs were installed, utilizing both available scroll-type viewers, in February 1977. By May, the library was sufficiently confident of its acceptance by staff and public and its effectiveness as a service tool to commit fixed-asset funds for COM catalog viewer purchase in the final budget process. Also as a result of the initial test experience, the number of viewers to be acquired was increased to five hundred from the

Table 6.5   **Microfilm Master Catalog: Viewer Test Site Libraries and Activity Index**

| Test Site | Group | Library | Number of Viewers | Activity Index Test Site | Activity Index Group | Activity Ratio |
|---|---|---|---|---|---|---|
| 1 | A | Iacoboni | 10 | 902 | 902 | 6.14 |
| 2 |   | Lancaster | 10 | 809 |   | 5.50 |
| 3 | B | Culver City | 10 | 791 | 746 | 5.38 |
| 4 |   | Montebello | 7 | 640 |   | 4.35 |
| 5 |   | Claremont | 8 | 562 |   | 3.82 |
| 6 | C | Compton | 8 | 488 | 503 | 3.32 |
| 7 |   | Hacienda Heights | 6 | 460 |   | 3.13 |
| 8 |   | Temple City | 4 | 370 |   | 2.51 |
| 9 |   | La Canada | 4 | 352 |   | 2.39 |
| 10 | D | San Dimas | 4 | 323 | 331 | 2.20 |
| 11 |   | San Vicente | 4 | 314 |   | 2.14 |
| 12 |   | Bilbrew | 4 | 299 |   | 2.03 |
| 13 |   | Manhattan Heights | 2-3 | 222 |   | 1.51 |
| 14 |   | Canyon Country | 2 | 218 |   | 1.48 |
| 15 | E | Bell Gardens | 2 | 214 | 194 | 1.45 |
| 16 |   | Hollydale | 2 | 205 |   | 1.39 |
| 17 |   | La Verne | 2 | 160 |   | 1.08 |
| 18 |   | South El Monte | 2-3 | 147 |   | 1.00 |

original estimate of four hundred, with the additional quantity generally slated for small libraries, where the only nonpeak hour queueing problems had occurred (table 6.6). Specifications for purchase of the required hardware were developed in May, and a contract for five hundred viewers to be installed over a three-month period was awarded at the end of June.

Table 6.6   **Microfilm Master Catalog: Viewer Overload Proportions**

| | Number of Samples | 100 Percent Use | Percentage Overload | Number of Viewers |
|---|---|---|---|---|
| Library | | | | |
| 1 | 189 | 1 | 0.5 | 10 |
| 2 | 192 | 8 | 4.0 | 10 |
| 3 | 177 | 1 | 0.5 | 10 |
| 4 | 208 | 5 | 2.0 | 6 |
| 5 | 240 | 1 | 0.5 | 8 |
| 6 | 185 | 0 | 0 | 8 |
| 7 | 188 | 2 | 1.0 | 6 |
| 8 | 186 | 6 | 3.0 | 4 |
| 9 | 228 | 23 | 10.0 | 4 |
| 10 | 196 | 19 | 10.0 | 4 |
| 11 | 147 | 2 | 2.0 | 4 |
| 12 | 222 | 12 | 5.0 | 4 |
| 13 | 164 | 41 | 25.0 | 2 |
| 14 | 150 | 74 | 49.0 | 2 |

*Table 6.6 Continued*

| | | | | |
|---|---|---|---|---|
| 15 | 176 | 42 | 24.0 | 2 |
| 16 | 196 | 52 | 26.0 | 2 |
| 17 | 120 | 45 | 37.0 | 2 |
| 18 | 152 | 94 | 62.0 | 2 |
| *Group* | | | | |
| A | 189 | 1 | 0.5 | 10 |
| B | 192 | 5 | 2.0 | 9 |
| C | 204 | 1 | 0.5 | 7 |
| D | 196 | 12 | 6.0 | 4 |
| E | 160 | 58 | 31.0 | 2 |
| TOTAL | 188 | 15 | 8.0 | 6 |

At the same time, the library's current catalog services vendor, interested in an evaluation of the book catalog package generally and the utility of the COM catalog in particular, contracted with a consultant to conduct such an evaluation, utilizing the Los Angeles County COM test. The consultant worked with the library to define evaluation procedures. Several questions were to be addressed, including the following:

What access tools are used? Which are used successfully?

Is the COM catalog a viable instrument for public use?

If a COM catalog is used, how many viewing stations are required for a library of a specified size and activity?

What is the effect of the COM catalog on total catalog use?

If the catalog is divided, is there measurable difference in volume of use of author-title and subject catalogs?

An interim report of the evaluation has been submitted by the consultant. Among the conclusions reported are the following:

1. With 120 viewers distributed around eighteen libraries, regional and system headquarters, over 80 percent of the test sites reported usage rates between 40 and 48 percent, based on hourly observations during the first four weeks of use (table 6.7).

Table 6.7  **Microfilm Master Catalog: Microfilm Catalog Viewer Use**

|  | Percentage of Catalogs in Use | Number of Viewers Available | Average Number of Viewers in Use |
|---|---|---|---|
| Library |  |  |  |
| 1 | 41 | 10 | 4.1 |
| 2 | 50 | 10 | 5.0 |
| 3 | 34 | 10 | 3.4 |
| 4 | 42 | 7 | 2.9 |
| 5 | 43 | 8 | 3.4 |
| 6 | 41 | 8 | 3.3 |
| 7 | 39 | 6 | 2.3 |
| 8 | 45 | 4 | 1.8 |
| 9 | 40 | 4 | 1.6 |
| 10 | 42 | 4 | 1.7 |
| 11 | 40 | 4 | 1.8 |
| 12 | 48 | 4 | 1.9 |
| 13 | 73 | 2-3 | 1.7 |
| 14 | 68 | 2 | 1.4 |
| 15 | 51 | 2 | 1.0 |
| 16 | 44 | 2 | 0.8 |
| 17 | 66 | 2 | 1.3 |
| 18 | 74 | 2-3 | 1.7 |

*Table 6.7 Continued*

| Group | | | |
|-------|------|-----|-----|
| A | 41 | 10 | 4.1 |
| B | 41 | 9 | 3.7 |
| C | 41 | 7 | 2.9 |
| D | 43 | 4 | 1.7 |
| E | 62 | 2 | 1.2 |
| TOTAL | 46 | 6.4 | 2.7 |

2. Smaller libraries with few viewers available (because of low activity indicators) had heavier rates of microform catalog use (an average 62 percent) than larger libraries with more viewers and more overall activity (table 6.6). Catalog use in small libraries did not drop off as sharply as anticipated from other activity indicators.

3. Based on hourly observations, COM catalog sites showed 9 percent more total catalog usage than control sites.

4. Hourly observations also tracked the type of catalog use (patron, staff, patron and staff, multiple patrons). Small libraries showed a higher percentage of staff use of the catalog and higher patron-to-staff and multiple-patrons levels (table 6.8). Over the entire test group, however, 76 percent of the total use was by patrons.

Table 6.8   **Microfilm Master Catalog: Type of Viewer Use**

| | Observed Uses | One Staff Member (%) | One Patron (%) | Staff Member and Patron (%) | Multiple Users in Line (%) |
|---------|------|----|----|----|----|
| *Library* | | | | | |
| 1 | 622 | 11 | 80 | 3 | 7 |
| 2 | 747 | 3 | 85 | 6 | 6 |
| 3 | 753 | 3 | 94 | 1 | 2 |

*Table 6.8 Continued*

| | | | | | |
|---|---|---|---|---|---|
| 4 | 432 | 10 | 78 | 2 | 10 |
| 5 | 795 | 19 | 73 | 2 | 6 |
| 6 | 280 | 0.4 | 96 | 0 | 4 |
| 7 | 347 | 0.6 | 94 | 4 | 1 |
| 8 | 162 | 15 | 78 | 2 | 4 |
| 9 | 321 | 8 | 84 | 3 | 5 |
| 10 | 325 | 8 | 77 | 3 | 12 |
| 11 | 196 | 18 | 70 | 10 | 1 |
| 12 | 290 | 10 | 72 | 17 | 1 |
| 13 | 139 | 12 | 74 | 0 | 14 |
| 14 | 199 | 15 | 58 | 0.5 | 27 |
| 15 | 135 | 8 | 61 | 11 | 19 |
| 16 | 166 | 25 | 49 | 10 | 16 |
| 17 | 139 | 22 | 41 | 16 | 21 |
| 18 | 206 | 10 | 13 | 16 | 62 |
| *Group* | | | | | |
| A | 622 | 11 | 80 | 3 | 7 |
| B | 644 | 5 | 86 | 3 | 6 |
| C | 474 | 7 | 88 | 2 | 4 |
| D | 259 | 12 | 76 | 7 | 5 |
| E | 164 | 15 | 49 | 11 | 27 |
| *AVERAGE* *TOTAL* | 433 | 10 | 76 | 5 | 10 |

5. The first patron opinion data showed 68 percent of the patron responses were very positive (31 percent) or somewhat positive (37 percent); only 10 percent were very negative. Many of the negative reactions can be addressed with better directional signs. Some patrons were concerned about the energy consumption of the viewers, and an informational reply was distributed to all libraries:

### "Saving Time and Your Taxes"

The Library's two-month test of our new catalog viewers has been a real success with the public—seven out of ten people who gave their opinion liked the new viewers better than the old books.

But some people felt this system might be more expensive. Actually, these viewers use microfilm to publish the catalog instead of paper, and a page of microfilm only costs about one *tenth* of a cent, while the printed pages cost almost ten times as much.

The energy we use in the motors and lamps is much less than the energy and expense used in printing the paper pages of the old catalog. Each viewer uses about $2.25 of electricity in a whole year—that's less than the cost of binding *one volume* of the 35 printed books the viewer replaces!

The new catalog viewers pay for themselves in less than two years, and make it possible to publish the catalog more often and still save enough money to publish the special catalogs such as the *Subject Guide.*

Several less formalized but nonetheless significant observations were made. First, children had no difficulty using the catalog, even though adult and juvenile titles were interfiled. At age nine or ten, children could use it reasonably well; indeed they often instructed their parents. Even for younger children, it was an almost invariable fascination. Second, related to that, COM catalog gamemanship is clearly an inevitable by-product— with races between neighboring viewers seeming to be the most frequent game. Third, as others have reported, there is a marked tendency for users to browse the COM catalog, although figures on average length of catalog use are not yet available.

The *Master Catalog* was cumulated October 1, 1977, and film for system-wide distribution is currently being duplicated. Table 6.9 outlines essential *Master Catalog* facts. Several other points need to be emphasized. First, adult and juvenile titles are interfiled. Second, the decision to use a divided catalog, author-title and subject, was an access decision, not a hardware requirement. Third, the economics of the COM catalog allowed expansion of the entries, most notably the display of tracings; but the real (as opposed to assumed) utility of the expanded entries has yet to be evaluated.

*Browsing Lists* While the inherent flexibility of a computer-supported catalog has long been recognized, it has only rarely been utilized to produce

Table 6.9    *Master Catalog*

---

*Scope:*  All cataloged titles.

*Frequency:*  Quarterly.

*Format:*  48X 2.0 mil roll film.

*Organization:*  Divided catalog: author-title entries interfiled; subject entries.

*Contents: Main entry:* author, title (including subtitle), edition, imprint, collation, all note fields, tracings, call number, bibliographic access number (BAN).
    *Added entries:* omit collation, note fields, tracings.
    *Subject entries:*  omit collation, tracings.

*Use:*  Staff and public.

*Distribution:* 250  copies  (community-regional-institutional-mobilibraries, regional offices, systems headquarters).

*Cost:*  Production: $.251 per frame.
    Delivery to SHQ: no charge.
    Cost per copy at 55,000 frames: $55.22.

*Publication Status:* Effective October 1977.

---

## Divided Catalog Use

|         | Author-Title | Subject |
|---------|:------------:|:-------:|
| Group A | 52%          | 48%     |
| Group B | 45%          | 55%     |
| Group C | 52%          | 48%     |
| Group D | 52%          | 48%     |
| Group E | 49%          | 51%     |

selective catalogs. Under the heading "browsing lists," the county library is producing selective catalogs based on format (films, periodicals), user needs (large-print books), or subject interest (Californiana). Lists in the first category are basic tools, for which this is a convenient means of publication; those in the second and third category mark an extension of traditional book catalog access.

Browsing lists exist as a generic category in the book catalog budget. Individual lists have not thus far been itemized. As specific lists, such as a *Periodicals Union List*, *Film Catalog*, and *Books in Large Print*, become regularly scheduled, they may be individually calendared and budgeted. Other products will continue on an irregular basis; some products (*I Can Read It Myself*, a catalog of primers) may well end up as one-time-only experimental products. Lists are staff defined on the basis of user need. Once a list is defined, republication is based on demonstrated utility. Frequency of publication relates to the volatility of that collection subset. One increasingly clear aspect of the specialized lists such as *Californiana* or *Books in Large Print* is that their size, narrow focus, and relatively low cost make their wide use outside the library attractive. Many branches are circulating copies of these catalogs, particularly *Books in Large Print*. Demand for copies from other community organizations or service agencies —local historical societies, Braille Institute, nursing homes—is climbing rapidly. The distribution of the first of the special catalogs to be republished, *Books in Large Print*, has been doubled from five hundred to a thousand, with most of the additional quantity to be distributed to nursing homes, hospitals and organizations serving the visually handicapped. Table 6.10 outlines current products on the constantly changing list.

Table 6.10    *Browsing Lists*

---

*Scope:* Variable:

    1. *Books in Large Print:* Titles with subject heading "sight-saving books."

    2. *Californiana:* Titles with collection code "Californiana."

    3. *I Can Read It Myself:* Primer titles selected by bibliographic access number.

*Frequency:* Variable:

    1. *Books in Large Print:* annual.

    2. *Californiana:* biannual.

    3. *I Can Read It Myself:* one-time demonstration list.

*Format:* Print (photocomposed). Column widths, type size, and face variable:

*Table 6.10 Continued*

      1. *Books in Large Print:* 2 column, 18-point type.

      2. *Californiana:* 4 column, 8-point type.

      3. *I Can Read It Myself:* 3 column, "primer" type.

*Organization:* Variable, e.g.,

      1. *Books in Large Print:* author-title entries, interfiled.

      2. *Californiana:* Main entry; title, subject.

*Contents:* Variable, e.g.

      1. *Books in Large Print:* Author, title, publisher, publication date, call number, bibliographic access number.

      2. *Californiana:* Author, title, edition, imprint, collation, all note fields, tracings, call number, bibliographic access number.

*Use:* Intended as primary, not supplementary, tool for specific user groups (for example, the partially sighted) or special parts of the collection (Californiana).

*Distribution:* Variable, usually five-hundred. *Books in Large Print* quantity increased to a thousand copies and distribution expanded to cover other community agencies.

*Cost:* Production: $375.00 set-up.

                  $4.00/page for copy one.

                  $10.92/page for multiple copies.

    Examples:

      1. *Books in Large Print* (122 pages, 500 copies): $2,326.95.

      2. *Californiana* (322 pages, 500 copies): $5,836.19.

*Status:* 1. *Books in Large Print*—Originally published June 1976. Republication November 1977.

      2. *Californiana:* Published June 1976.

      3. *I Can Read It Myself:* Published June 1976.

      4. *Periodicals Union List:* Scheduled March 1978.

      5. *Films:* Scheduled January 1978.

*The Subject Guide* While covered in the catalog services contract as a browsing list, *The Subject Guide to Books on the Shelves* is substantively different from any other browsing list and must be considered and evaluated separately. The fundamental premise is that a significant number of library users prefer to go directly to the shelf area where titles on the desired subject are located and browse among immediately available items. However, while patrons may—often do in fact—know a few classifications or shelf locations, their command of shelf arrangement is clearly limited. Observing patron use of subject volumes of the 1974 *Master Catalog*, it was clear that many used the subject catalog as a means of relating an unknown shelf location to a known, or at least discoverable, subject term—paying little or no attention to specific authors or titles.

The observation of catalog use habits, not in itself new or startling, gains added significance with the shift to a COM master catalog. Both the county library's test use and the experience of other libraries suggested that without careful management of the entire access system, queueing can become a public relations problem of significant size. First, on the basis of test data, catalog usage appears to increase slightly. Second, the average length of catalog use seems marginally longer as the access speed of the COM catalog is offset by an increased tendency to browse. Third, at the same time, physical access points are reduced, it being a reasonable assumption that the number of viewers will be fewer than the number of bound catalog volumes or card catalog trays. Even before test experience, it seemed apparent to the library that some catalog use must be shifted from the *Master Catalog* to other access tools. A subject guide to class numbers had been used at the Baltimore County Library since early 1976. Both on-site observation and the condition of the volumes indicated wide acceptance and heavy use. The Catalog Advisory Board specified that, in light of experience at Baltimore County and elsewhere, a subject guide be produced before beginning test use of the COM *Master Catalog*. The product was defined and published in December 1976.

*The Subject Guide* is a listing of terms used by the county library and of Dewey classifications associated with each term. Table 6.11 outlines essential facts. Public and staff reaction to the tool has been positive, although initial staff reaction was one of dismay at the use and misuse of subject cataloging. Over 50 percent of the subject term-class number pairs included in *The Subject Guide* are unique. The Catalog Advisory Board is currently reevaluating the guide. The distribution quantity will be doubled to a thousand copies, based on observed utility and demand. The first *Subject Guide* showed, in parentheses following the class number, the number of titles (if greater than one) in the collection with that subject term-class number combination. That information, useful to staff, has seemed confusing to patrons. Alternate display schemes are currently being evaluated by the Catalog Advisory Board. Frequency of subject term-classification number pair occurrence will still be available to staff in the as-used subject authority list, published in microfiche format. Ways of reducing the number of terms are being considered. In part, this will be dependent on a long-range reexamination by the library of its cataloging practice. Finally, the *Guide* will be set in larger type with more leading between lines to facilitate rapid browsing.

*Location Index* The microfiche *Location Index* provides each unit of the county library system with copy location data. Addition of current location data to the data base began in February 1976, and conversion of four million retrospective records began two months later. The first *Location Index* is currently being produced and is scheduled for distribution by December 1, 1977, containing locations for all titles held in five of the six regional libraries, about 16 percent of the bookstock, as well as systemwide holdings of titles added since January 1976. Cumulation and republication are scheduled on a quarterly basis, along with the COM *Master Catalog*. The retrospective conversion is scheduled for completion in late 1978, and until that point is reached the location file will grow rapidly.

Table 6.11   *Subject Guide to Books on the Shelves*

---

*Scope:* Entire data base, excluding juvenile titles, biographies (Dewey 92,920), and fiction. A list of subject terms appearing in LACPLS data base with associated classification numbers.

*Frequency:* Undetermined. Annual proposed.

*Format:* Print (photocomposed).

*Organization:* Alphabetical by subject heading. Classification numbers listed after subject heading, currently in ascending numerical order.

*Content:* Subject heading, classification number, number of times subject heading/class number pair occurs in data base.

*Use:* Staff and public use. Intended to give patrons appropriate stack location for browsing. Used by staff in directional reference.

*Distribution:* 500 copies (community-regional-institutional-mobilibraries, regional and systems headquarters).

*Cost:* Production: $.0039 per record.
$10.92 per page publication.
$4,016.63.

*Status:* Published December 1976. Republication scheduled January 1978.

---

Using staff made available through work simplification in various units, the retrospective conversion is a two-part process. Branch shelf-lists are matched against a printed and perfect-bound list of the entire collection in shelf sequence. Copies of this tool were produced in December 1975 under contract with the county's book catalog vendor. Shelf-list matches are indicated, as are the number of copies held by the branch, if greater than one. Completed volumes are forwarded to the catalog input unit for OCR keying. The location code (branch number) is keyed once on each input sheet, followed by packed lines of bibliographic access numbers, followed by copy quantity if greater than one. Input sheets are not proofed.

The decision to convert from branch shelf-lists was based primarily on a sample taken of location files at system and regional headquarters and branch shelf-lists, which showed a 15 percent loss of accuracy between each level in the hierarchy, moving from the branch to the system. Because the greatest percentage of titles would be held by regional and large community libraries and hence the greatest impact on the staff and public could be gained from publication of their holdings, the conversion schedule proceeds from branch to branch roughly in declining order of collection size. Conversion has also been deliberately spread across the county rather than completed region-by-region, to distribute the impact of increased collection access. The exception has been North County libraries, where conversion staff must be locally hired; driving distances (seventy miles from system headquarters to North County regional headquarters, for example) effectively prohibit use of centrally based conversion teams. At this point, field teams have accounted for 35 percent of system holdings; keyboarding lags behind that with 16 percent keyed, but the rate of key conversion has been increasing steadily (figure 6.1).

The location file uses a register index format, listing the bibliographic access number followed by location codes and, when greater than one, number of copies at a location. This sequence requires that the user (usually a staff member) know the bibliographic access number, which is obtainable through any other access product—a major staff education task because the staff has historically regarded the access number as nuisance data. Table 6.12 summarizes essential information.

*Bibliographic Register* A weekly noncumulative edit list, *The Bibliographic Register* includes a register of records added the previous week, an error list, and the scanned input list. Computer printout is used directly, instead of the photoreduced version originally proposed, to decrease turnaround time. This is a no-cost fallout of normal update routines.

*Authority Lists* Lists of all name and subject terms appearing in the master file at each cumulation cycle are displayed, along with frequency of use and associated classification numbers, on 48x microfiche. Used internally by the processing, government publications, and audiovisual sections, the distribution of terms facilitates catalog control. The list is billed as a browsing list—a useful category.

*File Interrelationships* Accustomed to the rigidity of the traditional master catalog plus supplement and with a long exposure to less manipulable catalog production systems, most library staff found it difficult to distinguish between the data-base and the output products and to handle overlapping, nonexclusive products. Figure 6.2 illustrates the conceptual structure of the catalog publication system. System boundaries have been

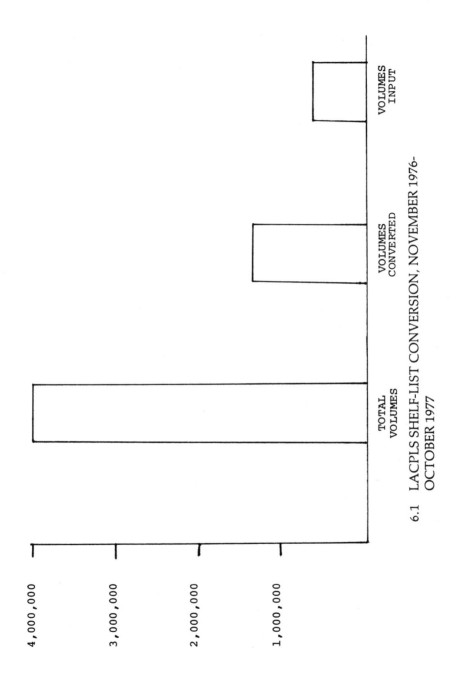

6.1   LACPLS SHELF-LIST CONVERSION, NOVEMBER 1976-
      OCTOBER 1977

extended to encompass delivery of data more often associated with acquisitions or inventory control systems.

Table 6.12   **The Location Index**

---

*Scope:* All items included in the *Master Catalog* (the retrospective conversion is in progress).

*Frequency:* Quarterly.

*Format:* 48X microfiche with header. Data displayed in continuous columns (not frames).

*Organization:* Bibliographic access numbers (BAN) in ascending numerical sequence.

*Content: Header:* Report title, distribution date, fiche number, first BAN in each column.

         *Entry:* BAN, location code, number of copies (if greater than one).

*Use:* Internal (reserves, interlibrary loan, patron referral).

*Distribution:* 120 copies (community-regional-institutional-mobilibraries, regional offices, system headquarters).

*Cost:* Production: $.1254 per frame.
      Delivery:    $35.00 set-up plus postage.

*Status:* Initial production November 1977.

---

## ORGANIZATION AND PROCEDURES

Over the past two years, the library systems group has performed a series of studies aimed at reducing technical services costs, integrating access system products in the internal operations of the sections, and speeding delivery of library materials and necessary access information to the end user. Two studies are of particular significance here.

*Acquisitions System Study* In July 1975, the Library Systems Group was directed to study procedures, files, forms, and staff positions involved in the selection and acquisition of books. Its objectives were to develop procedures to handle increased volume without increased staff; streamline operations to speed delivery of materials to the public; recommend a way of decentralizing selection responsibility, to make collection development more responsive to community needs, improve professional staff development, and minimize acquisition delays; and decrease the overhead associated with book selection and acquisition.

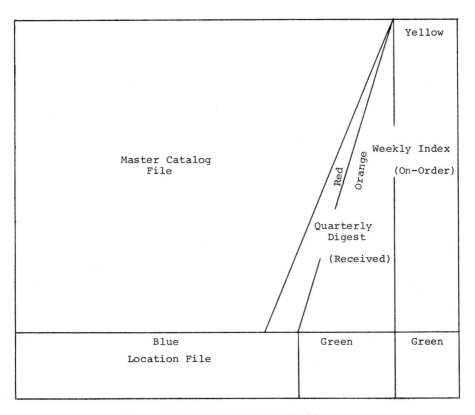

6.2   COLLECTION DATA BASE

Study recommendations, implemented by July 1976, touched all aspects of selection and acquisition. A systems headquarters book evaluation unit in technical services was eliminated, and a smaller acquisitions unit was created to consolidate and clarify acquisitions efforts. Book selection was redirected to public services, with strengthened central coordination but broad decentralization of decision-making responsibility. Some professional and paraprofessional staff were released for direct public service activity, decreasing politically sensitive overhead costs. Several files were eliminated, forms revised, and both work flow and administrative control improved.

*Request Systems Study* In fall 1975, a staff committee, chaired by a member of the Library Systems Group, was appointed to study procedures for processing overdue notices, claims for damaged books, and reinstatement of presumed-missing books. The major recommendation of the committee was that those procedures be performed, as modified, in branches, not at system headquarters. Implementation of that recommendation in February 1976, coupled with implementation of the access study recommendation to close the system headquarters location file, permitted the restructuring of a large interlibrary loan and overdue processing section into a small interlibrary loan section, releasing staff for conversion of four million location records. To accommodate closing the headquarters location file and gradual conversion to a distributed computer-supported location file, interim procedures were developed for intrasystem requests and interlibrary loan, again by a staff committee chaired by a member of the Library Systems Group.

## CATALOGING SYSTEMS STUDY

In spring 1976, the systems group began a study of cataloging and book processing sections, guided by the following objectives:

1. Reconsider all book processing operations in light of the access study, acquisitions study, and change catalog publications program and recommend procedures to facilitate the development of an integrated process.
2. Speed delivery of processed books to community libraries while maintaining or improving the quality of the bibliographic data base.
3. Increase productivity and define statistical measures for ongoing administration.
4. Strengthen the vertical organizational structure of the section and define clear lines of supervisory responsibility.
5. Recommend appropriate, effective use of available technology and of current network and commercial resources.

Study recommendations fell into three major areas:

1. Reorganization of the cataloging and book processing sections into a single processing section with reconstituted and strengthened lines of authority.
2. Redefinition of all major procedures with consequent reevaluation of staffing requirements.

3. Freezing of some and elimination of other files and forms.

Thus in a two-year period, the county library has undergone a large number of fundamental changes that affect every organizational unit in it. While many of the changes relate only peripherally to the access system, others stem directly from it. Several of the changes in the access system have had particular impact on the structure and day-to-day processes of the library: creation of a record in the data-base supplement file at time of order, recognition of the data base and computer-supported catalog as the authority for bibliographic control of the collection; utilization of network and commercial resources in conjunction with the internal access system; and addition of location records to the data-base and systemwide distribution of that information.

The extent and interrelatedness of the changes can be illustrated through a major example: the *processing section reorganization.* The catalog study recommended reorganizing the catalog and book processing sections into a single processing section, with three subunits: cataloging/classification, catalog input/editorial, and book preparation. In recommending a major, and in some details unorthodox, reorganization, the study team was concerned with strengthening the vertical structure of the section, improving coordination between units, and defining meaningful supervisory roles; and facilitating more rapid delivery of processed books to community libraries without sacrificing, indeed while attempting to improve, the quality of the catalog data base. The second goal is germane to this discussion.

Both the book and the data-base record describing it are, in some measure, the responsibility of the catalog/classification unit. The work of that unit is performed with book in hand and, in fact, generates data used in the physical preparation of the book for community library use. In addition, the unit creates data, chiefly a classification number, which substantially changes the existing data-base record. Thereafter the data-base record becomes the responsibility of the input/editorial unit and the physical item of that of book preparation. Name and subject authority control are a catalog editorial (not cataloging) responsibility. They are seen as relating essentially to the bibliographic record. The impact of this organizational redefinition is best amplified by the catalog study procedural recommendations.

Two procedural recommendations stand out. The first is that Library of Congress MARC descriptive cataloging should be accepted without further edit other than a limited, defined review of name and subject authority to ensure integration with the as-used authority. The second is that on the basis of county library experience, it can be assumed that Library of Congress cataloging will be available for 85 percent or more of the titles processed. Since Library of Congress descriptive cataloging is not to be altered by the county library, it need not be reviewed with the book in hand. The work flow of the processing section should therefore reflect the overwhelmingly probable availability of precedent copy. That is, new titles should be presumed to utilize precedent cataloging and to require local classification and, as appropriate, annotation only. Those local additions will be made before precedent copy is actually received. Books will then continue immediately through book preparation. Classification and any annotation will be added to the data-base record, which will be replaced by the MARC record, except for local classification number and annotation, when available. At that time name and subject authority will be reviewed, as necessary, by catalog editorial. Only if no precedent copy becomes available is the bibliographic work recycled through the cataloging/classification unit, to search first through BALLOTS shared cataloging or, as a last resort, supply original cataloging. While it is necessary to have the book in hand for those processes, implicit in this recommendation is a preference for recalling from a community library, after a reasonable period of new book use, one copy of 10 to 15 percent of the titles processed rather than needlessly holding up the distribution of all copies of all titles.

Several conditions make this cataloging cycle possible: the ease and relatively low cost of updating data-base records, a costly proposition with a card catalog; the establishment of a "short" or "acquisition-level" record at time of order, providing basic bibliographic access before the cataloging process is completed; and the standing search features of both the commercial and network resources being used by the county library.

The fundamental issue being addressed by this change is that of speed versus cataloging quality. On the one hand a primary goal of the processing section is to make library materials available to the end user through the community libraries as rapidly as possible. On the other hand, the long-term utility of the collection is in part dependent on the proper application of cataloging rules and standards, particularly authority control. Evaluation of requests and complaints from community libraries, a tour at a busy reference desk, or examination of a compact list of as-used subject terms with occurrence frequencies indicate clearly that, certainly at LACPLS and, one suspects, many other libraries, the first objective tends to be sacrificed in the name of the second—without, in fact, achieving the second. With a card file, usage patterns and frequencies are difficult to observe. Further, the cost of changing authority terms, implying a subsequent requirement to alter individual bibliographic records, has been virtually prohibitive.

A final condition of making the revision of the county library's update cycle not only possible but desirable is the development of commercial software for the analysis and maintenance of authority files. Coupled with the ease of updating data-base records, it now becomes possible to review and improve the use of subject headings. The edit cycle currently being implemented in fact encourages such review, without delaying distribution of new books.

STEPS ALONG THE WAY

Three of the key steps in moving the catalog from fixed to flexible format stand out: standardization of the record format, revision of the contract specifications, and development of staff interest and involvement.

*Format Standardization*  To take maximum advantage of developing network resources, the county library's data base, which existed in a pre-MARC and non-MARC-like structure, needed to be revised. Using some of the funds released by delaying publication of the print-form master catalog scheduled in 1975–1976, the library requested the vendor to retag fields, replacing application-unique tags with MARC equivalent tags and, where possible, analyzing fields and inserting appropriate subfield tags. This was about 75 percent successful. Standardization of tagging, and insertion of appropriate and useful indicators are now being continued by catalog editorial, a process of indefinite duration. Records are upgraded to meet specific needs. For instance, the ongoing need to select Spanish-language titles for a special catalog will result in the addition of the appropriate language indicator.

*Book Catalog Services and Products Specifications*  In September-October 1975, specifications were developed for what was to be an almost entirely changed book catalog services and products contract. Changes in specifications were aimed primarily at standardizing structure and processing as much as possible, allowing broad flexibility for ongoing product development and change during the life of the contract, providing the library with cost detail, and defining expected vendor performance. A major effort was made to review the direction of change with all possible vendors prior to development of specifications and to develop a truly competitive bid. The result was responsive quotations from almost all qualified catalog vendors. The bid and emphasis on the county's position as the largest library customer for those contract services and products resulted in receipt of bid prices actually lower, in some instances, than previous contract prices negotiated in 1972 (tables 6.13 and 6.14). A new contract was awarded in February 1976.

*Catalog Advisory Board*  Finally, in addition to a continuing series of reports, staff meetings, and outside meetings, the Catalog Advisory Board was developed into a successful tool for staff development and involvement. The 1975 catalog bid specifications require a monthly meeting (at the county library) of the vendor's representative and appropriate library staff to ensure ongoing vendor-customer communication, to benefit both. The group selected by the library for these meetings is the Catalog Advisory Board, plus selected managers and operating staff from both technical and public services. The tasks assigned the board, working with the vendor, are the review and resolution of implementation or operating problems (with

Table 6.13   **Projected Access System Contract Budget and Schedule,
September 1975**

| Publication | FY 1975–1976 | FY 1976–1977 | FY 1977–1978* | FY 1978–1979* |
|---|---|---|---|---|
| Weekly index | $ 24,000 | $ 39,000 | $ 44,000 | $ 51,000 |
| *Location index* (BAN) | 0 | 57,000 | 64,000 | 73,000 |
| MiniCat | 22,000 | 44,000 | 44,000 | 56,000 |
| *Master Catalog* | 0 | 146,000 | 146,000 | 187,000 |
| BAN register (and 1975 shelf-list) | 60,000 | 6,000 | 7,000 | 27,000 |
| Browse lists | 20,000 | 20,000 | 10,000 | 26,000 |
| Supplements (est.) | 40,000 | | | |
| Software and management | 20,000 | 45,000 | 45,000 | 58,000 |
| Equipment | 27,000 | 0 | 0 | |
| Special services | 40,000 | 0 | 0 | |
| Parallel operations | 68,000 | 0 | 0 | |
| TOTAL budget | $321,000 | $357,000 | $360,000 | $478,000 (est.) |

*Figures include an annual 3 percent increase in file sizes and a 10 percent inflation cost-increase contract.

a report to administration of those not resolved in a timely fashion), and the definition of products within the broad limits of the contract. Initially the board was heavily weighted with technical services staff—a balance that has steadily shifted over the two years of its existence. The board is chaired by the special assistant to the county librarian.

**Table 6.14  Projected Access System Costs, September 1975**

| | |
|---|---:|
| *Book catalog input* | |
| a. 20,000 titles/year × 85% MARC = 17,000 MARC | |
| @ $.15/MARC record from vendor | $2,550 |
| + $.05/Library of Congress number or key input directly | 850 |
| b. 3,000 titles/year original cataloging input | |
| @ $.60/record direct input keying OCR | 1,800 |
| + $.15/record input processing (vendor) | 450 |
| Total | $ 5,650 |
| | |
| *Vendor catalog contract* | |
| Publications and equipment as specified in study recommendations | 350,000 |
| *Book catalog distribution* | 4,850 |
| *Catalog supplements* | 6,000 |
| *Card catalogs (government)* | 18,000 |
| *System location files* (year 1) | 52,900 |
| *Library shelf-lists* | — |
| Subtotal, catalog access system | $437,400 |
| (Subtotal, current catalog access system) | (546,800) |
| NET ANNUAL SAVINGS        $109,400 | |

Early meetings were exercises in frustration for all participants—monologues interspersed with lengthy silences and line-by-line reviews of weekly edit sheets. About six months later, however, the discomfort began to fade. The vendor developed reports, suggestions, proposals, and background information. Technical services began analyzing edit reports, discerning patterns where they existed, and preparing suitable documentation. In perhaps the most striking change, public services representatives discovered the catalog as a set of public service tools to be defined by librarians in response to specific user needs. Public service representation doubled, and then tripled, as service specialists came in with product proposals and critiques. At present, an editor is appointed for each catalog product, to be responsible for development of the product proposal (goal, contents, format, distribution) and coordination of those production details internal to the library (such as writing text for user instructions), and consultation with appropriate staff. Editors may be from either technical services or public services units. To get both vendor representatives and technical services staff into community libraries and to enable staff in widespread locations to observe and participate on at least an irregular basis, board meetings are held variously at system headquarters and in community libraries. While initially the meetings in community libraries seemed to have no impact, during the next year local meetings had consistently been attended by nonmembers. In part because of increased understanding and encouragement from regional administrators, staff within the host library and region have prepared questions and suggestions in advance and have been able to participate effectively in the discussion.

## PLANS FOR TOMORROW

Today, while product development continues, the library is evaluating the changes that have already taken place and examining requirements and preparing new specifications. Among staff at all levels there is a new sense of the catalog as a flexible tool. There is a growing awareness that, given a sound collection data base, developed and maintained in accordance with recognized standards, the catalog product is a tool for today, for a specific need or group of needs, among a specific set of users, large or small. As those needs and client groups change, the products can change also. It is a view at once burdensome and liberating. Undoubtedly that view of the catalog implies an ongoing commitment to discover the bibliographic needs of the end user and to define and redefine tools to meet those needs. At the same time, while a responsible management must consistently seek the best product possible with the available resources, a product that can be changed does not have to be perfect. That fact has at times been immensely valuable in getting products produced and distributed at all.

Undoubtedly many factors—network development, budgetary changes, and population shifts, among others—will alter, in varying degrees, the appearance of tomorrow's catalogs. It seems more pertinent to examine just two recent Los Angeles County catalog developments that will be significant in defining near-term changes: the ongoing experiments with linkage between book procurement and catalog production, and the implementation of the microfilm catalog.

## BUYING BOOKS AND CATALOGS

One recommendation of the 1975 Library Systems Group study of book selection and acquisition was that the centralized book selection process be decentralized, with specific responsibilities assigned to both regional headquarters and individual libraries. In reviewing various ways of accomplishing this, particularly of involving geographically distant community libraries in new title selection without excessive travel and without cumbersome paperwork at all levels, the library decided on a trial use of a vendor-supplied, monthly, annotated catalog of selected new titles scheduled for publication within the next month. Catalogs are mailed directly to each of the ninety-three libraries, and the libraries individually prepare and return an order to the vendor. Fully processed books are shipped directly to the ordering library. The bills are processed and paid centrally. Processing charges of $.79 per volume (versus approximately $3.00 library unit processing cost) are paid through the book catalog contract.

This program was made more attractive in February 1976 through the chance of the bidding process; the library found itself contracting with one vendor for both supply of books and of catalog products and services. Branch orders are not centrally compiled, and no copies of the titles ordered are received by technical services. Cataloging data are transferred from the vendor's order fulfillment system to the book catalog system. Short records appear in *The Weekly Index* as soon as the order is processed and are updated as full cataloging becomes available. Once the cataloging record is in the data base, any essential changes or additions required to maintain internal consistency are made by catalog editorial.

To date, there are both pluses and continuing minuses. Unquestionably the libraries are receiving new titles faster. Reports from libraries have been uniformly favorable on that point. Central County, the region committing the largest percentage of book budget to that program, reports a dramatic decrease in the backlog of unfilled new title reserves. On the other side, in addition to the anticipated fiscal office work-load impact of handling ninety-three individual accounts, the processing section is adjusting more records—in many cases classification numbers. There are several reasons. First, individual orders are, in fact, individual. They are not compiled by the library or the vendor into a systemwide order. Only in the addition and updating of the catalog record are the separate order records united. Variations in data on spine labels, pockets, and circulation cards are possible from library to library. Second, the software does not allow the library to add a local class number to the technical processing, as opposed to the book catalog, record. Thus, local classification policy would always be a problem, albeit fortunately limited. Beyond that, however, variations between CIP and later Library of Congress cataloging have been troublesome. Processed books received by the libraries reflect the cataloging available at the time each library's copies were processed. While titles may not be back ordered, variations in the speed with which libraries return orders and the variable efficiency of the postal service create a sufficient time span for some copies to reflect CIP and some Library of Congress cataloging. The operating procedures necessary to resolve this problem are being developed by the vendor and the library.

In assessing the importance of this project for planning catalog services, the value of being able to transfer machine-readable data from the book supplier to the catalog services supplier was clear. That data need be handled only once by the library. Further, where both decentralization and maximum delivery speed are primary goals, the addition of the record to the catalog data base by the catalog vendor, based on acquisitions data from the book supplier, avoids a significant amount of centralized record creation, which would only slow the ultimate delivery of processed books. For these reasons, it seems probable that the library will attempt to build links between the book purchase and catalog production contracts, both due to be re-bid before the end of the fiscal year. At minimum, for instance, it is probable that the book contract will require the jobber to subscribe to the MARC distribution service and select a MARC record to use in processing a book or to supply the MARC record to the library or the library's catalog vendor; and to be able to supply a record of library orders, in a specified machine-readable format, to the library's catalog vendor.

## COM CATALOG IMPACT

The other current development that can reasonably be expected to have impact on future catalog planning is the systemwide installation of the microfilm catalog. That impact must result from the radical difference in cost, compared with that of a card or even book catalog; the probable impact on overall catalog usage; and the pattern of peak hour queueing reported by most COM catalog users. These points have been touched on earlier, but it may be useful to review some of the relevant questions. First, the shift to the COM catalog does free dollars previously committed to the print-form master catalog. To what extent can and ought those dollars be directed into other catalog products? If, as seems probable, the shift from book to COM catalog increases total usage while reducing physical access points, what is the most effective solution to the queueing that must result? How much master catalog use can beneficially be shifted to other products? How much use must there be of an alternate product costing, say, $4,800, to provide more access than three more copies of the master catalog (including hardware), totaling the same dollar amount?

## ONE MORE QUESTION

A continuous concern through all the changes to the access system, especially to the published catalogs, has been to keep the end user clearly in mind. Particularly in catalog product development, the constant question—not always asked often enough—is, who is the end user and does this product address that user's needs? In the management and use of tomorrow's flexible catalog, that should still be the basic question.

# Management Experience with COM Catalogs in a Large Academic Library

**7**

Robert H. Blackburn

This paper is addressed to librarians who have decided not to go on building their card catalogs but to use some form of computer-based catalog instead, and also to those who may come to that decision in the next few years. It may even be of interest, as a source of comfort or corroboration, to some who have already acted on that kind of decision. It sets down in some detail our experience since making that decision at the University of Toronto in the spring of 1975. It begins by describing what our catalogs were at that time, and goes on to say how we went about preparing for the change, what we decided about the new catalogs, and what we have learned during just over a year of operating and using a COM catalog of roughly 1.25 million bibliographic records.

## WHAT OUR CATALOGS WERE

In 1975 our university library had card catalogs representing roughly four million volumes held in the central library, the thirty-one departmental libraries, and the libraries of six federated and related institutions that border on the campus. I say *catalogs* because there were many. The main catalog (in the Humanities and Social Sciences Research Library) was in two parts: the old and the new, the new being much the larger and containing the cards for all titles acquired or reclassified since May 1, 1959. The old and new sections were based on different authority files and different filing systems. Each section was divided into a subject catalog and an author-title catalog; the new author-title catalog included hundreds of thousands of campus union catalog entries, edited from reports submitted by campus libraries that do some or all of their own cataloging. The central library also maintained a number of special catalogs and subsidiary catalogs in card form for rare books, maps, documents, university archives, technical reports, theses, microforms, duplicate copy collections, and branch libraries, and a computer-produced book-form catalog for its Science and Medicine Library. We also had (and still have) an official catalog in the technical services area, as well as other authority files. We also owed (but had been unable to provide) full copies of our main catalog to two suburban colleges, founded in the early 1960s, which were limiting their local college libraries to teaching collections on the understanding that their staff would have ready access to the research collections of the central campus. The two suburban campuses account for about ninety-four hundred arts and science undergraduates in a total enrollment of roughly forty-five thousand, which includes about twelve-thousand enrolled in graduate studies. This debt of catalogs owed to the suburban colleges was a good illustration of the fact that in spite of the number and variety of card catalogs we had, and the effort we put into maintaining them, they did not serve the whole university as a handily available key to the collections. Although this shortcoming was quite obvious and was aggravated by the history and geography of our university, it was not unique, but was a shortcoming shared by the library catalogs of most other large universities.

We also had about 1.2 million records in machine-readable form representing all the titles that had been cataloged in our central processing departments. We had been converting our records to machine-readable form for some years for a number of reasons, mainly because we saw a mechanized file as the best hope of integrating our various catalogs and making them more widely available, and as the essential basis for mechanizing many of our operating routines and eventually superseding most manual records. By the spring of 1975 the converted records covered both our old and new catalogs. About that time, we also began making full MARC records for our current cataloging and using them to produce catalog cards. In our budget planning we were reaching a point at which we would no longer be able to go on building a complete card catalog plus a machine file that was being used only for special purposes.

To begin preparing for that time, in February 1975 we appointed an implementation team for data base integration and application under the chairmanship of the systems librarian. (I will use the first person plural to signify the library and its staff; actually the implementation team was appointed by the acting chief librarian, as I was happily spending a sabbatical year in another part of the world.) The nine members of the implementation team were chosen for their expertise in the operations of their areas (acquisition, technical services, reader services, automation) and had, among their terms of reference, these two major ones: to analyze our requirements and priorities for data-base products and services, for machine-readable record completeness and update; and to oversee the successful transformation and machine translation of our machine-readable records from their present formats to one integrated MARC format. The second charge was necessary because our file conversion had begun in 1965, before the Library of Congress and the National Library of Canada and the Office of Library Coordination in the Council of Ontario Universities had announced even their initial MARC formats. Consequently our conversion project had gone through an evolutionary process and had given us at least five separate files that had strong family resemblances but were not really compatible. They had to be put together into one integrated base that would be adequate to meet all the important requirements. It was a tough assignment, but the implementation team went at it with a will in their weekly meetings. Within about four months, it had completed most of the planning connected with translating the various files into a single MARC-structured base.

Then in June 1975 the university's budget letter notified us of a 5 percent cut in operating funds for the following May. The time had come to make a choice between our card catalog and our data base; we chose to close the card catalog, and we had just under twelve months in which to do it. We did not know of any academic library of our size having done such a thing before, but we were prepared to move in what seemed to us the right direction.

## HOW WE PREPARED

There was a great deal of planning and preparing to be done, and all parts of the library operation would be affected by the outcome. Fortunately our implementation team had the right mix of expertise among its members and had shown that it could work as an effective team on this kind of problem. Its assignment was extended or particularized to include preparation for the orderly closing of the card catalogs and provision of an adequate and economic alternative.

As the team identified the specific tasks to be performed, it began to set up subcommittees with the necessary talents and with deadlines to fit the timetable. Eventually there were seven such subcommittees. The team was also advised by three advisory groups, each appointed by one of the advisory councils in each of our three operating divisions of the library.

The implementation team explored, recommended, and carried out plans within the boundaries set by existing policies and budgets. Its work generated the need for a whole series of complicated decisions to be made in order for the work to proceed. As chief librarian, I already had a large advisory council to consult on matters of policy, and I established a smaller planning decisions group to help me deal with other questions raised by the implementation team. We also established an implementation team on orientation and training, to plan and carry out a program of information directed at the library's staff and users and (as one of its terms of reference stated) to minimize the spread of wild rumors. The object of this apparently complex organization was to ensure that the outcome would be based on wide discussion of the best information we could muster and to meet the deadline. It worked fairly well, and if we had the same job to do again, we would organize it in much the same way.

## WHAT WE DECIDED

Although our long-term objective was a fully automated on-line catalog, it was clear from the beginning that our immediate alternative to cards would at least include some computer-output microform. We knew that it was not yet a practical proposition to have our full data base and all its indexes on-line, and we were not even sure how the users of our library would react to the idea of an on-line catalog. This last point we did experiment with during the year by mounting four public terminals with direct access to an abbreviated shelf-list of our Library of Congress–classed collection. We found that many readers, professors as well as students, used this particular on-line file with enthusiasm and wanted little or no help beyond the half-page of printed instructions. In fact the response was so positive that right up until the final estimate of costs, we did plan to include some on-line component in our first alternative to cards.

We had enough previous experience with book-form catalogs made from computer printout to know something about the production time, duplication costs, and update timetables and to know that we did not want to go that route with the full catalog, though paper printout might still be a possibility for certain limited purposes. But whatever hard-copy or on-line components might be included, it soon became clear that COM would have to be the mainstay in our initial alternative to cards.

Any talk of an alternative to the card catalog raised various degrees of dismay and panic in various quarters, and some predictions of doom. However, we had decided to close the catalog. By our definition, closing meant to stop making additions and to remove and discard full card sets when any change was made to a record by way of correction, added copies, transferred copies, and so on. The catalog would remain correct, though shrinking, and all changes and additions would be reflected only in the computer-based products. This is a criterion now being reconsidered, but it is the one on which we proceeded. We had to go on adding cards for categories of records that were not yet in the data base, such as humanities serial holdings, records not in the roman alphabet, and union catalog entries based on reports sent in by other campus libraries. The whole card catalog would continue to stand in its usual place, without any chains or padlocks on it, and we thought most people would prefer to go on using it for a long time as their first place to look.

Because the COM catalog was to be our new mainstay, we wanted it to be as complete and as easy to use as we could make it, and we wanted it to have at least some advantages over the old card catalogs. I will not attempt to recount the debates about whether to divide and how to divide the COM catalog; in the end we agreed to have four separate divisions so that we could watch and see which parts were used most often. We decided that the full bibliographic record (FBR) would be arranged by call number, thus providing a kind of classed catalog that had not been available to the public in our cards. In addition there would be three indexes: author, subject, and title. The initial letters in the names of these four files happened to provide the acronym FAST; this could be taken as a good omen and eventually was used as an acrostic in some of our publicity.

In the indexes, each record displays author, title, short edition statement, date of publication, call number, locations and holdings, and the computer-assigned sequence number of that record (RSN). All titles and series are access points, whether or not they are traced in the manual catalog sense. We hoped that this amount of information in the indexes would give most users all they wanted to know without having to look in a second place.

The frequency of updating the microcatalogs was planned in the light of what our timing had been in card production and filing, what seemed reasonable, and what we could afford. It was agreed that each of the four sections would be updated once a month by issuing a supplement and that the supplements would cumulate monthly until the next full edition was ready.

Deciding on the number and distribution of microcatalog sets was not easy. For our library departments, having their own set or sets was one of the best selling points for COM. The same was true for all our branches and departmental libraries and for other libraries attached in any way to the university. We were eager to take advantage of this fact, since it represented a real breakthrough in bibliographic access, but we had to consider how many sets would really be used to good effect and how many we could afford to supply and maintain. Eventually we agreed to have thirty-two catalog stations in the parts of the library system that are administered within the budget of the chief librarian. These stations varied from large ones with up to seventeen viewing machines, down to small ones with a single machine and some part of the COM catalog.

For other established libraries within the university, we offered one fiche viewer each, as a free introductory offer, if they would undertake to buy copies of the fiche catalog at cost. By the end of the year there were thirty-five such additional catalog stations on campus, making sixty-seven in all.

The question of whether to use microfilm or microfiche was related to the anticipated distribution and use and to the size of the file. The first edition would come to about 1.2 million records with 5.4 million access points. In physical form, at 48X reduction, with 68 characters per line, this would come to 514 sheets of COM fiche or 5 reels of 16mm film, each about 700 feet long. For the busiest catalog stations, where use would justify several sets of the microcatalog, there would be obvious advantages to having each film locked inside a mechanized viewer, ready for the user to switch it on and press the buttons that run the file forward or back. The ease and speed of it, and the security from misplacement of the file, seemed to justify the cost of mechanized film viewers, about four thousand dollars per set of our first edition, each set consisting of five machines. On the other hand we wanted to establish catalog stations in many places in which a set of the catalog plus the supplements could be served adequately by a single fiche holder and viewer, at about one-tenth of the equipment cost. Also, if the supplements were to be issued on film, they would require at least one additional film viewer per station, and each supplement would have to be mounted in each machine by trained staff. In the end we decided to use film for the main file at the busiest stations and fiche for the smaller stations and for all supplements. We eventually installed eighty-one Bell and Howell SR-IV viewers for diazo fiche, equipped with a 17mm lens giving 50X magnification, and sixty-six ROM-3 film readers made by Information Design, with 39X magnification and with internal adjustment to remove the large shadow that covered part of the screen on our first test of a reel large enough to hold 700 feet of 2.5 mil vesicular film.

Concerning the arrangement and spacing of the data displayed in each record, there were two main schools of thought—the first in favor of following the forms people were accustomed to and might therefore accept with ease, the other in favor of devising new forms that would make full use of the flexibility and freedom offered by the computer. The latter view prevailed in the long run, after many sample printouts had been studied, and none of the COM records look much like the face of a Library of Congress card. For example the main entry, wherever it appears in the record, stands out in capitals. In the three indexes the call number is low down in the record, and it is preceded and followed by a solid square block to flag it. And in any of the four sections of the catalog, the end of the last line in each entry is marked by the eight-digit record sequence number in parentheses. The display format is wraparound, and there is no blank line between entries. Planning the format of the data was especially complex because we wanted it to be identical in film and fiche. We wanted it so partly for the convenience of users but also (and especially) for reasons of economy; we wanted to do only one computer run from which both fiche and film would be produced. Nobody seemed to know of the two forms having been produced from one tape before, but we were assured it could be done, and we made that an important aspect of our decision to use both fiche and film.

In the filing order of entries, we had no clear pattern to use as a model— or rather we had too many. Our old and new card catalogs were filed differently, one word by word and the other letter by letter, with an overlay of special conventions. For the COM we chose a strictly alphabetic arrangement, except that leading articles and honorary titles are disregarded. Persons and places are interfiled, saints are interfiled with bishops and kings, and abbreviations filed as written rather than as spoken. Roman numerals in personal names file according to their alphabetic value, and numerics file according to their numeric value (preceding letters of the alphabet) rather than according to their spoken value. Punctuation, being neither numeric or alphabetic, is disregarded.

There were many other details to be decided and arranged within the timetable, which led up to final confirmation of the cutoff date and hour, the time at which we would cease to produce catalog cards and would begin to produce a COM catalog from the data base accumulated up to that moment. The time we chose was 5 P.M. June 30, 1976, one month later than our initial target. The moment arrived all too quickly, and for a few weeks we went through the sensation of waiting for the parachute to open.

## THE TECHNICAL PREPARATION

Preparing for the leap had been not only a matter of making a series of decisions; there also had to be somebody to make the parachute and even to build and fly the airplane. When we began, there was no vehicle readily available for the huge task of data-base integration and COM generation. Our library automation systems division, an ancillary operation that provides an on-line cataloging support service and related products to a whole network of libraries, had to find new techniques for us and apply them without disrupting its regular service to other users. At one point, while the relationships of bibliographic records in our various old files were being sorted out, there were more than three billion characters on magnetic discs and tapes waiting to be assembled and translated into one coherent MARC file. And well before the translation cycle was completed, there had to be a new file opened to receive current entries, geared to mesh with the translated file.

While this integrated file was being built into a live data base, our implementation team and the library automation systems division began to work on the next phase, COM generation. Sorting was the biggest problem; we had four major sorts to do, the largest involving about 1.75 million records, and this was far beyond the capacity of any conventional method of sorting. It could not have been done at all without designing a special multilevel highly compressed sort key. Each major sort involved eight steps and seven merges, each step taking four to eight hours of running time, evenings and weekends, on the Sigma 6. For the second edition, the sort is even bigger, but meanwhile a Sigma 9 has been added and can handle the work more quickly. After the sort, there remained the formating for paragraph, page, and fiche frame, another three hundred hours or so on the Sigma 6.

Meanwhile a vendor had to be found and educated to carry out the final phase: the creation of film and fiche masters and production of copies. Our requirements were pushing against the limits of capability of the vendor's capacity and equipment in a number of ways. For instance, at that time there was no ready-made package to generate the wide range of diacritics required, and library automation systems had to develop a method by which an existing facility could be made to do this. Also, going from the standard 24X reduction to 42X for the film and 48X for the fiche revealed some problems with standard production programs and called for very close quality control in the mechanical and chemical aspects of production. The fact that the images created were to be viewed on two types of readers, with 17mm and 51mm lenses, posed a new problem in coordination. The sheer size of our catalog had led us into a number of special problems and risks that would not have existed otherwise.

## WHAT WE HAVE LEARNED SO FAR

The parachute did open that first year, and by dint of hauling on a few of the cords, we landed safely on firm ground—not on the territory we expect to dwell in forever, but firm ground nevertheless. The first year has confirmed most of our expectations and has also given us some anxious moments and some pleasant surprises.

### COM PRODUCTION

We had obtained some short runs of film and a few sample fiche to see how the programs were working, but they could not possibly give us the feel of what problems would turn up in a full production run. While waiting for the first sections of COM catalog to be delivered, we held weekly progress meetings and began to hear about a whole succession of production problems. Our suppliers had never handled such a large order and had never actually produced film rolls more than six hundred feet long, or film and fiche from the same computer tape, or output adapted to our rather complicated requirements, which included diacritics and 48X reduction. It seemed that everything that could possibly go wrong was doing so, and the beginning of the fall term was looming up very fast; those of us who were not lucky enough to be on vacation were having anxious days and nights.

The first print to arrive was the first supplement on August 24, covering all changes up to August 13, and this at least gave us something to go on. By the beginning of term, we had received two sections of the fiche catalog and distributed them to the key locations. Each full set contained 514 fiche, and as sets were delivered, they were mounted and put into use.

In ordering the fiche, we had specified color coding of the various parts so that they would be easy to keep in order. The main file and the supplements were to be distinguished by having one on black film, one on blue. In looking at sample fiche beforehand, we had seen some with header strips in various attractive colors and thought that it would be worth the slight extra cost to have a different color for each of the four sections (author, title, subject, and full bibliographic record). We had therefore chosen four colors and specified them for the header strips; unfortunately in our innocence, we had not specified that the color should be a tint or dye in the film itself. What we received, to our dismay, were headers on ordinary film with a strip of rather opaque paint applied to the back of the header. Instead of making the fiche easier to use and file, the paint made the headers fairly difficult to read at all. Luckily the stock of painted film that we had ordered ran out, and we were able to switch to ordinary stock for the balance of the year. For our second edition we again want to use color-coded headers, but this time we have been careful to specify dye, not paint. And this time the headers will have reverse printing, which produces clear black characters on the dyed strip.

Production of good microfilm copies, five reels to the set on seven-hundred-foot rolls of 2.5 mil vesicular film, turned out to be almost beyond the limits of existing technology, and the machine that made the first satisfactory copies for us had been shipped from California to Michigan by the time we could inspect the first run and ask for more. The first film was not in place until early October, a month behind schedule, and it was another three months before the initial order was finally completed on equipment in Canada. Along the way we had rejected a number of reels because of their low quality, and we had accepted some rather poor ones, under protest, simply because we needed something.

These production problems suggest the hazards inherent in an undertaking that involves doing a number of things that have not been done before, or not on a large scale. They also indicate the kind of difficulties our COM catalogs had to overcome in order to be accepted as a good alternative to cards.

PERFORMANCE OF VIEWING EQUIPMENT

The acceptability of microcatalogs depends not only on the film or fiche but also on the machines in which they are used, and this was a point that had worried us a good deal. Card cabinets can look worn and dirty, but they seldom break down. We had seen some microform installations, but they were very new, or smaller and quieter than ours, or used equipment not available in Canada, and so there seemed to be very little information to help us. We simply had to look closely at the available models, guess at their performance under heavy use, and make out choices. So far, we have not regretted our choices.

Our fiche viewer, the SR-IV, has been almost trouble free, except that bulbs need replacing every three months or so in the busy locations. We did have the power switch rewired to operate on the low setting only, which is quite satisfactory, and no doubt this increased the life expectancy of the bulbs. We also had the top glass of the fiche carrier modified to prevent its being removed accidentally by inexperienced users, and there have been two instances of the glass being broken. Otherwise the only maintenance required has been a daily cleaning of the glass flats by the local staff and the exchange of old supplements for new ones in the fiche holders.

The ROM-3 film viewers, being motorized, have more parts that can and do go wrong. They are also more vulnerable to abuse, both deliberate and accidental, and the performance history of machines seems to relate closely to the degree of supervision available at the different stations. However, we had provided for regular maintenance and competent repair service, and on the whole the machines have performed very well. In the first eleven months, five machines did not require any service at all, and one machine was repaired or adjusted sixteen times. During a test period of several weeks, fifteen machines in the main public catalog area had an average rate of one failure each per 7.5 weeks, while three unsupervised machines, which stand in the hallway near the entrance to the cafeteria, had an average of one failure per 1.3 weeks, and these failures were of a type which indicated misuse. The average number of service calls per machine in the first eleven months was 5.7; the median was 5 or not quite 1 call every two months. About half the calls related to failure of a machine, and the rest were for adjustments, routine maintenance, or problems with the film. The most common failures have been in the drive belt (sixty-six times), the gears (forty-six times), and with film spooled off the reels (twenty-two times); these may all be related to the fact that our films are exceedingly long. Only twenty-one lamps have burned out, or about one in three machines during the whole period, an astonishingly small number.

Because the ROM design is still evolving to overcome problems encountered in the field, our sixty-six machines are not all the same, and none are the same as they were when we received them. For instance, the breaking of lens pins was the most frequent problem in the first half of the year, but this weakness seems to have been eliminated in recent versions of the machine.

All service and repair of our COM viewers is part-time work for two library technicians who have had the necessary training. Their timetables cover sixty-five hours a week, our busiest hours, and during term they spend about three-quarters of their time on preventive maintenance and repair. Between terms they spend about one-quarter of their time in this way. Since the machines are kept in good condition, we do not foresee any startling increase in service problems, and in fact there may be a decrease as machines continue to improve, as users become more accustomed to them, and as we switch to shorter films. We are convinced that efficient and available service is an essential part of a good microcatalog installation and has to be figured as part of the cost.

## CUMULATIVE SUPPLEMENTS

The ease with which additions and corrections can be inserted has always been counted as one great advantage of cards over any other form of library catalog. Of course card catalogs in an active library are never really up to date, but most users have found it comfortable to assume that whatever does not appear in the card catalog does not exist. A microcatalog, on the other hand, is obviously a by-product of a data base into which new information is being fed every day, and in which that information resides for some time unavailable to most users before it appears on fiche or film.

In order to keep the COM catalogs as up to date as possible, we planned for monthly supplements, fully cumulated, in four parts, corresponding to the main edition. After the first supplement, which covered six weeks, we set the second Friday of each month as a cut-off date and a delivery date ten days later. Thus the new data in each supplement were from ten days to six weeks old, and this was judged to be a fair equivalent to the timetable we had experienced earlier in the production and filing of cards.

On the basis of the number of additions and changes we had been making in the main card catalog, we reckoned that in twelve months the full bibliographic record supplement would grow from one fiche to twelve, and each index from part of one fiche to four. The monthly sets would begin with four fiche partly filled and grow gradually to twenty-eight by the end of the year. This was to call for the formating and production of a total of 256 fiche to cover the year, and this was what we allowed for in our budget. But the supplements grew twice as fast as we had expected, mainly because of corrections.

We recognized in advance that there would be errors of various kinds, and to disarm potential critics we invited them, in our publicity, to help us by reporting any mistakes they found. Many users responded to this invitation with enthusiasm. Their reports included not only the anomalies that were the result of faulty input, bugs in the programs, production flaws, or differences in coding that had not been eradicated in the mechanical integration of our files; they also reported spelling errors and other oddities that had gone undetected for years in the card catalogs. It seems that mistakes, along with other kinds of data, are more easily scanned and spotted in a sequential column than on cards.

As errors were corrected, they were fed into the supplement. At the same time we were beginning to put some new categories of records into machine form, such as our special listing of government publications, and these too went into the supplement. These were all in addition to our regular catalog input and adjustments; and once into the supplement they were repeated each month. After the third month we decided to economize by omitting the blank line that we had allowed between entries. Later we decided that minor corrections that did not affect filing should not be fed into the supplements but displayed first of all in the second full edition. Even so, by March the production of supplements had exceeded the total we had set for the year; we cut off the first supplement at that point and started a second one. At the beginning of the new fiscal year in May, we reduced the second supplement to a bimonthly cumulation; even so our total production for the year overran the original estimates by about 60 percent. If we had continued with monthly cumulation as planned beforehand, the overrun would have exceeded 100 percent.

Perhaps the rapid expansion of our supplement was brought about by circumstances peculiar to our library at that time, but I suspect that other libraries at the time of closing their catalogs may have a similar experience, and should allow for it.

THE CLOSED CARD CATALOG

The supplements were related rather closely to the card catalogs because we had decided that sets of cards were to be withdrawn when any change was being made to a main entry, and the updated entry was to go into the supplements. This meant withdrawing about two thousand cards a week, and that has created some problems; readers who were still using the card catalog sometimes missed cards that they knew they had seen before, and they complained. Occasionally their complaints were quite justified; there were times when cards had been withdrawn before the COM supplements were printed, and the records were not available anywhere. Our temporary answer to this was to delay the withdrawal of cards, but it is not a very good answer. Our effort to close the card catalog down systematically, keeping it correct by withdrawing altered records, is not appreciated by the readers and is costing staff time. The whole question of card files is under review again, and our handling of them is likely to change.

COSTS

We have no clear-cut before-and-after cost comparisons to make, no detailed accounting of a sudden shift from manual methods to full mechanization. We have mechanized the access to the catalog, but we still use manual files for bibliographic control. We are still working on the card catalog itself, closing it down, still adding certain things to it, still keeping up some special card files, still planning to convert some of them to machine form. And of course we are still learning how to reduce the cost of running the COM catalogs and learning how to use them more effectively. And there are so many complicated interactions between the COM catalogs and other changes that have been made, or are in process, that it is not possible to say precisely what the COM has cost or how many dollars it has saved or will save.

We can put a price on certain things. As a very minor instance, the reference department eliminated one of the two telephones at the catalog information desk because the main catalog is now available in so many other places. A more significant saving arose out of eliminating the production of something like four hundred thousand catalog cards a year for our roman alphabet acquisitions; this process had been automated for some time, and so the saving was simply transferred to a different kind of computer output. Another sizable saving grew out of the fact that cards that are not produced do not have to be filed; this fact was so obvious so early that it typifies the special management problem posed by savings that involve people. The staff in our filing section began to feel insecure as soon as our intentions were known and competed for transfers to any suitable openings in other parts of the library. As transfers were made, we had more and more of our filing done by student help and other part-time staff. We had assured the regular staff that those left in the section would be offered equivalent jobs elsewhere in the system, without loss of pay, and given whatever retraining was needed. When the time finally came, there were only three filers left to be resettled in this way, and their retraining would count as a minor cost of the microcatalogs.

I have already said something about the problems of processing mechanized records into a usable file and producing the magnetic tape from which COM can be made. During the first year of operation, our library automation systems division improved the process so that data processed once in this way do not have to be processed again every time they are to be included in a COM output; they can be stored and then merged with new or altered data that have been newly processed. This cut-and-paste process, as we call it, is considerably cheaper than processing the whole file each time. It has already made a unit-cost reduction in our supplements and will make a big difference to the cost of our third full edition. At the moment we pay for the processing of merged data, which has not been changed since a previous processing, at the rate of seven-tenths of a cent per entry plus four cents per page column; this is significantly less than the price of processing new data, which is also four cents a page-column plus 1.2 cents per entry plus two or three smaller components.

Using price quotations such as these, applied to an estimated throughput and a year's experience, our library's planning and budget committee has fitted the various aspects of COM production into a tight automation budget that includes several other operations and preparations and is less than we spent last year. For COM production our budget is $139,000, or roughly ten cents times the number of shelf-list records we shall have by the end of the year. To summarize last year's costs, we absorbed a 5 percent cut in total operating budget of the library, closed our card catalog, opened a full-scale COM catalog and adjusted to it, and distributed it on film or fiche to sixty-seven stations in the campus library system, and survived.

## ORIENTATION OF USERS

Adjusting to the idea of COM catalogs began as soon as we decided to close the card file. It began with the staff, especially those who might feel their jobs were threatened and all those who could not really imagine life without a foundation of 3 x 5 cards. We put the early announcements into our weekly staff news sheet but soon realized that something more was needed.

About eight months before the target date for the great change, our implementation team for orientation and training began to issue a special news sheet to the staff whenever there was progress to be reported. Their publicity built up to an hour's meeting with all library staff, in four sections, to review the whole project and prepare them for their first chance to use samples of our catalog on fiche and film. Training sessions were then held for a number of people who acted as instructors; they in turn gave practical instruction to the whole staff in groups of five or six people at a time. I went to one of these sessions and began to wonder whether our information program had really made the whole business seem too formidable. When they finally got their hands on the viewing machines, the people all seemed amazed and relieved at how simple it was. I suspect their reaction was more desirable in the long run than the opposite one that might follow from too little advance information.

The same implementation team worked out a schedule of publicity directed at library users, carefully planned to give out basic information and not to create either alarm or unreasonable expectations. When one major teaching department showed signs of alarm, it was visited and reassured by two members of the team. There were two special mailings to all teaching staff, a succession of articles and notices in the university's weekly bulletin, and a few paid advertisements in the student newspapers. There were also signs, posters, leaflets, and an audiocassette that could be mounted in strategic spots to offer users a short lecture; there was also a very handy little instructional flip-chart designed to stand on the table beside the viewing machines. Although these things could be planned in advance, some of them had to be produced very late in the game, when details of the text could be filled in. Distribution and mounting of them was an essential part of the action as the microcatalogs came into use, and helped to bring about a smooth transition.

## ACCEPTANCE OF COM BY LIBRARY USERS

Our staff had good reason to be anxious about how readers would react when actually faced with a COM catalog for the first time. We know something about the difficulty of introducing new patterns of use and about the degree to which signs, announcements, and leaflets are usually ignored. We were therefore braced for a sharp hand-to-hand engagement of explaining and training. Our staff were girded for the attack, but it never came; most readers simply walked past them to the COM viewers and went to work. The readers seemed much less aware than we were of the problems, or at least less concerned, and most of them took to the new catalogs quite naturally. Of course there were a few people who despise machinery and always will, but it was soon apparent that the card catalogs were nearly deserted. When I visited the undergraduate library, I usually saw ten or twelve people standing at the COM catalogs, and one or none at the nearby card catalog, which was almost as up to date and should have been easier to use because it was limited to the holdings of that particular library. In the humanities and social science research library, the majority of users switched quite quickly to COM, even though it lacks the campus union catalog and nonroman records. We had invited all users to help us by reporting any errors they found, and they did that, but complaints we received were less often about the catalog itself than about its distribution. For instance, one reader complained that the fiche viewer in his part of the stack, up on the thirteenth floor, was often in use when he wanted it and he had been obliged to walk down a flight to use the machine on that level; he seemed to have forgotten that until a few weeks earlier there had never been any catalog in the stacks. Perhaps one of the hazards of starting a microcatalog is that it creates a demand that can never again be filled by card catalogs.

## USE PATTERNS

One pleasant surprise, which became visible quite early, was that the circulation of our "old class" books jumped to about three times its former level, as a result of the "old" and "new" entries being interfiled in the COM catalog. Apparently a majority of readers had not been bothering to look at the "old class" part of the card catalogs.

Queues at some machines, and neglect of others, soon showed that we had been wrong in some of our preliminary guesses about the popularity of various sections of the catalog, and we adjusted the distribution as quickly as we could.

To help us lay plans for the second edition, we felt the need for more in-formation than could be got from casual observation, so during the first five weeks of the spring term, the staff carried out a study of the micro-catalog environment. Hundreds of questionnaires completed by the users of catalogs were analyzed, users were interviewed, some staff recorded their own uses of the catalogs, and the use of particular stations was observed and recorded over sample periods. Thus we learned something about what users were really doing, as well as what they thought they were doing. There was no time for a study to be carried out with great scientific elegance, and certainly more comprehensive studies are needed, but we did obtain helpful answers to a number of questions that were important to us just then.

We found that the simple alphabetic filing pleased the readers. Typical responses were "new system more logical—like it—simpler" and "not hard for the eye to zero in on what is wanted." Even the library staff, accustomed as they were to traditional library filing, indicated little or no difficulty in using the new order.

No category of user reported much difficulty in using the film or fiche, though film appears to be slightly more popular. There were many com-ments such as "marvelous idea," "fast and easy to use," and "you have made bibliographic work much easier." There were also many helpful suggestions about "crowded image" and "dirty screens," the need for more checks on the misfiling of fiche, and the need for more legible headers on the fiche. Fortunately these were problems that could be remedied to some extent. People also complained of some difficulty in keeping track of their place on the screen, and we are experimenting with thin guiding lines applied to the outside of screens. Besides the many enthusiastic or con-structive comments, there were also some others, of which the briefest and most sweeping was "ugh."

Users tended to overestimate their use of author and subject as access points and to underestimate their use of the title index. In 2,066 uses by library staff and 6,088 uses observed at public stations, there was the fol-lowing pattern:

|                           | Staff Use | Public Stations |
|---------------------------|-----------|-----------------|
| Author index              | 33.25%    | 36.23%          |
| Title index               | 27.69     | 33.06           |
| Subject index             | 6.87      | 20.52           |
| Full bibliographic record | 13.65     | 7.44            |
| Supplement                | 18.54     | 2.75            |

The time spent per search shows no significant difference between fiche and film.

The amount of information given in the indexes was sufficient to satisfy most searches by library staff and by others. The title index, which includes all titles, is used about half as much again as the subject index. There was a variation from station to station, but in more than eight thousand recorded uses, the traffic at the three indexes was in the ratio of 35 (author) to 32 (title) to 17 (subject). On this basis, the number of subject indexes at the larger stations can be cut down.

Use of the full bibliographic record (FBR) was surprisingly low and was mostly by library staff. Accordingly the number of copies has been reduced at some stations. Departmental libraries across the campus, which bought full sets of the fiche catalog at a somewhat subsidized rate in the first year in order for them to try the whole thing, have been charged a more realistic price in the second year, based on the full add-on cost of extra sets, but they have also been allowed to order only those sections they want. This year they pay $275 for the full edition plus $100 for the supplements, but quite a few departments have ordered only certain parts rather than full sets. If we had made copies free to all university departments, then all would expect to receive a full set of everything; the charge has proven to be a simple way of matching the demand to the budget, and I do not think it has inhibited distribution unduly. For instance, one teaching department, which has no departmental library and is just across the street from the central library, bought its own viewer and a full set of the fiche catalog.

We are not at all sure that the classed arrangement is best for the FBR, at least in our circumstances. It breaks into a number of separate sequences: one for the Library of Congress classification, another for records that were included from the Instructional Media Centre, a special one for government publications, several rare-book sequences, and so on, and each section has its own distinctive label. This means that a person who has used our index and wants to look up the full record using the call number must take care to look in the appropriate part of the FBR. This particular kind of search, which would seem to be the most usual, would be greatly simplified if the FBR were in one sequence arranged by the arbitrary record-sequence number, but we might then have some demand for a separate classed index, at least for the major part of the collection that the Library of Congress classed. There are also good arguments for arranging the FBR by author or by title. This is a question that could not be resolved in time for our second edition, but I do not expect that our third edition will have the FBR in classed order.

In our second edition the FBR will be on fiche only. The three indexes, having grown, will take two films each, but the films will be much shorter than seven hundred feet.

The greatest surprise for many of us was the light use of the supplements. We know that use is spread over the whole collection and is not concentrated on the recent acquisitions, but we were still exceedingly concerned about keeping the catalog up to date. Although the supplement was the first microcatalog to be mounted for use, our survey five months later showed that many of our readers were unaware that it existed, and those who did know about it used it only occasionally or never. Hardly anybody used it except the library staff, and in the survey it accounted for only 17.8 percent of their use. For budget reasons we have reduced the supplement to a bimonthly cumulation, and this appears to be still more than is needed by most of our readers. On the other hand our staff members who need to use the supplement in their business would prefer to have immediate access through a computer terminal rather than having to wait for any kind of printout on paper or film, and it now appears that the need for this kind of access is far more localized than we had thought.

The second year of full-scale operation, with most of our readers quite accustomed to microcatalogs, may modify our initial impressions; but it seems to me now that the wide distribution of COM supplements may not be the best way to provide short-term updates. The need might be met more effectively by having the last year or so of additions and changes on-line, available to library staff mainly through terminals that would be available in any case for other purposes and available to the public at only a few strategic points in the library system. Long-term updates for wide distribution will still require periodic new editions in microform. The precise form that this combination should take, the practical economics of it, and precisely how it should be brought about still require a great deal of analysis and planning, but after a year's experience with COM, we can proceed toward it with greater confidence in the outcome.

## SUMMARY

I hope these details of our experience at Toronto, in a year of preparation and the first year of living in the world of COM catalogs, will serve other libraries as useful hints for prospective settlers and not as discouragement. I am convinced that microcatalogs have an essential role to play in the transition away from cards and a continuing role in the management of catalog records for quite a long time to come. To end on a cheery note, I quote from a brief message that came to me last winter from a reader I had never met, a visiting professor from a distinguished foreign university: "Your microfilmed catalog must surely be second to none in the world. I today carried out a literature search in under an hour—which would (I am certain) have taken several weeks of eyestrain, frustration and sore feet at my own university." That sort of letter, I assure you, was never elicited by our card catalog.

# Constituency Concerns in OCLC Management: User, Library, Network, OCLC

# 8

Glyn T. Evans

It is my intention in this paper to review the relationship among the parties in an on-line shared cataloging network and to examine the environments within which each operates. These two steps are necessary precursors to a review of the constituency concerns held by each partner in the relationship. Finally, I will briefly discuss my perception of the long-range and short-range futures of the constituents.

Three preliminary statements are necessary at the outset. First, the paper is not concerned with the decision whether to join OCLC or not. It addresses the issues that follow that decision. Second, although cataloging and the catalog are central to library operation, it is not possible to view them in isolation. Changes in the management, and in the economics, of cataloging have a direct impact on all other services and functions. Always true, this is particularly apparent in an on-line environment where it is easy, and more obviously cost-efficient, to surround the bibliographic record with other data (for example a register of locations for interlibrary loan) normally considered the purview of other library departments. Third, when I use the term OCLC I am really talking about a national library network. I do not try to make claims from which even OCLC would shrink; and I am certainly not advocating that OCLC is, or should be, the national network, at the expense of say BALLOTS, or RLG, or University of Chicago, or firms such as SDC, Lockhead, or CLSI, although it is true that a thousand libraries in the same network is a compelling number.

Many of the problems faced by OCLC and its users were and are inevitable, no matter who built and designed the network of acceptance. They were the unavoidable consequence of a major technological revolution. OCLC, network, and libraries alike are learning on the job, particularly in the social and administrative areas, as well as the technical. A network is a complex social organism more than it is a communication-computer achievement. New questions, latent or unrecognized in other environments, are revealed. New problems are created by change.

There is a fundamental reason for the success of networks like OCLC, quite apart from their historical and technical inevitability, and that is their nature as a grass-roots organization. OCLC was designed, built, and supported by librarians working in the field, with other jobs to do. It is being maintained almost totally by libraries paying for service from their own budgets. Its committees and task forces are librarians who daily face operational reality. Under such conditions, even with all the stupidity and anxiety, frustration, egotism, and delay, a network must succeed. Heaven protect us from remote monoliths projected from above.

## RELATIONSHIP AMONG THE PARTIES

There are three types of relationships among the parties—OCLC, the network, and the using and sharing libraries—all of which are shown in figure 8.1. The contractual relationship (in the first instance) is between OCLC and the network.[1] Members of networks will then have subsidiary contracts with the individual network.[2] The type and content of each contract will vary with the type of network and the different individual library requirements, or rather the requirements of the parent institution of the library. Some will be private academic, some federal agencies, some civil agencies, and so on. The provision of legal services is not an insignificant part of network activity. The same is true of the fiscal arrangements through which libraries are billed for OCLC services.

Essential as the above are, the reason for the network's existence is to provide service—primarily training and educational services, and the start-up services, such as catalog card profiling, terminal installation arrangements, and work-flow consultation.

The functions of regional networks are contracting, marketing, education, evaluation, surveys, accounting, maintenance, and research and development.

Indirect participation in OCLC through regional networks provides the following advantages that cannot readily be achieved through direct participation: contractual service, fiscal service, telecommunications, training, local knowledge, local sensitivity, geographic proximity, and headquarters staff.

The following list of services provided to network participants is typical of the services offered by all regional networks headquarters, although local conditions and needs may dictate different structures and emphases.

| Training Type | Target Group |
|---|---|
| Information | Enquiring libraries |
| Phase I | Library administrators |

|                          |                          |                    |
| ------------------------ | ------------------------ | ------------------ |
|                          |                          | O = OCLC           |
| ▰▰▰                      | = Service relationship   | N = Network        |
| ⫼⫼⫼⫼⫼⫼⫼⫼⫼⫼                | = Contractual relationship | U = Using library  |
| ■▮■■■▮■■                 | = Fiscal relationship    | S = Sharing library |

### 8.1   NETWORK RELATIONSHIPS

| Phases II and III | Cataloger, operators |
|---|---|
| Basic | Staff that needs this as prerequisite to subsystem training |
| Subsystem | Staff responsible for utilizing subsystem |
| Library school | Faculty, students |
| Phase IV | Participating libraries |

### Additional Services: System Operation

Update sessions
Workshops
Profiling and profile changes
Error report, screening, analysis, and correction
On-site consultation on request
Continuous liaison re problems, questions
Library of Congress hot-line service on cataloging
Card reruns
Data set relocation
Terminal purchase and installation
Authorizations
Reclass projects
OCLC-MARC distribution tape service
Accounting

### Documentation

Lending service for videotape or cassette instructional material
Provision of PALINET and AMIGOS manuals
SUNY/OCLC implementation memoranda series
Support material distributed at training sessions
Occasional reports as appropriate (for example, printer survey, public service
  terminals)

### System Development

Participating in task forces engaged in design of new subsystem
Participation in OCLC and SUNY/OCLC advisory committees regarding
  operational systems and subsystems
Task forces currently active: AACR2, audiovisual material, music, maps,
  ILL
Advisory committees currently active: cataloging, serials, acquisitions
SUNY/OCLC staff attends and represents SUNY/OCLC
  participating libraries at meetings of Council of Computerized Library Net-
  works, OCLC board of trustees, OCLC regional directors, OCLC network
  coordinators

Figure 8.2 illustrates the structure of the training program outlined
above.

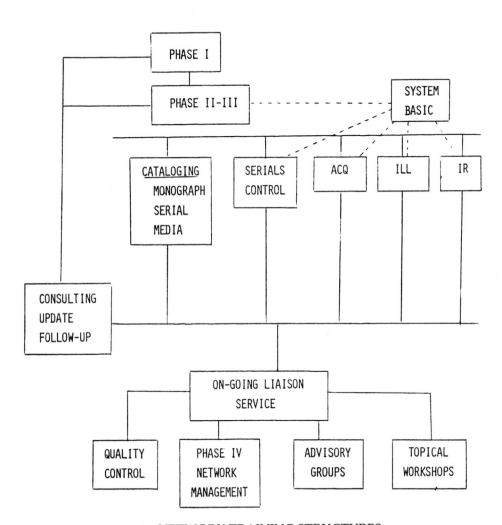

8.2   NETWORK TRAINING STRUCTURES

## THE NETWORK ENVIRONMENT

The environment within which the library-network-OCLC interaction takes place is extraordinarily complex, which in part explains some of the problems, concerns, and frustrations of the different constituents. The omnipresent questions are, "Why did . . . why hasn't . . . why . . . why not . . . ?" They are the staple diet of network activity.

Figure 8.3 shows library, network, and OCLC at the center of a very complex set of interacting forces. The listings are not intended to be complete but rather indicative of some of the groups that force or inhibit action by any one of the three components.

The four main headings are finance, governance, standards, and the library profession, and the interactions exist among the four. A pair of examples will suffice to illustrate these interactions.

External forces have an impact on the library operation in a very immediate and dramatic way. For instance, the international standard requirement of ISBD punctuation made participating libraries change their input procedures to accommodate that requirement. The CONSER requirement for full fixed-field coding had a similar impact on libraries. On the other hand, user request for new fields or codes, which may require a change in the MARC format, cannot be implemented until they have received the approval of the ALA MARBI committee and until they are accepted by the Library of Congress as a change to the MARC format.

Other brief examples are the impact of the withdrawal of NSF support of ANSI Z39, the impact of the Kellog Foundation grants on system and network growth and operation, and the extent to which OCLC's fiscal stability affects its research and development implementation ability.

Finally figure 8.3 is concerned only with the administrative components of the environment. The rapidly developing technological environment, the technical needs of the developing National Plan for Library and Information Service, and the gradual convergence of computer and communications techniques are not represented.

## REVIEW OF CONSTITUENCY CONCERNS

### LIBRARY CONCERNS

*Service Standards* Response time has been the omnipresent problem. The success of OCLC has been its greatest weakness, and we have all contributed to the problem. It was probably unreasonable to expect that OCLC and its data base could grow as rapidly as they did, and the system has had to play catch-up with the customer. It has had to cross technical hurdles to do so. For OCLC to go from a Sigma 5 storing fewer than one million records in 1974—when the State University of New York (SUNY)

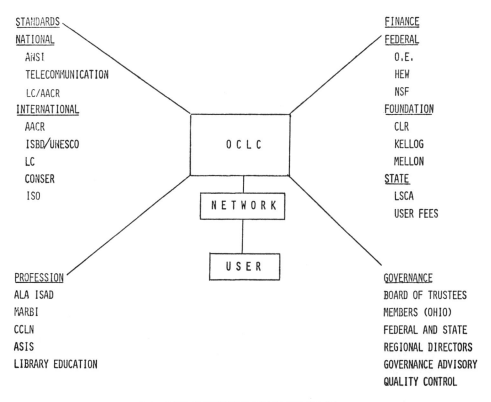

STANDARDS
NATIONAL
 ANSI
 TELECOMMUNICATION
 LC/AACR
INTERNATIONAL
 AACR
 ISBD/UNESCO
 LC
 CONSER
 ISO

FINANCE
FEDERAL
 O.E.
 HEW
 NSF
FOUNDATION
 CLR
 KELLOG
 MELLON
STATE
 LSCA
 USER FEES

O C L C

N E T W O R K

U S E R

PROFESSION
ALA ISAD
MARBI
CCLN
ASIS
LIBRARY EDUCATION

GOVERNANCE
BOARD OF TRUSTEES
MEMBERS (OHIO)
FEDERAL AND STATE
REGIONAL DIRECTORS
GOVERNANCE ADVISORY
QUALITY CONTROL

8.3   NETWORK ENVIRONMENT

joined OCLC—to four Sigma 9s linked together to store 3.2 million records in 1977, when no one had previously linked even two, is a considerable technical achievement.

In addition, there is now a battery of eleven minis in front of the Sigmas. Yet when SUNY joined in 1974, the first mini was an object of curiosity in the test tube. Current plans will place minis between the Sigmas and the data base, creating a unique system architecture.

Part of the cost of that achievement was disappointment and disillusion in the member libraries. OCLC has such optimism that it failed at first to admit to itself that it could not maintain performance standards at such an accelerated growth rate. The frustration and cost to the libraries was high. Productivity dropped and projects slipped. Staff morale was hurt, and difficulties were created for administrators in scheduling and other areas.

The saving force, ironically, was that the drop in library productivity also caused a drop in OCLC revenue. The way to pay the bills was to improve service. These are the facts of life when there are no grants or subsidies to fall back on. The monthly statistical reports of OCLC activity demonstrate the impact of response time on revenue.

Strong action was eventually taken by the board, when it imposed moratoria on growth if average response time exceeded eight seconds. Following that action, two more moratoria have been imposed, and growth is now very carefully controlled.

The quality of products is another area of concern. Production errors occur in the various products—catalog cards, accession lists, distribution tapes—and they are an expensive nuisance. OCLC has, however, established policies under which it will replace defective outputs provided libraries notify their networks within a specified period of time.

OCLC terminals manufactured by Beehive are protected by a ninety-day warranty and service maintenance contracts. The terminal has proved to be very stable; the maintenance service charge has decreased from forty dollars to thirty-nine dollars to thirty-three dollars per month in two successive years. Breakdowns caused by carelessness, such as coffee spilled in the equipment or paperclips in the keyboard, are excluded from the service contract.

There are three other products from OCLC that do cause concern, however. The first is documentation, which leaves much to be desired, as demonstrated by the almost universal adoption of the PALINET cataloging manual and the AMIGOS serials control manual for OCLC users. Second is statistical reporting. There is a mass of valuable management information latent in the system that would be a boon to administrators if it were organized and published. There has been one improvement in reporting this year, almost vitiated by a concurrent change in the method of computation during the year. Summing up twelve monthly reports does not equal the annual report, although in future years the reports will be consistent. Third, unexpectedly, is the billing process. The development of administrative procedures at OCLC has lagged behind growth both in size and in technical ability. Only the card invoice from OCLC is computer produced; everything else is a manual record. The sooner this is improved, the better. Many networks are well able to handle machine-readable accounts records, to everyone's advantage.

These are relatively minor problems, and OCLC is aware of them. But they are concerns, and they are irksome.

Another large problem for user libraries is the overoptimistic implementation dates set up by OCLC. For example, four years to produce serials catalog cards is too long if you have been expecting them within months and if you have changed your internal procedures in anticipation of their advent. This is a minor if blatant example, and one that would not really inflict much hardship on a library. But a really major reorganization delayed for a year—such as serials control with automatic check-in—can cause much distress.

*New Products* New products and services are closely related to research and development performance. Libraries make a significant (if largely unrecognized) contribution to and investment in new product design and implementation and to the establishment of new-product priorities. First, the letters, comments, and telephone calls to network headquarters are carefully studied for new suggestions and ideas. These may then be referred to a specific advisory group or task force, such as the reorganization of holding symbols for interlibrary loan or the development of "all-produce" for public-library systems. Alternatively a new advisory group may be created to address a specific topic—perhaps music cataloging or manuscript cataloging. The library may have delegates to specific task forces either within the region or within OCLC itself. Even if travel expenses are paid by regional networks, there is local investment in staff time.

When the advocacy and advisory moment has passed, the library makes a real investment in start-up costs in training, staff reorganization, and perhaps the acquisition of more terminals to accept new services. Each case is different; each has to be assessed on its own merits; each has its own personnel, administrative, and fiscal problems. It is not idle to stress that the most important component is training, retraining, and the development of competent staff.

Finally it is necessary to monitor the performance of a new system facility. How efficient is it? How effective? Can it be improved? Am I getting my money's worth? These questions always follow the introduction of a new service.

And, always, the omnipresent and extraordinarily complex question of timing must be considered. Is it possible to synchronize the efforts of

OCLC network, and individual library? OCLC does not want to invest in services that users are not ready or able to use, any more than libraries want to invest time, money, and emotion in a service that does not yet exist.

*System Charges* The service has to be paid for, and management has to assess what it will cost. The work is in two phases: examination and justification of the decision to use the service, and then annual budgeting thereafter. The first phase (and to some extent the second) is hampered by a general ignorance of one's pre-OCLC cataloging costs, and even a reluctance to admit to the existence of real costs in a local environment. When that hurdle is jumped, however, one discovers that OCLC costs have remained remarkably stable in the last few years, despite steep inflation elsewhere in the economy. A terminal cost $3,700 in 1974 and in 1977; the monthly terminal maintenance charges actually dropped from $46 in 1975 to $39 in 1976 to $33 in 1977; the FTU charge to networks rose just nine cents between 1975 and 1977 (from $1.11 to $1.20); and the cost per catalog card remained constant at $.034 from 1974 through 1976, rising only to $.039 in 1977.

*Internal Management* OCLC brings new demands to management at all levels. Because OCLC is a novelty and because few member libraries had previous experience with automation, implementation of OCLC often took place in a goldfish bowl, with everyone from president to clerk interested and anxious, some praying for success, some hoping for failure.

The fundamental issue is staffing. Involvement of staff in planning, sensitive allocation of work, competent training, and faculty development are essential. Successful implementation demands a total rethinking of the entire library operation. Merely plugging in a terminal does not solve anyone's problems.

*System Stability* Once the library has made its commitment to OCLC and has changed its staffing patterns, work flow, and management procedures accordingly, it has the right to expect system stability: that is, that the system will be available during the hours when OCLC says it will.

Many years ago, I wrote that I did not believe library on-line systems needed redundancy in hardware systems in order to maintain continuity of service. I was wrong. The sheer size of OCLC changes the game. If OCLC is down unexpectedly for one hour at peak time, bringing fifteen hundred terminals down with it, it also brings down fifteen hundred catalogers all over the country at perhaps eight dollars per hour, for an *hourly* cost of twelve thousand dollars. It does not take too many hours at that rate to make system backup economically attractive. Libraries are trained to schedule staff for nonterminal activity in case the system goes down, but that is still not a complete solution.

Systems come down for a variety of reasons. Lightning does strike twice, and Thurber was right to worry about floods in Columbus, Ohio. Users bring the system down too. With sixteen million holdings records, the system is beginning to get the one-in-ten-million occurences that demonstrate the validity of Murphy's law: if something can go wrong, it will. Programmers bring the system down; so do operators and engineers.

One major crash, and the only one where records were lost from the data base, occurred at OCLC when five independent occurrences, none of which could "ever happen," all happened in a swiftly concatenated sequence.

Nevertheless I am pleased to state that OCLC is exceptionally stable. Normally the system operates in excess of 95 percent of its scheduled time. Furthermore, the design of the new generation terminal and new system architecture seek to alleviate the downtime problem totally.

Library planners can schedule terminal work with a fair degree of confidence, although it is true that OCLC occasionally brings the system down for some engineering purpose without giving adequate notice.

NETWORK CONCERNS

Network offices exist only to serve their members. Their job is to provide or facilitate services that will improve the efficiency and effectiveness of library operation. They seek to buy such services at favorable rates or develop them if necessary. They must advocate and protect the needs of their members. Their concerns, therefore, are primarily the concerns of their libraries, even though they have well-defined operational problems of their own.

Networks play a pivotal legal and administrative role in library service within their region. Further, they are the repositories of skills that are sufficiently rare and expensive that the costs are best spread among many libraries.

Network headquarters are usually staffed by activists who have a well-developed philosophic base and knowledge of the kinds of services that a library should be able to have access to on-line, and who understand the compelling economic forces underlying librarianship today. They also work unconscionably long hours. They therefore speak to, and are concerned about, the library problems already addressed; OCLC service and product performance; OCLC research and development performance; OCLC system charges; training and implementation problems, including guidance on internal management problems; and system stability.

Each network is the legal interface between a library and OCLC, and it negotiates contracts with OCLC, receives invoicing from OCLC, and provides training and general liaison service.[3] The only reason a network user contacts OCLC directly is to resolve technical failure problems with the terminal or the telephone line.

Each network does its job differently. Each has its own training procedures, implementation procedures, governance and advisory structures, and so forth, and all of these are the result of local choice and local conditions.[4] (*Local* is an awkward word to use in regions as large and diverse as the ten states of SOLINET, or the six of New England, but you understand its context.) These bring their own local problems and concerns, particularly regarding funding of the network. Most networks are financed through service charges to members, although the techniques of assessment vary from network to network. There is little private, state, or federal direct funding of network operations. Another problem is the governance of the regional network. This will also differ with the location, the politics, and personalities involved. The only useful comment here is that all networks have these problems, and no network wants them.

At SUNY headquarters 80 percent of our staff time is devoted to training: either directly in face-to-face sessions, or indirectly through the writing of implementation memoranda or training materials, for example. Advisory and consultative groups are also a vital operation, which takes the next largest amount of effort.

The network's jobs are to catch new materials and changes coming from OCLC and from the library environment, and translate them and retrain the library staffs; to catch the failings of OCLC and the ideas generated by our libraries; and to advocate and undertake action on both sides to improve the situation. This includes being aware of such long-range but urgently pressing problems as AACR2 and the Library of Congress catalog closing, trying to understand and assess their import, and preparing to help libraries through the inevitable period of change.

Networks do go to bat for their members against OCLC, sometimes winning, sometimes not. One of the abiding problems networks and libraries face is the somewhat capricious nature of OCLC policy—or rather something called policy by its staff members. It takes a long time for new staff members at OCLC to understand the nature of this problem. It also takes them a long time to understand the relationships among center, network, and library. Attempts to bypass networks and go directly to a library, whether by accident or design, can result only in more work for OCLC. The center could not survive the onslaught of correspondence and queries it would receive without the filter of the network office. The network offices do fulfill a need for OCLC, as demonstrated by OCLC's creation of its own Western Service Center to function as the regional network in California.

There is one final important role that the networks play, and that is in the development of the national network, and in their membership on the Council for Computerized Library Networks.

It would be incorrect to create an impression that OCLC is not responsive to the suggestions of networks. For example, network proposals currently being examined at OCLC include the ability of one library to examine the local data records of another and suggestions for the design of the next generation of on-line terminals.

## OCLC CONCERNS

OCLC is in business to sell service and products to members. It has to survive in a hard world; it has a massive investment in facilities, hardware, and staff. It has an eighteen million dollar annual budget. It has received less than a million dollars in grants during its existence. It survives by selling service; its budget is predicated on increasing service (and thus generating more income) by increasing both the number of members and the range of its services. It is a research-centered organization, which immediately turns the results of its own research into a directly salable product, an interesting economic phenomenon in itself.

It is driven by its own aim of slowing the rate of growth of library costs and promoting library resource sharing rather than making a profit. Hence it is in a strong competitive position. It is successful. It is not perfect and it knows, probably better than any critic, what its imperfections are.

OCLC has to be concerned with maintaining or increasing its income; improving its fiscal stability; improving its service; satisfying the needs of its members both in Ohio and in regional networks; and bringing its mode of governance into line with its development as a major component of the national bibliographical network.

In order to satisfy these concerns, it must maintain and improve its research and development component and performance; improve its administrative services and physical plant; and improve service relationships with networks and member libraries. At times it is its own worst enemy.

## TWO GENERAL CONCERNS

The emerging National Plan for Library and Information Services and the quality control of bibliographic data overarch the entire network and transcend the constituency concerns of the participants.

### THE EMERGING NATIONAL PLAN

Network participants, regional networks, and OCLC are all vitally concerned with the emerging national plan and with the planning process itself. Regional networks are fully supportive of this important work and indeed participate— either individually or through the representation of their own organization in the Council for Computerized Library Networks (CCLN)—in the work of the Library of Congress's Network Advisory Committee.

The great contributions that the regional networks bring to this task are their vast and unique experiences as operating components of a network and their very nature as grass-roots organizations. CCLN's view is that if it had not been for the various initiatives in the individual states and regions, the networks would not be the reality they are today; and that the same initiatives and experiences are the essential component of a successful national plan.

Members of the OCLC network should immerse themselves in the issues, inform themselves on the problems, and participate fully through regional networks in the planning process. Individual libraries are the primary end users of the network, and participation now will be to the benefit of all later.

QUALITY CONTROL OF BIBLIOGRAPHIC DATA

The quality of the on-line data base at OCLC is the other basic issue that all must address. Participation in on-line shared cataloging has brought to the fore the question of the quality of cataloging in individual libraries and the efforts that should be made to build and maintain a quality data base. The work of individual catalogers, which previously entered only the library's own card catalog, is now examined by peers all over the country, and, if errors are found, corrections are made. The more effort made when the record is created, the more cost-efficient is the total system.

The State University of New York Office of Library Services held a two-day workshop recently to address the problem of quality control of bibliographic data. No one expected that there were easy answers or that answers would be found at the workshop; but the issue was aired, and the result was the following list of questions. The questions are in need of further refinement, but they do serve to put the problem in focus.

1. What are the differences in efficiency and procedures between inspection control and quality control?
2. How can we solve the problem of acquiring definitions of authority standards in a timely, acceptable manner (for example, the AACR2 problem)?
3. What are acceptable performance standards for cataloging data by record, and by field within a record, and what are acceptable costs for meeting these standards?
4. What is the appropriate sanction and reward procedure to attain quality data, and what are the appropriate network practices in administering the procedure?
5. What are the National Library and Information Service Network implications for quality control of bibliographic data—for example; cost of poor-quality data; loci of responsibility (and their relationship to industrial "lot inspection" procedures); and communication among levels?
6. What is the role of authority files in the quality control of bibliographic data, and what procedures should implement the role?

7. What are the implications of quality control for individual library personnel policies and practices?

8. What are the appropriate error correction procedures in on-line quality control, and who has authority to correct the file?

9. What are the future roles of the Library of Congress and other national libraries, and the international bibliographic network, in the maintenance of quality control of bibliographic data?

10. What are the future roles of other producers of bibliographic data (such as the publishing industry) in the maintenance of quality control of bibliographic data?

11. What is the appropriate investment pattern to ensure the generation and maintenance of quality control procedures, and high-quality data, for the national library system?

## CONCLUSION

The grouping of libraries into regional networks, in order to acquire OCLC services on a cooperative basis, is an astonishing success story. Perhaps the most important outcomes, even more than the efficiencies realized by the libraries, have been the breaking of artificial barriers between the types of libraries in regions and the emergence of a new national pattern of library cooperative service.

The most interesting developments of the next decade will probably center around these phenomena as more libraries join networks and as they add their contribution, and their voices, to the developing national network. One of the tests of the viability of existing administrative structures will be the way they respond to the changed environment. Will the responses be conservative and defensive, or open and creative? The forces that created and built networks will continue to strengthen networks so they can in turn make a major contribution to the developing national library network.

## NOTES

1. Ronald M. Miller, "Negotiations between Networks: OCLC/New England Board of Higher Education (NELINET)," in *Proceedings of the Fourteenth Annual Clinic on Library Applications of Data Processing, 1976* (Urbana: University of Illinois, Graduate Library School, in press).

2. Glyn T. Evans, "Regional Network Contracts with Libraries for OCLC Services," in *Proceedings of the Fourteenth Annual Clinic.*

3. Miller, "Negotiations;" Evans, "Regional Network Contracts."

4. Teresa Strozik, "Training and Staff Development," in Anne Marie Allison and Ann Allan, eds., *OCLC: Its Impact on Librarianship* (Boulder: Libraries Unlimited, in press); Glyn T. Evans, "The View from Regional Networks," in Allison and Allan, *OCLC.*

# Shelf-List Conversion: Management Pitfalls and Opportunities

# 9

John Kountz

Libraries are not eleemosynary, but they *are* institutions that do not have to show a profit. In sharp contrast to their commercial neighbors, the book sellers, where a dollar saved is a buck in your jeans, I suspect the majority of libraries would not know what to do with a profit it it stood on their desks begging for reinvestment. This is not to chide librarians for their lack of dollar sensitivity. Rather it is a simple observation of a void in our experience and education. I also believe many of us are aware of our lack of business exposure. But awareness of an issue in no way implies its solution.

Being a librarian myself, I think it only appropriate to mention a book concerning a technological revolution similar to the one now going on in libraries. Its title is *From Tin Foil to Stereo*. Today this book is technically outdated, having been published in 1960; however, it poses a provocative analogy to the current situation in libraries.

Basically the book traces the confrontation between artistically bent technologists and bottom-line managers. Public contact services (theatre owners) and their suppliers (the emerging talking film industry) were pressed into a profit-making battle by such financial forces as the Rockefellers and the Morgans. In our own situation today, the public contact services (libraries) and their suppliers (the book and media industry) are pressed into a cost reduction battle by such financial factors as taxpayers and their elected spokesmen.

Nor does the parallel end at that point. The thrust in movies was to use the highest technology available at that time and to convert struggling silent and burlesque theaters into attractive cinema palaces that consistently yielded net revenues in nine-figure numbers for several decades, including the depression years. Despite their strong and widespread resistance to

change, most libraries are being pressed by funding agencies into the arena
of the highest technology to reduce costs and provide a more viable and
attractive service mix.

The common link between the movie industry of the late 1920s and
libraries today is simple: modernize and reduce costs or languish. There
are several attractive approaches to modernization, to the use of high,
current technology. But as elsewhere in our free enterprise system, the
marketplace is glutted with adult and corporate technical toys. Some of
these are as bizarre as a stuffed horsehead mounted on the front of a
motorized buckboard, while others offer quantum leaps into a yet-to-be
formalized world of library service beyond the wildest dreams of Dewey,
Cutter, or even Art Brody. The market offers automated typewriters
that produce a set of archaic catalog cards from typing a title, concurrent
with powerful data bases supporting patron-computer dialogs to retrieve
literally a physical copy of a desired item: on time. The range of approaches
that has evolved in reality panders to the degree of commitment the individual library wishes to make to the past or to the future.

In this context the future means moving toward a real world in which
individual libraries are functionally interdependent, and away from a
phantom world in which each library strives for independence. Inter-
locking specialism might best describe the objective; the starting point
today is isolated generalism.

Thus to ignore the future objective and opt for corporate toys that
promise participation in the future, but in reality do little more than
fortify the past, is, at best, a futile ghost dance in the guise of professional-
ism. It may salve the soul, but it denies the existence of reality. In short,
if funding agencies are of a mind to support modernization, there is a
single activity that will propel you the farthest into the future with the
least amount of wheel spinning in the present: convert your shelf-list
file data to machine-readable form and maintain it in that form. The
benefits are bountiful. From acquisitions to weeding, a mechanical shelf-
list file (in the electronic data-processing sense) and its computer maintenance system are the most powerful and service-supporting tools you can
add to your library. But the journey from manual to machine files has perils
and can be likened to the egg-hatching ceremony of the Galapagos turtle.
Having survived three such journeys directly and others by way of pro-
pinquity, perhaps I can point out the more subtle snares and traps that
festoon the path to tomorrow.

## BEFORE THE ACT

At a minimum, ask yourself this question: What are you going to convert? Costs, time, and level of perturbation all depend on this decision.

For this one, take your time. Be sure to involve everybody, everywhere, and be sure to document in specific detail the results of your deliberations, considerations, and lost arguments.

Naturally the shelf-list is the file that you are going to convert because, characteristically there is less dross, there is a closer correlation to inventory; and patron service is not disrupted as conversion proceeds.

Naturally you are going to convert the whole file. If you do not, you will be a victim of the second law of library automation. "Don't do today what you can put off 'till 'illo anno qui nunquam veniet.' " As a result of the dabble approach, you will end up with a piece o' this and a hunk o' that and the job will not be finished, costed, manageable, or satisfactory since two processing systems will be required . . . forever. It is perverse fun to play mystical games by telling patrons, "If the book was purchased after January 14, 1973, it's in the printout;" or, "All materials cataloged by the Library of Congress (MARC) are listed;" or, "If it has circulated, you can search it on the terminal." But those games are not service oriented, and the typical library user does not have the slightest idea of when the item was published, let alone when you bought it, or if the Library of Congress cataloged it, or if it has circulated; in fact, could you answer those questions? Ah, yes . . . let us be service oriented. Convert the file and get it over with.

Naturally you know what uses you are going to make of the converted file. There is a book catalog, a circulation system, new book lists, specialized bibliographies, a search tool for acquisitions, lists supporting inventory, and so forth. Wrong. Be specific! Even Jason had an objective, albeit a golden fleece. If you are not clear at the outset, your golden fleece will turn into a golden fleecing. For example, not so many years ago, a conversion usually meant all data for all entries. I would hate to contemplate the dollars spent on keyboarding "23cm," "illus," or whatever. Similarly, output from those seminal systems typically was a string of regurgitated catalog card images.

Due to some fluke of rationality, other, more people-oriented displays are currently in vogue. As a result, many of the traditionally required bits of information may be suspect. I am not going to begin even to allude to the slightest hint of a tentative suggestion that any of the numerous, carefully thought out, and very carefully specified data elements in a bibliographic citation are dross; I shall shout it. Outside of a few hundred catalogers, who cares about how many unnumbered pages the book has, or its height, or that the endpapers are illustrated, or that George Sand's thumbprint appears on the verso of the tipped-in plate on page 372?

For years, the greatest catalog producers in the world, telephone companies, have evolved layouts and contents of their catalogs determined, in large measure, by the balance between cost and amount of data required to satisfy the bulk case of the general public. How about letting the user designate the content and layout? The user is, after all, paying for it.

Your preconversion decision should reflect such thoughts, since the actual cost of conversion will be affected by them. The relationship is quite straightforward: more data mean higher costs for conversion, file maintenance, and production of various outputs. It is not necessary to capture everything. But you should have the following:

1. The Library of Congress card order number (LCCN) where available.
2. The international standard book number (ISBN) where available.
3. The international standard serial number (ISSN) where available.
4. Any other mechanical key to a larger, more bibliographic complete data base (OCLC, Inforonics, Inc., Blackwell North America, for example).
5. An indicator for each title that identifies which larger, more complete data base the complete bibliographic data is resident on (MARC, OCLC).
6. In the absence of the above, a local control number.
7. In the absence of items 1 through 5, text consisting of separately identified fields for full author, full title, full subtitle, publisher, and date of publication. And codes for the format of the material (book, periodical, film), the language of the item; does it circulate? Is it a reference book?
8. The call number for each represented copy affiliated with each unique description prepared in accord with items 1 through 5 and 7 above.
9. A count of the copies for each call number including their location where not explicit in the call number (branches, locked cases, the director's desk).

Watch out for item 7. You must be firm in your criterion for what constitutes a new title. First, a title is new only if it is not on the machine-readable file. Simple enough. And then the fun begins. And tempers ignite. For example, is it a new title if the entry on the mechanical file reads:

Albert, Solomon Naphthali, 1916–
Blood Volume, by Solomon [*sic*] N. Albert. Springfield, Ill.
Thomas [c 1963], 175p. illus. (American Lecture Series, publication no. 517. American Lectures in Anesthesiology)
1. Blood Volume.

while the shelf-list card presents:

Albert, Solomon N.
Blood Volume, Springfield, Ill., Thomas [1963] 175p. illus.
24cm.

or:

Albert, S. N.
Blood Volume. Springfield, Ill., Thomas [c 1963]
175p. illus.

I think you get the idea. Depending on your decision, each of the above will be either a separate "new" title, a variant edition, or an additional copy of the "old" title. Since you will have to pay for the conversion (and the maintenance and the products), you may wish to begin thinking about this particular criterion now! In any event, first clear the air of ambiguity regarding what is a new title.

Before the act, you should also spend a few minutes contemplating how you are going to convert the file. Are you going to hire a press gang of Hessians, use existing staff, use a mixture of both, or contract the whole thing out and be done with it? I have a personal preference for the contract approach. Your gray hair quotient is constrained to monitoring the progress of a single, responsible agent. This approach stands in sharp contrast to snapping the whip over a group of people and being called on the carpet yourself. Believe me, contracting is sheer delight—contracting by competitive bid, I might add. That contract should specify penalty clauses for taking too much time; schedules of payment and of deliveries; the rights to any software for which the vendor might charge you; a firm understanding of who is responsible for what; what is to be handed to the vendor (besides money) and what the vendor will give you (besides excuses); and your criterion for what constitutes a new title.

Whatever the actual approach, you will want statistics relating to the file in terms that may be foreign to some of you. For example, the number of unique titles is as important as the number of copies. Remember the criterion for new titles? It will apply here immediately. Also, depending on the amount of data (such as completeness of the bibliographic citation or description) you wish converted, it is essential to measure the conversion effort by the number of characters or lines to be converted. Such statistics will aid you in preparing your bid document to communicate with the potential vendors and, for those who would inflict the effort on themselves, to form a basis for "how many people over what period of time" budgeting.

Integral to how you might proceed is the question of conversion site. Regardless of who does the conversion, you must decide where it is to be done. If you can tolerate twenty additional people over a six-to-nine-month period in your technical processing area, then you could conceivably do the job *in situ*. But those additional folk may just pose problems: for example, where do they park their cars? In partial relief, you might microfilm the entire shelf-list (both sides of each card) in jig time and for a nomimal fee, and thus liberate your technical processors from a nine-month bout of Buskashi as they try to find "that missing drawer."

The resultant microform version of the file can be used anywhere; all those drawers cannot. Besides a vendor can use microform images too. Some of you may wonder why both sides of each card would be filmed. It is difficult to conjecture what is hiding in the shelf-list files of all libraries. However, if, for your library, all data relating to the copies of an item represented by a single shelf-list entry appear on the front of that card, you need only film the fronts of those cards. But I suspect you will end up filming both sides. Remember, you will convert not just titles but copies as well. Why bother to convert at all if you do not capture and maintain your inventory data on a copy-by-copy basis within title?

Finally, you must think about errors and error correction, because costs and errors are directly related. However, the relationship, in certain instances, is subtle. Presumptuous as it may seem, the errors begin with the data already in your manual file. Onerous factors like typist fatigue, last-day-on-this &$OXZ jobitis, and "I told you to edit Helen's work" have been active for years. Your first decision, then, is to fix or live with the content of your files. Guiding you in this decision will be your earlier specified criterion for a new title and the knowledge that additional written instructions to the convertors can effectively winnow a lot of chaff. Also guiding you will be a first-hand review of the actual file with your own eyes in keeping with the ancient adage of library automation, "Know thy data."

The second source of errors will be in transcription, or keyboarding. Here, errors relate to character transpositions, miskeyed (wrong) characters, omitted characters, and the like. The operative term is *character*. For example, let us assume you have a file of a hundred thousand titles with an average of four hundred characters per title, including flags, tags, indicators, and so on. With an additional 20 percent for luck, somebody is going to have to push at least forty-eight million buttons to get the job done if you do not take advantage of existing data bases. At a keying error rate of 1 percent, you will have a half-million mistakes in the finished product, which is probably about one-tenth the aggregate error rate of the data in your manual files.

There are keyboard techniques that reduce errors, however, and you should be aware of them. If you keypunch, have the date verified (each punch card is rekeyed by a second operator using the same text, or source document used to prepare that punch card originally). Verification also applies to most computer input operations including key-to-tape and key-to-disc. The difference between these last two and keypunch is that keypunch produces a deck of punch cards, which in turn must be converted to computer usable form, while the other techniques yield computer-usable forms directly (typically magnetic tapes).

If optical character recognition typing is your forte, then errors sensed at the keyboard can be corrected by the typist in a variety of ways, usually as long as the paper has not been removed from the typewriter.

Are there other, viable conversion techniques? Well, if you find one that works, is reliable, and eliminates pushing buttons, buy stock in it and then tell your friends.

## DURING THE ACT

Depending on earlier decisions, the politics of your organization, and the way you held your mouth, you are now converting happily or not happily. Without reference to your course of action or the selected technique, there are some other things you might wish to contemplate now.

It was assumed that a documented plan of action resulted from your before-the-act machinations. Included in the plan were a tentative schedule, rates of conversion, bogey quantities of entries to be converted by estimated dates, and manpower loading or cost estimates. Since you have this plan of action, you can now use it as a road map to be followed through the swamps and deserts of conversion.

The first thing you will notice is the slow pace. How about the learning curve? Depending on how complex (or complete) you have made the entry to be converted, you may find you have saddled yourself with a learning curve that may be several weeks long before your employees hit full production. So monitor production. You will find that several minor peaks will be achieved before the group is in full swing—full swing being less than 10 percent day-to-day variation in units converted.

Take note that the longer the conversion period has been estimated to be, the longer it will take per unit converted. This observation is based on human beings. For a long conversion, there will be more personnel turnover. For each person lost, there is another learning curve. Lesson: beware of long conversions. Gear up for it and get it over with.

No one can be of greater assistance than a grizzly chief clerk. You know the type—hard as nails. That's the one you put in charge. And authorize and make him or her responsible for the job (if you do it in-house). To your chief petty officer you should provide a Gantt chart, a table of organization, the estimated number of volumes to be converted by which dates, the arbitration of parking spaces, and the telephone numbers of all affected parties (their *real* ones). From your chief petty officer you should receive gripes, messages of praise and damnation, estimates of time remaining to completion, and weekly status reports (the last item over lunch on Fridays).

By this time your match criteria should have evolved into a practical procedure and the wheels are turning in high gear. In fact, everything *should* be rosy. But expect notification from the group under the stairwell (after they see their first printout) that you are not capturing data they think they absolutely require if you expect them to do their job efficiently in the future. Perhaps the notification will not be from the group in building 307, perhaps the notification will relate to some data that would be nice to add. Perhaps you will discover the missing data element yourself. Remember, conversions take time and we all change in time.

Now, what do you do? Understand, it is assumed the omitted item is relatively minor—like illus, bibliographic notes, third subject headings. Should there be a real problem (say, the author field has been truncated to two characters), then it is best to resign and omit the experience from your résumé as you enter another profession.

At the risk of being casual, let me suggest a few alternatives, which, curiously, do not relate to the impact of the omitted data but rather to the size and paranoia factors of your organization. As you might intuit, the ability to recover rationally is in inverse proportion to these two factors—

and much exacerbated if your organization features both factors. I might mention that I drew upon my own childhood experience, in a big family of prima donnas, when I suggested that in determining what you are going to convert you should be sure to involve everybody, everywhere.

It is axiomatic that you shall overlook something in any event. If you did your homework and documented it, you can give the discoverer(s) of omissions hell for not revealing them at the time specifications were being drawn up, and plunge gracefully on. On that slim chance that you did not involve everyone, everywhere, all is not lost (completely). If you are contracting the work, request two cost estimates from the vendor—first, for backtracking to capture all occurrences of the omitted data, and, second, for capturing the previously omitted only on the entries remaining to be converted.

The resultant estimates will provide a series of extremely viable alternatives. Before you exercise any of them, however, be sure your computer system can accommodate the new data. If it cannot, it is time to take this information to the powers that be. If your system can handle the data, you can weight costs versus value of the data with the discoverer of the omission or the impacted functional group. Potentially you can defer to a later date, do it all now, do only the remaining entries now and the others later (not recommended), or drop the whole shot. And I'm sure when the realities of the situation are fully known, there are subtle gray things in between the four more blatant alternatives above.

For those doing the job with extra or temporary help, now is the time for the grizzly CPO to give you an estimate (just like the contractor). The CPO will probably give you a double whammy as well, since you are tinkering with the schedule and after twelve months those temporary people will be permanent, or whatever the ground rules inflict on the unsuspecting where you live.

You can also anticipate a series of finger-pointing exercises. Your data processors cannot make the vendor's tape run. Or the optical scanner cannot read your typing. Or everybody quits. Or the keypunch service has gone belly-up, and that last batch is locked up under court order. You can provide your own variations to this list; I won't try to predict what it will be.

By this time you are just about at the end of the tunnel. What had been a black opening in the rocks now has a little white window in the middle of it. This is the part you must be prepared for. It is the most difficult part of all. *How do you know when you are finished?* There will be a sudden burst of new files, piles of stuff overlooked, and (with but a slight warning, too slight to be remembered distinctly) editing. You are so close to being done at this point, that it is time to slip into the final phase since the excitement that begins with the end heralds, accompanies, and in large measure will constitute what you do after the act.

One final word: do not wait for someone else to tell you it is over. *You tell them.* As artists great and small will agree, "I didn't finish the thing; I just stopped doing it!"

## AFTER THE ACT

So now it's over . . . isn't it? Well, yes and no and maybe. The error reports have been reduced to nil. For those whose funding runneth over, thou shalt have converted on-line, kind-of-a-custom OCLC approach that does not track errors on the parlor carpet. For the rest of us, someone in the data-processing department, miffed no doubt because his name will not appear on the product or because he did not invent it, will have become perverse and in true cost-beneficiality require a batch approach. Thus the last card in the file you have just converted was spat out (intact) on a printout because the title was not delimited—I might add spat out with twenty thousand others, all labeled (in line with classic data-processing humor) errors. Getting those twenty thousand errors to stick on that magnetic tape (or disc) at the right place, then, is called editing or error correction. So your error reports are nil; so what is new?

In that case, how about your products? Are they all up to snuff? Have you checked all the dirty words to see that the malcontent clerk typist, who will now lose a job typing red-ribbon subject headings, did not slip you a few funnies? What about content? Machines are spiffy for telling you that such and such a thing should be a number rather than an alphabetic letter (typically zero for OH, L for one, S for five, B for eight, and so on). Machines, however, do not read plain text and have been known to sever common English prose at the seventy-eighth character, statements finished or not. Similarly, like passé ethnic jokes, one alphabetic letter looks just like all the rest to a machine, until it is time to sort things. Are there strange spellings? Weird words? Funky phrases? Disturbing diphthongs? Ludicrous liaisons?

You may be sure the above garbage will festoon your products, but don't panic! Meticulous care, very meticulous indeed, must be exercised only for items that are known to appear on the first page, frame, or sheet— but only the first. Few people will ever look closely beyond that point.

Clearly when the staff is in major revolt about the dross you are going to inflict upon them (as they point to that symbol of man's faint handle on perfection, the card catalog), you can agree and then urge all haste, that is up to the middle of the "A" in titles, authors, subject headings, call numbers, and the like. Once this is done, become rational. One person, part time, then is permitted to tunnel through Everest (with an ice pick). Else you will be back in the saddle again, and the conversion will be in full swing a second time.

And that's about all that can be said about the pitfalls of conversion.

## BENEFITS OF CONVERSION

A great deal more can and should be said now about the economic and service benefits one may expect to derive from a successfully completed conversion project. Our experience in converting the library shelf-lists on the nineteen campuses of the California State University and Colleges system points to such a wide range of service and cost benefits, I cannot cover them all in the narrow limits of this paper. But I can give some of the highlights under five major captions: circulation control, union shelf-list system, cataloging support system, systemwide circulation control network, and costs.

### CIRCULATION CONTROL

The automated shelf-list leads simply and naturally to automated circulation control on each campus. In libraries elsewhere, the increased ease of patron borrowing, made possible by an automated circulation system, has led to quantum leaps in the recorded use of collections—as much as 40 percent in some libraries—and we expect similar gains in the CSUC system libraries. Along with increased use will come the other now-familiar benefits of automated circulation, such as automatic and timely production of overdue and recall notices, generation of collection-use data for systematic weeding and duplicate-copy programs, and provision to faculty of library-use data in specific curricular areas.

### UNION SHELF-LIST SYSTEM

A near doubling of interlibrary loans of books within the system libraries is anticipated, based upon our experience with the computer-produced union list of periodicals, which brought about an 88 percent increase in the interloan delivery of journal articles. Taking inventories of monographs with the automated shelf-list will be a much easier task, and we expect the cost of doing so to be cut in half. Availability of the union shelf-list in all nineteen campus libraries is expected to lead to a substantial reduction in intrasystem purchase of low demand materials. Eventually we anticipate an average systemwide reduction of the purchase of such books on the order of a hundred thousand volumes per year. Finally, staff time devoted to interloan search procedures will be drastically reduced by the availability of human-readable union shelf-lists in each system library.

### CATALOGING SUPPORT SYSTEM

Availability of a comprehensive, systemwide bibliographical data base will allow many of the individual libraries to cease the very costly purchase of various bibliographic services to which they now subscribe, such as Library of Congress slips, the *National Union Catalog,* and various commercially produced microfilm services. Staff costs for preorder bibliographic searching can be reduced by about half. The ratio of clerical to professional labor time for cataloging will change from the current 90:10 ratio to a ratio of 99:1, indicating potential salary savings of great magnitude in the cataloging operation at each library.

## SYSTEMWIDE CIRCULATION NETWORK

The near doubling of interloan activity we predict will be greatly facilitated through this network, which will also substantially reduce the current unit costs of the manually run interloan system. The circulation network will eliminate the present system of interloan communication, 20 percent of which is handled by telephone and 80 percent by mail. Substantial savings in the labor and materials costs of interloan activity will begin to accrue when the systemwide circulation network becomes fully operational.

## COSTS

For the total automation system, whose bedrock and indispensable foundation is the automated shelf-list, we predict that the total investment in system automation will be amortized by fiscal 1982–1983. By that time, the cumulated annual operations cost savings will equal the total investment in creating the automated system. Thereafter, we predict that a total net savings in excess of three million dollars annually will accrue to the libraries in the CSUC system. These savings will in no way imply any curtailment of library services. The case is just the opposite: in addition to the fiscal benefits, we are quite certain that the automation program will bring large increases both in the quality and the quantity of the library services we have hitherto provided using conventional systems of library operation.

Like the movie moguls of the 1930s, who prospered even through the depression era by fully exploiting the most advanced technology then available to them, we expect not just to survive but to flourish through the lean years ahead because of our timely and comprehensive adoption of the best computer technology now at our command. Other libraries that successfully maneuver their way around the many managerial pitfalls that lie in the way of automated shelf-list conversion may expect to do at least as well as we have done, or better. Those fiscal clouds you see looming on the horizon are not lined with silver; they are packed with gold, and they should fill us all with hope rather than dread as they move steadily closer to us.

# The Great Rush to Automated Catalogs: Will It Be Management or Muddling Through?    10

H. William Axford

Management attitudes, vision, and resolve at individual libraries will ultimately determine whether the data bases we develop and the national information network growing out of them make rational and cost-effective use of computer technology. Our ability to achieve this goal may be jeopardized by a lack of interest within the profession for cultivating the skills and attitudes that will produce genuine leadership rather than more muddling through. Evidence supporting this concern is visible in the proto-type utilities that currently provide automated cataloging services. They are accurate barometers of management thinking in the libraries that created them.

Although generalizations are inherently unfair to their exceptions, there is a strong tendency within both administrative and operative ranks to view the automated data base as a deus ex machina for irrationally pre-serving many of the practices and concepts of the precomputer age of bibliographic control. In a sense, we perceive the emerging technology in the same sentimental way that General MacArthur perceived the Korean War: "God's last gift to an old soldier," and an opportunity to conduct another old-style campaign, as if a new day in history had not dawned.

Recognizing the strength of this attitude, and its effects, is necessary for any discussion of management issues in automated cataloging. I would therefore like to sketch a broad overview of the profession as it has developed in the last century, concentrating on those historically ingrained ways of thinking that still govern our responses to the challenges, oppor-tunities, and problems showered on us by explosions of technology and the rapid emergence of a knowledge-dependent society. One frequently observed attribute of our profession is its heavy absorption in daily crises, which inhibits reflection upon where the profession came from, how it got where it is, and where it ought to be going. Figuratively speaking, we do not climb, as did the American historian Frederick Jackson Turner, to a South pass in the Rockies in order to contemplate the onward flow of our history. We allow ourselves instead to be swept along by it. We do not critically examine our assets and our liabilities as one epoch emerges from another, substantively altering the demands on libraries and the people who staff them. Thus the full exploitation of our new assets is curtailed by our inattention to the deadweight burden of our old liabilities.

Libraries are both the products of and participants in the historical process. On the one hand, they cannot escape being molded by the fresh energies released by man's restless, curious, and imaginative mind. On the other hand, they could absorb these energies in such a way as to affect the course of events, if to no other end than sustaining the library's traditional role as the collective memory of man and as the wellspring of the historical process itself—which R.G. Collingwood has so aptly called "the human mind contemplating its own development."

Applying Collingwood's dictum to modern library history, one becomes aware of certain pivotal attitudes firmly lodged in our corporate personality. And it is to these attitudes that we must look for an understanding of the present state of the art in the management and use of automated cataloging, and for predicting its future course.

One of our most critical attitudinal liabilities is our widespread antipathy toward management per se. For a significant part of the profession, it is something to be fearful of or to be held in contempt. Or it falls into the category of the weather—something we like to talk about at seminars and conferences but prefer to do nothing about, even though our professional and institutional survival is becoming much more closely linked to our performance.

Contributing to this antipathy to management are *a priori* assumptions that were etched into the profession's corporate personality during the formative years of its modern history (roughly the seventy-five years preceding World War II)—assumptions that, no matter how noble in nature or enshrined in tradition, are anachronistic in their insensitivity to fundamental social changes of the last three decades, and to the new management imperatives these changes impose upon the theory and practice of librarianship. We are captives of a cottage industry mentality whose origins go back to the nineteenth century. It views librarianship largely as a matter of individual artistry rather than a coordinated institutional endeavor. In this view the determinants of institutional performance are the reference librarian sitting on one end of the log and the student on the other, weaving the complex design of a Platonic dialog; the cataloger in splendid isolation artistically divining main entries within the permissive and sometimes mystic guidelines of various codes; and the bookman-architect patiently and methodically building collections and dreaming of palaces in which to house them. These stereotypes have been the pillars of the profession in the past and will, with some variations, continue to be so in the future.

But this view fails to recognize that the growing complexity and inter-dependence of a global information community, declining economic sup-port for libraries, and the onrush of technology have created a situation where, for such artists to seek the outer limits of their virtuosity, there must be effective orchestration of both the human and material resources avail-able to us. Maintaining institutional productivity and vitality in a rapidly changing world requires a stronger leadership-management component within each library, and more attention to cost-effectiveness related to mission, than ever before. We are no longer a cottage industry and cannot continue so to regard ourselves unless we wish to see library management infiltrated by persons from other professions who have managerial creden-tials but may have no understanding of the need to employ advanced technology in a manner consistent with the library's historically human-istic role.

To argue for more effective management is not to advocate a return to the dictatorial era of library governance. It is, rather, to argue for the diffusion of management attitudes throughout the entire organization, which implies that important issues, such as automated cataloging, should be discussed within the context of empirically derived cost-benefit data rather than be settled by the enthusiasms and anxieties generated by the prospect of impending change.

The management of change, however deftly handled, inevitably causes some anxiety and distress, precisely because it involves subjecting en-thusiasm for the new to the realities of a cost-benefit analysis and to over-coming attitudes deeply rooted in emotion and canonized by tradition.

The anxieties aroused when the old confronts the spectre of the new are well illustrated in a letter published in the November 1976 issue of the *Journal of Academic Librarianship.* "Important and frequently irreversible decisions," says the writer, "such as reclassification, joining OCLC and closing the catalog are being made by administrators who may or may not be working catalogers. One shudders at the thought of decisions of such magnitude being made by those who do not fully understand their ramifi-cations and implications."[1] Encapsulated here is not only the artisan's loathing and inborn distrust of management but also a traditional conserva-tism, characterized by a sense of history in which time stands still. This is clearly seen in the writer's apparent unawareness of the fact that all three matters over which concern is expressed—reclassification, use of automated data bases, and the demise of the card catalog—are no longer matters for debate as to their desirability. That point has long since passed. The issues now center on how soon and under what circumstances the transitions can be accomplished. This letter reveals the soul of a dedicated artist, a true believer in the uniqueness of each library, writhing in agony as the forces of history propel us toward global library networks based on standardized bibliographic and communications protocols. Here we see the cottage industry mentality acting as the stoutest obstacle to our mounting the aggressive managerial initiatives required to maintain control over our own future and to provide the information services required by present and future generations.

I do not mean to deplore individual artistry. It has been a traditional source of strength for the profession and will continue to be so. But we cannot allow this artistry to dissipate its talents in trying to preserve a nineteenth-century bibliothecal Eden, instead of focusing them on a future that is constantly being massaged into new and more complex shapes by developing technology.

The continued vitality of attitudes twenty-five years behind the times is due largely to twenty-five years of annual budget increments large enough to increase institutional output without resort to new ways of doing things. The years of opulence following World War II draped the library cotter in a Brooks Brothers suit, thus creating the illusion that the suit itself had produced a new model manager, attuned to present and future, rather than past, realities. The unfortunate results of this illusion are seen in our frequent mismanagement of new technology and our misunderstanding of the new management concepts for institutions staffed by people whom Peter Drucker aptly calls "knowledge workers."

For example, where computer technology has been applied to library processing systems, its thrust has often been toward replicating manual systems rather than building entirely new information delivery systems. And participatory management theory, only superficially understood, has commonly been an impediment to achieving the increased institutional productivity which is its principal justification.

So much for a historical overview of the profession. What is its relevance to the future development and management of automated cataloging data bases?

For the sake of economy, most libraries will share catalog data bases rather than create and manage their own. The nature of these shared utilities will reflect the management vision, attitudes, and capabilities resident in the participating libraries. As libraries are drawn into networks where the cohesive element is an automated cataloging data base, they become consumers of services they formerly provided for themselves. And as consumers, they will determine the nature of the services and products offered. In such an integrated and interdependent environment, decisions about the kinds of services contracted for must take into account not only local needs but the needs of the larger community as well. The rapid emergence of a postindustrial information society brings with it the need for a kind of Copernican revolution in management thinking. The individual library can no longer be seen as the center of the bibliographical universe, and the cottage industry mentality is no longer adequate for dealing with present realities. The Ptolemaic view of the universe began its retreat the moment Copernicus unveiled his new cosmology.

Unfortunately, we have been slow to comprehend how far and how fast technology has propelled us from isolation to interdependence, and to a need to look to new management horizons. Attitudinal anachronisms continue to loom large in decisions that involve heavy institutional investments in the powerful technology that is becoming the backbone of library service.

Let me illustrate this point by some observations on the Ohio College Library Center, which is the highwater mark in the development of automated cataloging data bases thus far and which until fairly recently virtually monopolized the field. It is also the most conspicuous example of the limitations imposed by attitudes that are irrational but powerful vestiges of the precomputer era of librarianship. OCLC is essentially the creation of its member libraries; it is both a beacon into the future and, to some, the source of an illusion that we have already reached the promised land.

Because it was the first to demonstrate and dramatize the compatiblity of computers and libraries, OCLC has become the showcase of the library world—a modern wonder as seductive and compelling as was the Alexandrian Library, which reflected "the glory that was Greece and the grandeur that was Rome" and stood for two millennia as the archetypical library for scholars and librarians alike. Despite its brief existence, OCLC has already established itself as a rival to the Alexandrian legacy, exhibiting imperialistic ambitions and eliciting loyalties worthy of comparison with those of the Alexandrian Library. Yet in spite of its youth, it has begun to show signs of age. It is an innovator that has not been able to exploit the full potential of its innovations. As a consequence, it is in certain respects both conceptually and technologically obsolete, a fact that is sometimes obscured by the size and evangelistic fervor of its supporting legions—of which it is both creator and captive.

In the first place, there are no authority files in OCLC's software structure. This means that for thousands of titles in the data base, there are variant entries, causing confusion and needless expense at the local level, and raising serious difficulties for incorporating the files in a national data base. Second, the software does not include data-base maintenance and production packages, which would enable member libraries cheaply to provide multipoint catalog access, or to organize their files in a variety of ways beneficial to users—services not possible with the traditional card catalog.

Library users are increasingly frustrated by the physical limits to access imposed by the card catalog and by the inadequacy of subject access provided by Library of Congress headings. With the advent of the MARC

program and the linking of the computer with micrographics, these problems could be solved through the provision of multiple copies of the
catalog, supplemental catalogs organized in nontraditional ways (such as
by language or area), and catalogs produced in response to individual SDI
profiles. Beyond furnishing sequential history tapes, which can then be sent
elsewhere for processing, OCLC cannot provide these services. More
important, there seems to be very little pressure from member libraries to
move OCLC in these directions. In spite of its potential use in interlibrary
loans and its planning for serials check-in, acquisitions, and subject access
systems, OCLC remains essentially what it has been in the minds of its
member libraries since its inception: a utility designed primarily to produce
alphabetized catalog cards customized to local, idiosyncratic cataloging
practices.

This situation is by no means due to any lack of perspicacity on the part
of OCLC's creator and executive director. In mapping his strategy for
OCLC, he was surely aware of the attitudinal problems he would have to
deal with when he went to Columbus with the goal of creating the land-
mark institution that OCLC has since become. He knew that to insist
upon a level of sophistication requiring radical change in potential member
libraries would only guarantee that the project would never get off the
ground. Consequently he had to design a system in which the computer
supplemented rather than replaced traditional systems, providing primarily
for the customized production of catalog cards. It is within this context
that OCLC can be seen as both an innovator and leader in moving libraries
toward automation, and at the same time as a captive of attitudes that
inhibit the exploitation of the initial breakthroughs.

The attitudes that have thus far restricted the development and utilization of OCLC and other automated data bases are clearly revealed in the
results of a 1976 survey of the 106 libraries then comprising the SOLINET
network. The purpose of the survey was to identify membership priorities
in the future development of the network. Interestingly the survey was
undertaken at a time when the SOLINET libraries were "in near revolt, and
the full effort of the technical staff of the network was placed on planning
for complete and total independence from OCLC" (as stated in the 1975–
1976 SOLINET annual report). This situation arose from service problems
caused by the relocation of OCLC's computers and unexpected problems
involved in extending the network into an area served by a large number of
private telephone companies.[2] This was an ideal moment for reexamining
the purposes and capabilities of an automated data base in the light of
OCLC's performance, the existence of new technology, and the developing
momentum for creating a national network based on standard cataloging
protocols. Unfortunately this reexamination did not take place. What the
survey revealed was dramatic evidence of the extent to which the OCLC
model had dominated management thinking in the member libraries,

despite their dissatisfaction with OCLC's performance at the time.

The priorities expressed by the SOLINET libraries were, in order of importance, a cataloging system for monographs, a cataloging system for serials, a cataloging system for nonbook materials, a system for interlibrary loans, and, tied for last, an acquisitions system and one that incorporated authority files.[3] The last-place position given to authority files—and by implication to standard cataloging protocols within the network—was the most revealing aspect of the survey. It clearly indicated that management thinking in the member libraries had not progressed beyond the view that an automated cataloging data base is primarily a technological device for perpetuating cataloging practices and concepts made obsolete by the rapid pace of change in the past thirty years. If any opinions were expressed as to the desirability of data-base maintenance or production packages beyond alphabetized catalog cards, they were not numerous or strong enough to merit mention in SOLINET's annual report for 1976, which published the survey results.

Managerial myopia of this nature is by no means limited to libraries in the OCLC network. For instance, in the state of Oregon, the libraries of the state system of higher education have been inching for the past two and a half years toward a network utilizing the cataloging data base operated by Blackwell North America. This organization has sophisticated data-base maintenance and COM production packages that can provide, economically, vastly enhanced bibliographic access to collections both on the local campus and within a library system. To date, however, only one of the three university libraries in the system enters all current cataloging into the data base, and only two of them record all changes made locally to MARC or other records. This is a particularly bothersome situation because inaccurate call numbers in the data base result in needless delays and costs in borrowing and lending within the system.[4] Only one of the libraries in the system is employing the capabilities of BNA's software to begin the process of phasing out its card catalogs. At the University of Oregon, the production of subject cards ceased on June 30, 1977, and new COM subject catalogs representing approximately two and a half years of acquisitions made their appearance. The annual savings from this first phase of closing the card catalogs will be approximately thirty thousand dollars.

One final example of how cottage industry attitudes adversely affect the utilization of an automated cataloging data base is worth mentioning. It involves a medical library that is an OCLC member. The current cataloging procedure in this institution is to search for the entry in printed sources, copy it when found, paste the copy to a 3 x 5 card, edit it, and then attempt to find it in the OCLC data base. The result is that the library unnecessarily bears the costs of both irrational manual procedures and underutilizes the automated cataloging system at the library's disposal.

This is an extreme example of the mismanagement of resources, both human and material, that occurs when precomputer age attitudes are allowed to control the use of twentieth-century technology. But there is disturbing evidence in Barbara Markuson's survey of a large number of OCLC libraries that the situation just noted is by no means an isolated phenomenon. In her study, she was unable to establish among the responding libraries any clear trends in unit processing costs resulting from joining the OCLC network. This finding strongly suggests that the management of automated cataloging systems in the individual library is less efficient and effective than it should be, for it seems certain that the unit cataloging cost, for any medium-to-large library utilizing an automated data base, ought to be significantly less than manual costs if internal processes and procedures were properly tuned to take full advantage of the capabilities of the automated system. That they were not is illustrated, for example, by the fact that some OCLC member libraries still buy some of their catalog cards from commercial sources. They are thus paying the high fixed overhead costs of belonging to an on-line cataloging network and at the same time going to an alternative source for part of the basic service that the on-line network provides.[5] The management rationale behind this practice strains the imagination, as does that reflected in a recent news item in *Library Journal*, reporting the demise of a state centralized processing organization that subscribed to OCLC services through SOLINET. The article quoted the director as saying that the cause of the center's failure was not that its high processing costs were driving member libraries to commercial sources but that the state failed to subsidize the operation to the extent necessary to "keep its prices competitive."[6]

It is this lack of management perception that explains the general lack of enthusiasm within the profession for investigating alternatives to OCLC, even among libraries where the relatively high fixed-overhead costs of the system cannot be spread over a large volume of titles processed. The phenomenal growth of OCLC from a utility serving a consortium of Ohio libraries, to a network spanning the nation, may be similarly explained. From a broad historical perspective, it is hard to escape the conclusion that this remarkable growth phenomenon has been as much due to a kind of religious conversion experience as it has to strictly management considerations. The rush to be "saved," irrespective of cost, is clearly reflected in the NELINET and SOLINET price structures. For a NELINET library processing forty-five hundred titles a year, the annual costs of telecommunications, terminal maintenance, modem, membership, and network surcharges come to $1.23 per title cataloged. A similar library in SOLINET would pay $1.27. For a per-title expenditure not more than 10 percent higher, these libraries could get from BNA, for instance, alphabetized cards, spine and book pocket labels, BNA input of all original cataloging, data-base maintenance services, and the capability to produce a variety of COM packages organized on nontraditional principles.

Considering that around 46 percent of SOLINET members are libraries processing fewer than five thousand titles a year and that this ratio probably holds true for the entire OCLC network, Markuson's observation that "many library directors do not know how to go about [a study] to determine whether going to an on-line system will be cost effective" does not seem to be stretching the facts.[7]

Whether OCLC service is managed effectively in the local library, the fact remains that important fringe benefits have flowed from the rush to jump on the OCLC bandwagon. The rapid extension of the network through its brokerage agreements has provided a means for introducing libraries to the benefits of automation at a pace and on a scale that would have been hard to imagine ten years ago. In the process of this transition, large numbers of librarians and support staff have gone through an educative process that relieved their fear of the computer and enabled them to accept it for what it is: a powerful and valuable slave when it is properly managed. Finally, the extension of the network to nationwide dimensions has helped create an awareness of the interdependence of libraries serving a knowledge-dependent society—and, for that matter, not just libraries but the interdependence of what has come to be called the knowledge industry. With respect to this latter point, there is reason to believe that a strong causal relationship exists between the growing use by libraries of automated data banks (such as Lockheed, SDC, and the *New York Times*), and the rapid development of the OCLC network.

One further aspect of the spectacular development of the OCLC network may have serious management implications. Anyone interested in the behavior and performance of public service institutions should be intrigued by the eighteen or twenty satellite networks that orbit today around OCLC. Each of the organizations has a central headquarters and staff that have to be paid for out of membership assessments and surcharges. Because these organizations are the creations of a highly bureaucratized profession, one must speculate on the possibility that they will develop in the classic pattern of Parkinson's law—which is to say they will become entrenched bureaucracies whose primary purpose becomes survival rather than the performance of demonstrably useful services.

Two difficulties exist in investigating this hypothesis. In the first place the satellite networks have not been in existence long enough to demonstrate conclusively a trend in this direction. Secondly, historical data on their operational budgets, which might provide some clues either pro or con, are difficult to obtain. NELINET has not issued an annual report since 1972,[8] and the 1976 annual report of the Interinstitutional Council of the North Texas Area, which is the parent organization of the AMIGOS Bibliographic Council, contains no budget information at all. In 1975 and 1976, the Council for Computerized Library Networks surveyed its members to obtain information on headquarters, budgets, staff, and charges to members, but in neither year could it obtain these data.[9] Perhaps it is only my lingering paranoia in the wake of Watergate, but their reluctance to make such data public intensifies my curiosity as to its content. However, from other documents that are available, it is possible to piece together information that indicates that the growth of network overhead costs is something that will bear watching in the future, to determine to what extent these middleman organizations are subject to Parkinson's Law.

Budget growth in two of the largest regional networks tied to OCLC— NELINET and SOLINET—does not arouse much optimism. In NELINET, operating expenditures derived from membership dues and surcharges rose from approximately $90,000 in 1972-1973 to more than $280,000 in 1975-1976—an increase of over 200 percent in just three years. In SOLI- NET, they climbed from $52,000 in 1974 to $352,000 in 1976—an increase of 575 percent in just two years. What this means for a NELINET library processing 4,500 titles a year is $.68 per title in network overhead charges, and $.72 for a library in SOLINET. And these figures do not include the personnel costs to member libraries involved in a seemingly endless suc- cession of meetings devoted to network maintenance, governance, or operational problems.

In both cases the steepness of the upward curve is largely attributable to the fact that the networks were in a stage of rapid expansion until recently. However, from a management perspective, it will be important to see to what degree the curve flattens out as membership growth inevitably declines, and to what extent the future growth of network headquarters conforms to Parkinson's observation that bureaucracies tend to expand "by an inexorable rule of growth irrespective of the work (if any) which has to be done."[10]

This brings me full circle to my central theme, and that is the critical importance of the level of imagination and management capabilities in the individual library in determining the future development of automated cataloging data bases. Do we have the imagination and determination to exploit the free market situation now emerging with the appearance on the scene of some serious competition to OCLC? Can we muster the will to use the leverage inherent in a competitive market to move forward from the more or less static situation that now exists, or will the initial breakthroughs harden into a new and constrictive orthodoxy?

There is a widespread aversion among librarians to doing business with private industry. This prejudice, ingrained in managers of public service institutions, ignores the basic fact that all organizations that sell services take your money, and that what is important in terms of management is what you get in return, not the nature of the source of supply.

Decisions that involve large institutional investments in advanced tech- nology will be more and more rigorously scrutinized by layers of authority above us that are being pressed, as we are ourselves, to take more muscular management stances. They will demand sound cost-benefit studies of all available alternatives before approving investment, and ongoing performance studies of the source of services that is selected. Decisions and proposals larded with sentimental attachment to the old, or uncritical assessment of the new, will be rejected out of hand.

Fortunately, institutional executives are also looking to us for leadership as they themselves struggle into unfamiliar areas of management. And there is a bright side to the present period of budget austerity, for it offers unique opportunities to provide real leadership, as stable or declining budgets force concentration on real rather than ephemeral issues, and encourage bold decisions.

Not long ago, a colleague relayed a conversation she had had with her counterpart in another institution. The question was raised as to why her library was not fully utilizing the capabilities of the automated cataloging data base available to the system. The response was, "Well, we are willing to play around a little with the computer, but not willing to jump into bed." Coquettish relationships with new concepts or new technology are characteristic of the profession. When Joseph C. Rowell, university librarian at Berkeley, first proposed the adoption of the card catalog in 1876, he noted, "It has been suggested . . . that the use of the typewriter be made in making such a catalog . . . . If this be practical, no time will be lost on my part in gaining knowledge and power to handle the instrument."[11] Nevertheless, the typewriter did not enter the catalog department at Berkeley until 1902—twenty-six years after the decision was made to adopt the card catalog. Another case in point is the fact that over three-quarters of a century has elapsed since Ernest Cushing Richardson first proposed a national periodicals lending library, and we still do not have one.[12]

Writing in 1933, H.G. Wells observed that "in England, we have come to rely upon a comfortable lag of time of 50 years or a century between the perception that something ought to be done and a serious attempt to do it."[13] I think a comparable observation would apply to our own situation with respect to catalog data bases. We really do perceive at least the essential outlines of what must be done to exploit the initial breakthroughs. But the dead hand of tradition and management attitudes not yet congruent with the times stifle the will to move rapidly in the directions indicated. Unfortunately present economic conditions deny us the luxury of a prolonged flirtation with the new technology. We must quit playing around with the computer and consummate quickly what is now called a "meaningful relationship."

## NOTES

1. *Journal of Academic Librarianship* (November 1976): 222.
2. SOLINET, *Annual Report, 1976*, p. 4.
3. Ibid., pp. 17–18.

4. The system consists of three university libraries, four college libraries, and the Health Sciences Library of the University of Oregon. Among them, the three university libraries account for 90 percent of the system's acquisitions. Consequently the resource-sharing effectiveness of the system is dependent upon their full input into the data base and their maintaining accurate records in it.

5. In his *Annual Report* for 1975–1976, the executive director of OCLC, in commenting on the lower percentage of first-time uses for records already in the system for Ohio libraries than for the network as a whole, noted that some Ohio members "are not doing all their cataloging in Roman alphabets on the system." Whether any of these utilize other sources is unknown. However, the fact that some member libraries do not fully utilize OCLC is indicative of the generally limited conception of the purpose and capabilities of an automated cataloging data base.

6. *Library Journal*, December 1, 1976, p. 2418.

7. Barbara Evans Markuson, "The Ohio College Library System: A Study of Factors Affecting the Adaptation of Libraries to On-line Networks," *Library Technology Reports* 12, no. 1 (January 1976): 39.

8. Nancy Johnson, staff assistant, NELINET, to the author, May 31, 1977.

9. Charles H. Stevens, executive director, SOLINET, to the author, July 18, 1977; Mary Jane Pobst Reed, chairperson, Council on Computerized Library Networks, to the author, August 16, 1977.

10. C. Northcote Parkinson, *The Law of Delay* (New York: Ballantine Books, 1970), p. 1.

11. Quoted in *The University of California Libraries: A Plan for Development*, (Berkeley: Office of the Executive Director of University-wide Planning, 1977), pp. 57–58.

12. For a delightful account of the early history of this concept, see Basil Stuart-Stubbs's remarks on "Sharing Resources: National Centers and Systems" in Association for Research Libraries, *Minutes, 86th Meeting*, May 8–9, 1975.

13. H.G. Wells, *The Work, Wealth and Happiness of Mankind* (Garden City, N.Y.: Doubleday, Doran & Co., 1931), 2:616.

# Key Issues in Managing the     **11**
# Automated Catalog:
# A Panel Discussion

Peter Spyers-Duran, Moderator

*Panelists:* Bruce Alper, Richard De Gennaro,
Bela Hatvany, Lois Kershner,
Frederick Kilgour,
and John Kountz

MODERATOR: We are delighted to present to you our distinguished group of panelists, who will no doubt give you valuable information and good entertainment in concluding our program. After introducing the panel to you, I will ask each panelist to make a brief statement on a particular issue specified prior to this meeting. Later on, questions will be fielded from the audience.

The panelists are seated alphabetically, to avoid any dispute over rank and seniority. To my right is Bruce Alper, group computing director for Blackwell North America. Next to him sits Richard De Gennaro, who is director of the University of Pennsylvania Library; then Bela Hatvany, chairman of the board of CLSI; Lois Kershner, manager of the BALLOTS program at Stanford; Frederick Kilgour, executive director of OCLC; and on the far right is John Kountz, who is associate director for automation with the California State Universities and Colleges System.

Now, Bruce, you are first on the program, and I've asked you to address the question of the need for quality control of bibliographic data bases. Specifically, what role do you foresee for the business sector in providing quality control not only for cataloging but other data bases as well?

BRUCE ALPER: If we go back to Brett Butler's paper we'll recall that he talked about two different types of data bases: resource data bases and specific collection data bases. I will discuss only resource data bases, and these, of course, are not exclusively available from commercial sources. They are provided also by organizations such as OCLC and the Washington Library Network. So I prefer to couch my response in general terms, covering both the commercial and the not-for-profit providers of resource data bases.

My first concern is, Why would you edit a record coming into a data base for quality control purposes upon its receipt? Such records come from national libraries such as the Library of Congress and the British National Library, and it is clear that the users of resource data bases do not raise major quality issues with respect to these records. They do make changes because of local idiosyncrasies, but the fact is the records as received are of very high quality and do not require much editing. Most of the editing involves mechanical issues controllable through software. The important question is, Why edit records as they enter the data base? Remember that the resource data base will be used to generate someone else's specific collection data base, and until a record is used from the resource data base, it has no intrinsic value. When the record is selected for use, then it becomes important because the user indicates it has some value to him.

I think it is folly to maintain that every record in our data base deserves to be edited prior to any user demand for it. Now the records from the national libraries pose very few problems. But what about those that come from other sources?

We have heard repeatedly of the 80/20 rule: 80 percent of the use of a collection comes from 20 percent of the items in it. The same rule holds true for resource data bases. So the question arises, Should we invest money in editing all records as they come in from participating institutions? Well, the library that put the record in the data base obviously felt its quality was satisfactory, so the quality issue arises only when someone else utilizes the record.

My experience indicates that the investment in reediting such records is not merited by the benefits. But there are some things that the operators of resource networks can do to guarantee that data-base pollution is minimized. First of all, there is the question of setting standards for entering records. If minimum standards of content and structure are set for accepting a record in a data base, distress to future users will be minimized.

Second, resource data bases can provide for records of lesser quality to be input directly into a specific collection data base without having it pollute the resource data base. A library may thus have any quality record it wants in its own data base, without imposing the same standard on all other users.

Finally, there is the issue of education. If we work with our users and explain to them why certain minimum requirements are essential to ensure the quality and continued utility of the data base, then we can expect higher-quality data.

The policy I would advocate is that resource data bases should maintain records in the format received (except for obvious errors), and this also applies to authority forms.

Consider the problem of a resource organization, such as Blackwell North America, servicing several hundred libraries with various stages of authority in their own public catalogs. If the Blackwell North America data base were entirely consistent with the latest subject heading authority, how many libraries could use the data base when their catalogs do not reflect current, eighth-edition standards? Instead, we provide total authority control for the specific collection data bases extracted by our users.

To sum up, I don't think it desirable to edit records as they enter a resource data base. The national library records are of sufficiently high quality to make editing inessential, and records from other sources are not used often enough to justify the editorial costs. The Washington Library Network is, of course, undertaking to edit all original cataloging records, but one must ask whether the editorial catalogers can be relied upon to produce a record of higher quality, and wider acceptance, than the one they started with.

The last question I'll address is what the commercial firms can do to aid in library automation. The commercial vendors are already doing many things. What they provide is another alternative, as Dr. Axford said: another place to spend your money. When you look for a service or a product to accomplish some management objective, don't worry about the type of organization that provides it. Instead, worry about whether you're getting the best possible return for your money. The money you spend goes no further with a not-for-profit organization than anywhere else. It buys you a service, and the extent to which that service aids your library is the key. A cost analysis is the real issue. If you get quotes from all available services, tear off the top of the quotation sheet so you don't know who they come from, and make your decision based on content, capability, and cost, then the commercial versus noncommercial issue becomes irrelevant.

There are many commercial services that overlap, and there are many noncommercial services overlapping with them. Pick out the parts that fit best for you. I think you will find in one area, however, that the nonprofit organizations are lagging far behind the commercial sector: in providing local computer systems for support of local library consortia, or individual libraries, and in the production of microform catalog products from automated catalogs.

MODERATOR: Thank you, Bruce. Now we have Mr. Dick De Gennaro who will talk about why libraries have been very cautious in abandoning the card catalog, even though automation enables us to do so and has been with us for some time.

RICHARD De GENNARO: The closing of card catalogs in 1980 and making a new beginning with COM or on-line catalogs is not even a technical problem. It's a human problem, and a political problem, and it must be managed with the greatest skill and care.

There is often a great difference between the things that interest librarians like those of us who are attending this conference, and the things that interest the librarians in our cataloging departments back home, and the faculty and students we are trying to serve.

The large number of professionals and clericals in catalog departments can't be expected to welcome being told abruptly that in 1980 we are going to close the card catalogs and computerize the operation in the future. A good deal of preparation and education needs to take place before then, and, more important, a good many procedures need to be eliminated from our catalog departments between now and catalog closing time.

Our faculties—particularly those in the traditional disciplines like history, languages, and literature, who tend to be most interested and influential in the affairs of our central libraries with large catalogs—will not welcome being suddenly told in 1980 that we are closing the card catalog and starting again with a computerized version. Recently at a committee meeting I tried to give the faculty a preview of things to come, announcing that the Library of Congress was going to close its card catalog and telling them what this meant for us—and how we might possibly go to a COM version and then to some variation on the on-line catalog; and I held them spellbound for about fifteen minutes. And when the meeting ended, the chairman, a senior professor and personal friend, and a strong library backer, called me aside and said, "Can we talk for a minute or two in your office?" And he said to me, "You know, gee, I kind of like those card catalogs." So I reassured him that change would come in an orderly fashion, imperceptibly, and that he and his colleagues would love it once it was done.

Well, the users, and particularly the faculty users of our main libraries are very conservative. They'll have to be sold on the need for closing existing catalogs and going to separate files, the new one being COM, which most have never heard of, or on-line, which most are very skeptical of.

Our users, and particularly our senior humanities faculty, are not at all familiar with these exciting developments. They have not heard or seen Bill Walsh, John Rather, Henriette Avram, or the other stars of the Library of Congress dramatizing their need to close their catalogs and improve upon them with new computerized versions. They have not heard Fred Kilgour and other network people tell about the exciting things they have in store for us. We have a tremendous job of educating our users in the next few years, if we are going to overcome the powerful resistance a far-reaching change like this will engender.

It may be best to make the changes a step at a time in order to minimize both the human as well as the technical problems we are sure to encounter.

While it may be true that the technology now exists to put catalogs on-line, it does not yet exist in most libraries. There's a great difference between having a certain technology available in a few sophisticated centers such as the Library of Congress, Chicago, Toronto, and the New York Public Library and having the same technology available in scores of college and university libraries.

Most libraries do not have a staff with the technical competence to plan and implement on-line or even COM catalogs. We must turn to consultants and vendors with turnkey systems to obtain the expertise that we need to select and implement the appropriate systems.

These systems may not be ready for routine implementation in 1980, but in that case there is no technical reason why a library that feels it must close its catalog cannot simply do so and begin another card catalog on an interim basis, while capturing its catalog data in machine-readable form through OCLC and other systems. Other libraries may wish to go directly to a COM catalog, since they are commercially available now, even though they may presently lack the sophisticated components needed for authority control, cross references, and so on.

To go to an on-line catalog in 1980 will be nearly impossible for most libraries. Some libraries by then may have gained experience in using the brief-record catalog in an on-line circulation system and may even have in-house minicomputer capabilities and terminals required to deal with a full MARC entry catalog of recently acquired titles.

The problem of retrospective conversion of a large card catalog is something that few libraries will want to address before gaining experience with a smaller current file. Large libraries with old collections and mixed classifications will probably be wise to postpone that effort until conversion technology and procedures are more fully developed. Smaller libraries may well lead the way in putting their entire catalogs on-line.

Finally, I would like to question the assumption that when the Library of Congress closes its catalogs in 1980, the rest of us will have no choice but to follow suit quickly. I think this is nonsense. Libraries have an infinite capacity for muddling through, for fitting strange and wonderful entries into their already confused and inconsistent catalogs. AACR2 entries can be absorbed into our catalogs just as we absorbed those from all the other codes, and as the Chinese absorb invaders.

My advice to you is not to close your catalogs in the spirit of panic in 1980. But if you have done your homework and are ready, and feeling adventurous and innovative, you can use the Library of Congress's action as a rationale for closing your own card catalog and joining the future.

MODERATOR: Thank you, Dick. I am now going to ask Bela Hatvany a most difficult question: What is the current and emerging role of commercially owned data bases in the larger scheme of things? Is the profit sector competing with the nonprofit networks, or is there need for both? Can these two forces complement each other, or are they heading for a showdown?

BELA HATVANY: The whole solution is a compromise between conflicting concerns. It's an emotional issue, but for-profit and not-for-profit are just methods for accounting for sources of equity. Profit has nothing to do with evaluating a library automation service. You should instead be concerned with the firm's stability, and how it does the job. Does it even want to do your job? Can it do your job? Can it give you everything you want? What is its distinctive competence? Is it providing the service already, and what do its own customers say?

Ask who it is serving: libraries, stockholders, or government agencies. Does it employ knowledgeable professional librarians? And what does it do with profits: pay dividends, build reserves for a rainy day, or reinvest in improving library services? These are relevant ways of deciding which organization you are going to use to help solve your problem.

In the library automation industry there are several components that add value to the basic bibliographic data, but the most significant one is that which provides accessibility. OCLC, CLSI, and other organizations have actually managed to make data accessible to libraries in an economic manner. Accessibility is by far the most complex problem that faces any aspiring automator of libraries. There are no standard solutions to that problem yet. Airline reservations systems have been under development since 1957. They are now standard, and accessibility has been the focus of the value-added column.

When will standard automation systems appear in libraries? In early 1978, many of our current customers will install public access catalogs automated in conjunction with circulation control, and I think we must now focus generally on that combined approach. In that context, the on-line catalog is the most economic step to take next in the automation of libraries.

MODERATOR: Thank you, Bela. Our next panelist is going to address the question, Should automated catalogs make it possible for any library in the nation to know the holdings of all other libraries? Is this a desirable goal, or should such access be limited to smaller geographical regions?

LOIS KERSHNER: I would like to break the question into two parts and look at it from the user's point of view. First, is it a desirable goal to be able to have access to the holdings of all other libraries in the country? Certainly that desire is manifested in the various union catalogs scattered around the country. But even so, access to these resources is sometimes impossible because of geographical location. Access to holdings of other libraries is certainly desirable and valuable at the local level. In making a purchase decision, it is often important to know whether another library already owns the book, and union catalogs can provide that information.

As a library user, I would want to have not only local access but, if the need arose, progressively wider access to regional and national resources. My position here is consistent with the objectives of the national library network, which Henriette Avram spoke about [chapter 5]. There are, of course, many problems to be resolved in the grand scheme of providing access to the holdings of all other libraries. First, all holdings would have to be converted to machine-readable form, and some libraries may not wish to do that. Then there is the technical problem of standardizing access from one bibliographic utility to another so requests can be switched automatically when necessary. Then there is the problem of presenting bibliographical data to the user in standard formats, regardless of its source, and, finally, the problem of effecting delivery of the document once it has been located.

I think it's just a matter of time until all libraries and library users have access to the holdings of all other libraries, for the pace of technological development is rapidly increasing and shows exciting promise of fulfilling that goal.

The final question is, of course, will all these things be economically feasible?

MODERATOR: Thank you, Lois. Now Fred Kilgour has agreed to review the current state of the art and tell us where we are going over the next twenty-five years in the area of automated cataloging. I have specifically asked him to discuss whether libraries are using the best rationale for joining networks from a cataloging point of view.

FREDERICK KILGOUR: First, the future certainly holds most exciting developments for the cataloging networks. They will dramatically increase the provision of information to library patrons where they need it. Because the networks are restricted to on-line cataloging, it is in terms of this kind of cataloging that the future will arrive, in respect to making information available to patrons when and where they need it.

I was going to tell you that there are now 1,019 libraries on the OCLC system, and it was my belief that about nineteen of them made really intelligent decisions to join OCLC . . . and then elaborate on the good job they are doing. But there is just no end to them, so I'm going to talk instead about the questions to be asked in selecting a network.

You might be surprised to hear that the first question you have to ask yourself is how much the service will cost. How much are you going to have to expend on the network, and how much is it going to cost within the library to use the network?

Now these are two different terms: *expenditures* and *costs* are not the same thing. You are going to have to do costing within the library, preferably before you consider joining a network, so you can know what your costs are.

At a recent meeting I heard a nonlibrarian ask a question regarding cataloging costs, and a librarian responded by saying, "We don't know what they are"—implying that, if you've got leprosy, you just don't look in the mirror. Still you must make accurate estimates of your own cataloging costs.

As far as the networks are concerned, there are two ways of charging for services, and these can be confusing, but comparisons can be made. Network systems engineering in OCLC and BALLOTS is not the same, for instance, and this leads to two different methods of pricing that are not directly comparable. You can only make assumptions about the use you are likely to make of either system and get the experience of other libraries in order to make a comparison. It takes a considerable amount of work to get this kind of information. You should also discover the processes and products each network provides, list these, and do pricings on each one.

Once you have determined these costs, the next most important question is, To what extent is the network going to reduce the rate of rising costs in my library? This is an extremely important question to answer. There is no point in getting into a network and have either the price of the network, or the cost of the way you use it, increase the rate of rising costs in your library. Whatever you do, you've got to be sure you're going to reduce that rate.

The second question is, To what extent will the network make more library resources available to patrons of the library? I was delighted yesterday to learn that of the last twelve terminals we installed in Ohio, five were for the patrons, not the librarians, to use. This is a pretty small nonstatistical observation, but even so I hope it's significant because from my point of view, and OCLC's, the major focus has always been the patron of the library. You can't start with the patron, but eventually you must reach the patron.

So the questions you should ask are: Does the network have an on-line union catalog? Does it or will it have automated interloan requesting techniques? Then you've got to get some kind of answer to the question of quality control of the data base, and I can assure you that is not easy to do. In BALLOTS and OCLC, for example, you have two types of data bases. One is centrally produced and comes from national libraries. The other is cooperatively produced by the network participants. There is a surprising concern about the amount of error in the cooperatively produced records, but it's everybody else in the network who seems to be doing the dirty cataloging. However, last year we sent four thousand error reports to the Library of Congress to have their records corrected. But in the cooperatively produced records added to OCLC last year, the rate of error was 1.4 errors per record input. This is not a percentage but it's very close to a percentage, and the point is it's not enormously high. Nonetheless we are doing things to lower it, both from the technical standpoint and from the viewpoint of those who input the cooperative cataloging.

It is also desirable for you to know whether the network conforms to the standards for communicating bibliographic records. If you get records from the network to produce a COM catalog, will your commercial vendor's equipment be able to read the data the network produced? Technical standards must also be considered, as well as the network's financial stability. If all of its creditors should suddenly say, "Kenneth, pay me; Kenneth, pay the bills," could he do it? The one reason a profit or not-for-profit institution goes bankrupt is that it cannot pay its bills.

Finally, I'm going to bring up the problem of governance: not management, but governance. If it is important for you to participate in governance, you should find out whether your voice is going to be heard.

Let me conclude by saying that in deciding whether to join a network, you should do a trade-off of all the elements involved, under the following eight headings: types of processes and products currently available and planned for the future, cost, savings, increased availability of library resources, standards, viability, future development, and governance.

I want to raise just one question about future development, particularly with respect to Bill Axford's paper. Are we going to move increasingly in the direction of automating nineteenth-century librarianship, or are we going to use automation to produce a new librarianship totally different from both the past and present?

MODERATOR: Thank you very much, Fred. Our last panelist is John Kountz, who is in charge of shelf-list conversions with the California State Universities and Colleges System. I'd like John to comment on the role of simplified bibliographic entries in the conversion of a shelf-list and maybe touch on current Anglo-American cataloging rules, and whether they were designed primarily for teachers—and how they bear on automation.

JOHN KOUNTZ: Fred Kilgour characterized my response by alluding to a future librarianship. With reference to abbreviated or truncated data being adopted during a shelf-list conversion, I might observe that few studies have been made to determine what data the user requires to find a specific item. This statement applies to libraries. Government agencies have made such studies and found there was not much concern among users with what we call the main entry. The concern was rather with such things as contract numbers and descriptors along specific functional lines. This may be instructive.

If we would take a look at what we are providing to our users and what we do with our in-house data, as Mr. Blackburn is doing at Toronto, we could probably cut down on our COM costs by providing the full bibliographic record only to those few who really need it, leaving the general catalog unclogged with such data. Most users are hunting for the item itself rather than the description of it.

The data that we ceremoniously dub "the bibliographic description," with all its rules and regulations for development, including spacing, and number of carriage returns, is a foolish compromise. The people who create technical literature systems instead write abstracts—not just subtitles and bibliographic notes and collation lines. They write abstracts, add descriptors, look at the whole string of data (as BALLOTS is capable of doing), and imbedded within that string is the description itself. Here is a mechanical retrieval capability that far outstrips the formalized bibliographic descriptions we are continuing into the future.

I have heard a lot about authority files. But suppose I could enter a keyword into a terminal and use that word as part of a value string, passed across the whole string of data, then the terminal would tell me every time I have a citation met by the string I have keyboarded in. I don't have to have subject headings or authority files. Subject headings require me to refer to a formalized vocabulary. But the vocabulary I bring to the computer search does the job for me. And there you have an example of what I mean by a "future librarianship."

MODERATOR: Thank you, John. We are now open for questions from the floor.

PARTICIPANT: I would like to ask Mr. Alper what facilities Blackwell North America provides for transmitting data from a user library to your cataloging data base.

ALPER: I assume you mean for the purpose of producing a catalog of your own collection. At the present time we use something called the post office system. There are other ways of communicating, however, and my remark is rather facetious. A large percentage of the bibliographic data stored at Blackwell comes from OCLC. We also receive tapes from institutions developing their own data bases—for example, the Texas Registry—to give you an idea of how complicated these arrangements can be. Blackwell does not at this time produce or provide on-line, bibliographic network type access to its data base.

PARTICIPANT: I'm not sure if I have a question or a statement. Recent library use studies tell us that very large proportions of our collections are not being used. That raises a question as to what portion of a collection you should convert.

HATVANY: I would like to say that the 80/20 rule, which holds that a large portion of the collection is not being used, does not apply in the experience of the libraries we serve. A very much higher portion of the collection is used, especially in the public libraries. Experience varies, but in the first year of automated circulation in, say, a twenty-five-year-old library, it is very often 40 percent of the collection that circulates.

De GENNARO: I think the key issue is whether we're talking about public or academic libraries. In large university libraries a small proportion of the collection does indeed satisfy a large portion of users. The problem is, of course, that you don't know which 20 percent will be heavily used, and if you don't convert a substantial portion of the collection, you make it difficult to weed out the 80 percent that is not used. You are also stacking the cards against the use of that part of the collection that you do not convert.

HATVANY: Actually one of the best strategies, in a public library at any rate, is to convert first the books that are at eye level on the shelf.

PARTICIPANT: I don't think that anybody has ever claimed that only 20 percent of the collection would be used. The claim is that a small percentage of the collection will satisfy a large percentage of the users. Figures emerging from the Pittsburgh study show that only about 60 percent of the collection has a chance of being used even once, while the other 40 percent may never be used at all. And I suggest when you are thinking about conversion, you should be thinking about that 20 percent portion of your collection that will be heavily used.

KOUNTZ: The Department of Finance of the state of California asks us to be able to identify little-used books before we purchase them. Then we don't have to create bibliographic data for them, thus avoiding additional expense. And of course if you can answer questions like that, you have got an island in the Bahamas, and you'll take three phone calls a year . . . all from a publisher.

De GENNARO: Let me comment further on this same problem. I think in some ways you can predict which books are not going to be used before you buy them. Consider foreign-language materials, which major university libraries and the Library of Congress spend 50 percent to 75 percent of their resources in buying. And customarily maybe 15 percent of total library use is of these materials. We all know from experience that most Americans don't really read foreign languages. So for certain public and academic libraries, it might be a reasonable thing to refrain from purchasing most foreign-language publications.

KOUNTZ: Could I ask Dick what happens when the chairman of a language department at the University of Pennsylvania swears to God that that material is necessary for show?

De GENNARO: Well, that's a political question. I have responded to those questions, and I have eliminated eighteen languages that used to come into my library. And that is the appropriate thing to do.

PARTICIPANT: No mention has been made about the value of automation for special libraries and for special situations. We are merging with another special library, and I want to know if there are automated systems to help us.

ALPER: Special libraries are spared some of the overhead and limitations that the majority of libraries have to live with. Their population of users has a much narrower range of interest, and many of the political dilemmas of conversion are absent in the special library situation. Blackwell serves an incredible variety of special libraries, and most of them have been easily able to eliminate the overhead that they must and take a decision-making approach to automation. As to your particular merger problem, suffice it to say that many special libraries have handled such an automation problem successfully. Contact some of these people directly, and I think you'll be surprised to find out that conversion projects in special libraries are much more easily carried out than in other types.

PARTICIPANT: I would like to address this question to Fred Kilgour in reference to on-line catalogs. A recent report from OCLC indicated that the system was up 97 percent of the time. Now this is very good, I understand, for any on-line operation. But for an on-line public catalog, we need nearly 100 percent operability. One of the worst things that could happen to us is to have an on-line public catalog go down. The public relations problem would be terrible. Is there some technology coming along that would remove that risk?

KILGOUR: The answer is yes, but not a complete yes. For example, one of our greatest concerns is the physical security of the equipment operating our on-line catalog. The catalog itself is backed up thoroughly. We've got an extra copy in the machine room, we've got another copy in a vault off the site, and still other copies elsewhere.

But if a large aircraft collides with that machine room, we will be out of business for a long time. And this can certainly happen even though the probability is not very strong. And if it's going to put all the other catalogs around the country out of operation—you can't tolerate that, and we can't either. So we are developing multiple nodes of the network, and there will be enough redundant hardware in each one that if catastrophe strikes one node, the others can take over. But this is going to be quite a while in coming, and so is the complete on-line public catalog.

Also we are developing backup power systems for running the equipment, and a duplicate data-base dispatcher, so if one goes down, the system automatically shifts to the other. So we are inching ahead in the direction of attaining 100 percent up-time, which is absolutely imperative.

De GENNARO: What Fred is saying is fine for the networks, but if you are thinking in terms of a minicomputer and a local library, then you would certainly want to have some redundancy built in such as a COM catalog of the main file, and I don't see this as an impossible provision.

HATVANY: The downtime in a system is the sum of the downtime of the components. The more components there are in a system, the more it is down. It is very important that the number of components involved in a critical function be minimal. Any system should therefore be divided into segments in order to maximize reliability. We do not want to have everything being served through one central point, which can fail. The public-access catalog should be based, and will be based, on a small system dedicated to that function, and a CLSI version of the on-line public catalog will be operating in libraries in 1978.

Now that system will consist of a network of the central unit, which controls the data base for one library exclusively, and then satellite units, which contain status files in connection therewith, and will continue to function even if a central unit goes down, so the critical functions of the library will be maintained.

The big rule one has to keep in mind is that downtime is the sum of the downtime of the critical components. We must ensure that there are a minimum number of components that could possibly malfunction and that a function can be switched to another mode when a malfunction occurs.

The era when things were centralized around one computer for any function, however small, is now over. Vestiges remain only because the conventional wisdom dies hard.

PARTICIPANT: I would like to ask Mr. Kilgour what plans OCLC has for creating data-base products other than catalog cards.

KILGOUR: Well, as a matter of fact, we produce other things than cards now, including on-line public catalogs. At the moment they are union catalogs, but in the foreseeable future we will have on-line catalogs for individual libraries. The local call number will be attached to the record, so that when you bring it up on the terminal, you will know where the item is in the library. We also produce archival tapes and currently have 293 subscribers. Then there is the serials check-in service, and the interloan and acquisitions systems will also depend upon the data base.

Our income this year will be about two million dollars from the production of catalog cards, but we want to get out of the business of producing catalog cards.

PARTICIPANT: I would like to ask Mr. De Gennaro to comment on the future of in-house processing.

De GENNARO: I think that the catalog departments in large research libraries are going to diminish enormously in the next several years. Mine has already diminished in the last few years. We've had OCLC since 1972 and since then have eliminated a number of both professional and clerical positions. We never fill vacancies in the catalog department any more, and I think there will be a time when we may have just a few catalogers left to do local in-house work. And I guess within 10 years or maybe even five, many large libraries will be and should be out of the cataloging business.

PARTICIPANT: Why wouldn't you see just the opposite pattern, with the small public library no longer needing the catalog department or the cataloger?

De GENNARO: My answer is that I did not intend to exclude small libraries: there is no question that local cataloging will disappear from them too. I think we are heading for a very severe budget crisis in libraries, and it will compel us to change our traditional practices not just in cataloging, but other areas too.

PARTICIPANT: Only one speaker thus far has mentioned the connection between an on-line public catalog and automated circulation. Does anyone foresee the complete merging of the two functions, or does the catalog simply remain a bibliographic finding list?

KILGOUR: Traditionally we have maintained a series of catalogs in the library: a public catalog, an official catalog, a shelf-list, an order file, and a circulation file—and all are really catalogs, though we call them by other names. The way we are pursuing the design of automated catalogs is to merge all these catalogs and functions into one. As you know, even with manual techniques some efforts have been made to merge such files. But using manual systems, the marriage of files is very difficult, and the divorce even more so. But merging is relatively easy to do in a computerized system, once we recognize that these major bibliographic files are really just parts of one catalog. This is the attitude and design approach we are taking at OCLC, and I am sure that other on-line networks will do the same.

HATVANY: A central concept of our system, since it was first thought of in 1969, was that it should be centered around one bibliographic data base. A primitive version of our on-line public catalog shows the location status for each item entered in it. The terminal tells you whether a book is out, when it is due back, whether it is on order, combining all the functions of circulation control, acquisitions, and catalog access. That is a principal justification of the on-line catalog: integration of all the bibliographic systems and the elimination of manual activities to update the catalog when a book is acquired, or lost, or transferred.

KOUNTZ: This may be a slight variation on a theme, but it is also possible to envision a division of responsibility predicated on data in files, so that your major resource data base functions like the Sears & Roebuck catalog. Certainly the Sears catalog doesn't tell you which warehouse has the wanted item. And you don't really care where the item comes from as long as you get it.

Either BALLOTS or OCLC, for example, could describe for you books that are available somewhere and also give you a mechanical key that provides entry to a local inventory system, to determine first where the item is located and then whether it's available for loan to you. These are very high-volume dynamic files where, once you describe a desired item, it's not necessary to copy the description every fifteen seconds for other people to procure the item for you.

KERSHNER: On-line catalogs bring up possibilities for radical reorganization in libraries. We'll see not only changes in the way users get information; we'll see possibilities for change in what a library should be doing and in our techniques for delivering information. And the time is here now. Some users already have terminals in their homes to access library data bases, and we'll go directly to the home and find very exciting possibilities for changing the basic structure of library service.

KILGOUR: I would like to illustrate what Ms. Kershner just said with one example. In Columbus, Ohio, we have the first interactive cable television system, and OCLC is trying to use their equipment with ours so you can search your library's catalog at home. In effect, a television set could be made to function as a library catalog. The technology is all here, and I am sure that within five years you are going to see this type of access.

De GENNARO: I want to endorse nearly everything that's been said before about on-line catalogs and linking them with circulation systems, but I also want to remind you that this is not an either/or situation. Catalogs are used in various ways, and not every user wants to know immediately whether a book is available. In a research library a lot of people want to browse and also use the catalog, and I think there is going to be a place for an alternative catalog for a good time to come. The alternative will be the COM catalog. Scholarly users will approach it in special ways, and it could be used to provide special listings and also serve as a general back-up.

PARTICIPANT: I couldn't leave without saying something in defense of leprosy. The basis of all catalog automation has been the unique record created by individual catalogers and then entered into a central system. The advantage of OCLC is not so much that it has MARC data, but the input from catalogs all over the country. And as for the number of catalogers being decreased due to automation, well, somebody has to create the records for the data base, and those people who make the records should not be discouraged.

De GENNARO: Let me say I have not meant to discourage or disparage catalogers. I did not say they were going out of existence as a breed. I merely meant to say there's going to be a decreasing number of them in individual libraries. The Library of Congress and other sources for centralized cataloging will continue to create the records that are the basis of the system. But I don't think we can afford to pay for local cataloging on the scale we did in the past; certainly we cannot afford to do that much longer.

MODERATOR: We have come to the time when our program must end, and I wish to thank each member of our distinguished panel for helping us clarify the many puzzling issues of automated cataloging.

# Index

chicago

NOVEMBER 3 - 5, 1977

holiday inn

chicago city centre

# ACM CONFERENCE ON MANAGEMENT ISSUES IN AUTOMATED CATALOGING

## CONFERENCE CHAIRMAN

Daniel Gore, Library Director, Macalester College

## PROGRAM CHAIRMEN

Joseph Kimbrough, Director, Minneapolis Public Library & Information Center

Peter Spyers-Duran, Library Director, California State University, Long Beach

# PROGRAM

REGISTRATION DESKS WILL BE OPEN WEDNESDAY EVENING, NOVEMBER 2, 7-10 P.M., AND THURSDAY MORNING, 9 A.M. - 1 P.M., IN THE LOBBY, GALAXY BALLROOM.

## THURSDAY, NOVEMBER 3

(ALL SESSIONS CONVENE IN THE GALAXY BALLROOM)

1:15 p.m. Welcoming Remarks — Dan Martin, President of the Associated Colleges of the Midwest

1:30 p.m. The Key Question for Library Managers: Whether to Manage Your Own Automated Catalog Data Base, or Acquire Outside Services? — Brett Butler

2:30 p.m. Staff and Human Relations Issues in Automating the Catalog — Peter Spyers-Duran

3:15 p.m. The Disposable Catalog: A Survey of the Solid Virtues of the COM Catalog in Any Library Setting — S. Michael Malinconico

4:15 p.m. The Automated Catalog and the Demise of the Cataloging Mystique; or, Here Comes the Catalog the People Always Wanted · · · Maybe — Sanford Berman

THURSDAY AND FRIDAY EVENINGS, SEVEN UNTIL TEN O'CLOCK, THERE WILL BE AN INFORMAL GATHERING OF CONFEREES IN THE LOBBIES AROUND THE GALAXY BALLROOM, WITH COMPLIMENTARY REFRESHMENTS, AND OPPORTUNITIES FOR CONVERSATION WITH COLLEAGUES AND SUPPLIERS OF AUTOMATED CATALOG SERVICES.

EXHIBITS: VENDORS' DISPLAYS OF EQUIPMENT AND SERVICES WILL BE OPEN TO CONFEREES ON THURSDAY MORNING, AND THURSDAY AND FRIDAY EVENINGS.

## FRIDAY, NOVEMBER 4

9:00a.m. The Effect of National Networking on Catalog
Management Decisions

Henriette D. Avram

10:00a.m. The Flexibly Automated Catalog: Budgets, Services, and the Varied Catalogs at the Los Angeles
County Public Library

Mary L. Fischer

11:00a.m. Management Experience With the COM Catalog
in a Large Academic Library

Robert H. Blackburn

Noon -  Conference Luncheon
2 p.m.                    (no program)

2:00p.m. Constituency Concerns in OCLC Management:
User, Library, Network, OCLC

Glyn T. Evans

3:15-3:45 Coffee

3:45p.m. Shelflist Conversion: Management Pitfalls and
Opportunities

John Kountz

## SATURDAY, NOVEMBER 5

9:00a.m. The Great Rush to Automated Catalogs: Will
It Be Management or Muddling Through?

William Axford

10:00a.m. Key Issues in Managing the Automated Catalog:
A Panel Discussion, Chaired by Peter Spyers-Duran

Noon Adjournment (or thereabouts)

WE GRATEFULLY ACKNOWLEDGE THE SPECIAL CONTRIBUTIONS
OF THE FOLLOWING FIRMS, WHO ARE JOINTLY PROVIDING,
FOR YOUR COMFORT AND CONVIVIALITY, COFFEE AND PASTRY
SERVICE DURING THE CONFERENCE, AND REFRESHMENTS FOR
THE THURSDAY AND FRIDAY EVENING SOCIAL GATHERINGS:

AUTO-GRAPHICS                BAKER & TAYLOR
           BLACKWELL NORTH AMERICA
BRODART                                CLSI

**THE SPEAKERS**

HENRIETTE D. AVRAM is Director of the Network Development Office, Library of Congress

WILLIAM AXFORD is University Librarian, University of Oregon

SANFORD BERMAN is Head Cataloger, Hennepin County Library, Edina, Mn, and Editor of the HCL Cataloging Bulletin

ROBERT H. BLACKBURN is Chief Librarian of the University of Toronto

BRETT BUTLER is Director of Butler Associates, Los Altos, CA

GLYN T. EVANS is Director of Library Services, SUNY Central Administration, Albany, N.Y.

MARY L. FISCHER is Special Assistant to the County Librarian, Los Angeles County Public Library System

JOHN KOUNTZ is Associate Director, Library Automation Division, California State Universities and Colleges

S. MICHAEL MALINCONICO is Assistant Chief, Systems Analysis and Data Processing Office, New York Public Library

PETER SPYERS-DURAN is Library Director, California State University, Long Beach

**THE PANEL**

BRUCE ALPER is Group Computing Director, Blackwell North America

RICHARD DeGENNARO is Director of the University of Pennsylvania Library, Philadelphia

BELA HATVANY is Vice President of CLSI

LOIS KERSHNER holds a management position in the BALLOTS program at Stanford University

FREDERICK KILGOUR is Executive Director of the Ohio College Library Center

JOHN KOUNTZ is, as noted above, with the California State Universities and Colleges system

SPONSORED BY THE ASSOCIATED COLLEGES OF THE MIDWEST

DR. DAN MARTIN, PRESIDENT

MS. JEANETTE MC GRATH, CONFERENCE COORDINATOR

18 SOUTH MICHIGAN AVENUE, SUITE 1010

CHICAGO, ILLINOIS 60603

## ABOUT THE EDITORS

**Daniel Gore** is former Library Director at Macalester College in St. Paul, Minnesota. Among his earlier publications are *Farewell to Alexandria* (Greenwood Press, 1976) and *To Know a Library* (Greenwood Press, 1977). **Joseph Kimbrough** is Director of the Minneapolis Public Library. **Peter Spyers-Duran**, co-author with Daniel Gore of *Economics of Approval Plans* (Greenwood Press, 1972), is Director of Libraries at California State University, Long Beach.